ESTABLISHING CAREER LADDERS IN TEACHING
A Guide for Policy Makers

ESTABLISHING
CAREER LADDERS
IN TEACHING

A Guide for Policy Makers

Edited By

PAUL R. BURDEN

CHARLES C THOMAS • PUBLISHER
Springfield • Illinois • U.S.A.

Published and Distributed Throughout the World by

CHARLES C THOMAS • PUBLISHER
2600 South First Street
Springfield, Illinois 62708-4709

© *1987 by* CHARLES C THOMAS • PUBLISHER

ISBN 0-398-05285-9

Library of Congress Catalog Card Number: 86-14497

Printed in the United States of America
SC-R-3

Library of Congress Cataloging-in-Publication Data

Establishing career ladders in teaching.

   Bibliography: p.
   Includes index.
   1. Teaching — Vocational guidance — United States.
2. Promotions — United States.   3. Teachers — United
States — Rating of.   4. Teacher-administrator
relationships.   I. Burden Paul R.
LB1775.E78   1987   371.1'0023   86-14497
ISBN 0-398-05285-9

ABOUT THE AUTHORS

Robert **Alfonso** is Vice-President for Academic Affairs at East Tennessee State University. He formerly was the Dean of the College of Education and the Graduate School of Education, and Associate Vice-President for Academic Affairs at Kent State University. He started his career as a public school teacher. He has written numerous monographs, articles, and papers in the area of instructional supervision and leadership for improved instruction (e.g., in *Educational Leadership* and *ASCD Yearbooks*). He is the coauthor of *Instructional Supervision* (2nd ed.) published by Allyn and Bacon.

Paul Burden is an Associate Professor at Kansas State University where he teaches courses in leadership for improved instruction, classroom management, curriculum development, and teacher education. He has researched and written in the area of teacher career development. His publications include book chapters on career ladders for teachers (in *Merit, Money, and Teachers' Careers* published by University Press of America, 1985) and teacher career development (in *Advances in Teacher Education, Vol. II* published by Ablex, 1985), a monograph on helping beginning teachers start the school year (entitled *Before School Starts* published by ERIC, 1984), and numerous articles. He also is the coauthor of the 1985 Association of Teacher Educators monograph entitled *Developing Career Ladders in Teaching.* He previously was a public school teacher.

Judith Christensen is the Director of the Master of Arts in Teaching Program at the National College of Education in Evanston, Illinois. Previously, she was a public school teacher in Madison, Wisconsin. She has researched and written in the area of teachers' professional development. She is the coauthor of a Phi Delta Kappan fastback (No. 214) entitled *Teacher Career Stages: Implications for Staff Development,* an Association of Teacher Educators monograph entitled *Developing Career Ladders in Teaching,* and an ERIC monograph entitled *Stages of Teachers' Careers: Implications for Professional Development.* She has articles published in

Action in Teacher Education, Phi Delta Kappan, Journal of Staff Development, and other journals. She has two chapters in a book entitled *Career-Long Teacher Education* published by Charles C Thomas, Publisher.

Jean Easterly is Chair of the Department of Teacher Education at California State University, Hayward. She formerly taught at Oakland University, and served as area chair and coordinator of student teaching. Jean is a former elementary school teacher. She has researched and written in the area of teacher career development. Jean has articles in a number of journals including *Action in Teacher Education, Educational Technology,* and *The School Counselor.* She was the chairperson of the Association of Teacher Educators Commission on Master Teachers and is the coauthor of its monograph entitled *Developing Career Ladders in Teaching.*

Fenwick English is a Professor of Education at Lehigh University and has written extensively in the areas of career ladders for teachers, differentiated staffing for school personnel, and improved working conditions for teachers. He is the coauthor of *Strategies for Differentiated Staffing* published by McCutchan, and the 1985 Association for Supervision and Curriculum Development publication entitled *Incentives for Excellence in America's Schools.* He has other books published by Charles Merrill, C. A. Jones Co., Educational Technology Publications (3), and a book by the American Association of School Administrators entitled *Skills for Successful School Leaders.* He has five booklets published by ASCD, AASA, NSBA, and the Council for Basic Education. He has eight chapters in edited books published by Prentice Hall, Harper and Row, Saunders, and ASCD. He has 67 articles published in educational journals. He was the chair of the ASCD Task Force on Merit Pay and Career Ladders.

Russell French is a Professor of Education at the University of Tennessee, and since April 1983 has been the Executive Director of the Tennessee Career Teacher/Career Administrator Program (which has been involved in the development of the Tennessee Master Teacher Plan). Russ is a former high school teacher. His numerous articles deal with topics such as instructional improvement, educational communications, and career ladders for teachers (in journals such as *Educational Leadership, Research in Education,* and *Theory into Practice*). He has several book chapters published (e.g., by Interstate Publishers). Russ is the coauthor of the 1985 ASCD book *Incentives for Excellence in America's Schools* and is nationally known for his work in the area of career ladders for teachers.

Mary Hatwood Futrell is the President of the National Education

Association, the nation's largest (1.7 million members) organization of teachers, professors, and allied school employees. *Ms.* magazine named her one of the 12 Women of the Year for 1985, and *Ebony* magazine honored her as the outstanding Black business and professional person for 1984. *The Ladies Home Journal* named her one of the country's 100 top women in 1984. She has been secretary-treasurer of NEA, and served on the Board of Directors and on other national panels such as the NEA Task Force on School Volunteers. Futrell has served as President of the Virginia state unit of NEA. She has worked with the National Assessment of Educational Progress and is an active member of the Carnegie Foundation's National Panel on the Study of the American High School. She was selected by Virginia's governor as a state representative to the Education Commission of the States in 1982. She received the NEA Creative Leadership in Women's Rights Award. Futrell has served on a number of other national committees and has received numerous awards.

Carl Glickman is a Professor at the University of Georgia. Previously, Carl was a public school teacher and principal. He is a consultant to schools throughout the United States and Canada, a researcher of instructional improvement processes, and author of several books including *Instructional Supervision: A Developmental Perspective* published in 1985 by Allyn and Bacon.

Thomas McGreal is Professor of Educational Administration at the University of Illinois where he specializes in evaluation of educational personnel, supervision of classroom instruction, and teacher and school effectiveness. Tom started his career as a high school teacher. He has worked with over 350 schools in the U.S. to help them upgrade their teacher evaluation systems. His numerous publications include *Successful Teacher Evaluation* (published by the Association for Supervision and Curriculum Development in 1983). His articles are published in a number of journals including *Educational Leadership, The American School Board Journal,* and the *Peabody Journal of Education.*

Phillip Schlechty is the Executive Director of the Jefferson County Public Schools/Gheens Professional Development Academy and Professor of Educational Administration at the University of Louisville. Formerly, he was Professor of Education at the University of North Carolina at Chapel Hill and the Special Assistant to the Superintendent of the Charlotte-Mecklenburg (NC) schools. In Charlotte, he guided the enactment of the district's professional development (career ladder) plan for teachers. He has written extensively and is a nationally recognized expert in the areas of recruitment and retention of teachers, career ladders, and the professional development of teachers. He has served as the director or principal investigator in 14 federally funded and/or development grants. In 1985, Dr. Schlechty received the American Educational Research Associate Award for relating research to practice. In June of 1985, he received the American Federation of Teachers Quest Citation for Outstanding Contributions to the Professionalization of Teaching.

Albert Shanker is the President of the American Federation of Teachers, AFL–CIO, since 1974 with 610,000 members. He sits on the AFL–CIO Executive Council and is President of AFT's New York City local, the United Federation of Teachers. Since 1981, he has been President of the International Federation of Free Teachers' Unions, an organization of teacher unions in the democratic countries. He is President of the AFL–CIO Department of Professional Employees, is a member of the Trilateral Commission and the Committee for the Free World, and has served as an American delegate to several international conferences on Soviet Jewry. For the last 15 years, he has written a weekly column, "Where We Stand," on education, labor and human rights issues, which appears in the News of the Week Review in the Sunday *New York Times* and is picked up by some 60 newspapers across the country.

George Smith is Vice-President and Executive Director of the Center for Excellence in Education at Northern Arizona University. He previously was a school district superintendent for 35 years, including 17 years at Mesa Unified School District. He has received numerous awards for his contributions to education. He has served on the Arizona State Board of Education, including a term as its president. He founded the Arizona School Administrators organization.

Georgea Mohlman Sparks is an Assistant Professor in the Department of Teacher Education at Eastern Michigan University. Formerly, she was Vice-President of the Stallings Teaching and Learning Institute, and a classroom teacher. She has written in the area of staff development and teacher effectiveness with articles published in journals such as *The Journal of Teacher Education, Educational Leadership, American Educational Research Journal,* and the *Journal of Staff Development.* She is the author of two book chapters, and coauthor of two Association for Supervision and Curriculum Development videotapes—*Effective Teaching for Higher Achievement* and *School Improvement through Staff Development.*

Lance V. Wright is an Assistant Professor at the University of Georgia.

Previously, he was a school principal in Aurora, Colorado. His research interest is the role of the school principal in school-wide instructional improvement.

PREFACE

The primary purpose of this book is to provide information about career ladders in the form of background information, recommendations, and guiding principles. If people making decisions about implementing career ladders have this information, presumably they will be able to make decisions which will increase the probability of successful implementation.

To achieve this purpose, the book is divided into three sections. Section I provides an overview of career ladders and includes two chapters. In Chapter 1, Phillip Schlechty discusses the concept of career ladders and considers why they are being proposed. Russell French describes a number of common components in career ladders that are already being implemented in Chapter 2.

Section II includes 10 chapters that address implementation issues. For successful implementation of career ladder plans, the issues in each of these chapters need to be carefully considered by decision makers. In Chapter 3, Robert Alfonso discusses the process of change and how the implementation of career ladder plans requires careful attention to the principles of change theory. Fenwick English discusses career ladder features in Chapter 4. Judith Christensen considers the roles of teachers and administrators in Chapter 5. The issue of decision making is discussed in Chapter 6 by Carl Glickman and Lance Wright. Thomas McGreal examines the issues of identifying and evaluating teachers within a career ladder plan in Chapter 7. The issue of teachers continuing their professional development within the career ladder is discussed by Georgea Sparks in Chapter 8. Jean Easterly, in Chapter 9, examines factors in the work environment of teachers that should be altered with the establishment of career ladders. The issue of costs of a career ladder is considered by George Smith in Chapter 10. The support of teachers and the involvement of the professional teacher associations are discussed by Mary Futrell in Chapter 11 and Albert Shanker in Chapter 12.

Section III represents a summary of the ideas and recommendations that are provided throughout the book. In Chapter 13, Paul Burden discusses 58 principles that can be used to guide decision makers as career ladders are implemented.

CONTENTS

ESTABLISHING CAREER LADDERS
IN TEACHING
A Guide for Policy Makers

Section I

AN OVERVIEW OF CAREER LADDERS

Chapter 1

THE CONCEPT OF CAREER LADDERS

Nowadays, the term "career ladder" is commonplace in the parlance
of educators. As of September, 1985, 31 states had enacted legislation aimed toward creating some form of career ladder for teachers and
in some instances for administrators. In addition, many local school
districts have created or are in the process of creating patterns of differentiated staffing that have or are perceived to have characteristics of a
career ladder. The idea of a career ladder for educators has, in fact,
become so widespread that it has taken on some of the qualities of a
social movement. For example, there is now a career ladder network
with its own publication (**Career Ladder Clearinghouse**, Lynn Cornett,
Southern Regional Education Board, 1340 Spring Street, N.W., Atlanta,
Georgia 30309 (404-875-9211). Indeed, it is not uncommon to hear speakers
use the term "the career ladder movement."

Like most social movements, the career ladder movement has generated considerable emotion both pro and con. And, like most concepts
and slogans around which emotions develop, the idea of a career ladder
has come to take on many different meanings. In Tennessee where the
career ladder concept emerged as a substitute for a then less well received
idea (i.e., the idea of a master teacher and merit pay), the meaning of the
term **career ladder** is substantially different than in Charlotte, North
Carolina, where the term **career ladder** was not used locally. The Charlotte program is referred to locally as the Teacher Career Development
Program. Only recently has the term career ladder been accepted
(reluctantly) as an appropriate label for describing the nature and intent
of the Charlotte program.

Unfortunately, given the rapidity of the emergence of the concept of
career ladder in education (prior to 1982 this idea was not in the forefront of educational thought and discussion) and the wide variety of
responses to the idea, there has been a tendency to view the concept of

career ladder as a unitary notion and to assume that all career ladder programs are basically alike both in design and in purpose. The reason this is unfortunate is that there is growing evidence that the career ladder movement in America is in serious difficulty. Teachers are reluctant to embrace the concept; legislators are beginning to question whether realistic funding is feasible. Even some of the more outspoken proponents of the career ladder concept are beginning to raise questions regarding the feasibility of managing the complex evaluation procedures associated with many career ladder programs without creating an inordinate bureaucracy and an overwhelming amount of paper work.

It is not my purpose here to forecast the future, but I feel compelled to express my fear. As things now stand, it appears likely that negative sentiment toward the concept of career ladder is growing even while increasing numbers of states and localities are just now initiating career ladder programs. Should this negative sentiment continue to develop, it is likely that policy makers will abandon the idea of a career ladder. In some states, the career ladder movement may go out with a bang (for example, Florida). In other states and localities, it is more likely that the career ladder movement will disappear with a whimper.

PROBLEMS IN THE TEACHING CAREER

Should the career ladder movement be abandoned, it is also likely that this abandonment will be accompanied by a tendency to rationalize away some of the basic problems to which the generic ideas embedded in a career ladder program might appropriately be addressed. Among the more critical of these problems are:

1. **As the teaching occupation is now organized, teaching is a truncated career and a front-loaded occupation** (Lortie, 1975). For example, almost all of the salary gains that are made by teachers (other than those associated with cost of living) are made in the first 10–12 years. Furthermore, there is little difference in the status, honor, and responsibility afforded a beginning teacher and that afforded a more experienced teacher. The consequence of this condition is that persons who are career oriented (i.e., persons who want to pursue a particular line of work over a long period of time) find teaching discouraging. The negative effects of this discouraging condition are well documented in the literature. (See, for example, Schlechty & Vance, 1981; 1982.)

2. **As is often noted, teachers' earnings, when compared to equivalent**

occupations in other fields, are relatively low. Teachers' annual salaries are low, but more important, the potential career earnings of teachers (i.e., the amount of money a person can earn for pursuing teaching over a lifetime) are even lower. Thus, the longer one stays in teaching, the greater the economic cost to the teacher. Such a condition certainly discourages careerism. Equally important is the fact that such a condition probably discourages those who stay in teaching from maintaining a high commitment to outstanding performance. At a minimum, it does not encourage continued performance of outstanding quality.

3. **Teaching, unlike many other occupations, provides few opportunities for professional growth, development, and occupational variety.** Levine (1984) summarized the matter as follows:

> Schools have for a very long time imposed upon teachers a set of working conditions that can only be described as demoralizing and debilitating.
>
> It is one of the paradoxes of teaching that an occupation that is based on nurturing, developmental knowledge, motivation, reinforcement, incentives, and rewards should itself be so deprived of those characteristics in the organizational setting in which it functions.
>
> Clearly, too many excellent teachers do leave; many who might become excellent teachers if they had the appropriate environment for improvement and professional growth also leave, feeling themselves to be failures.
>
> But that is not all that happens. Some do not leave but adjust their behavior to the conditions surrounding them. They "compromise" (Sizer, 1984) or "make a deal" (Sykes, 1983). The net effect is less teaching and less learning or sometimes none of either.
>
> Teachers who have "defected" identify conditions related to a feeling of inefficacy. Those conditions are why they leave; if turned around, they may become why they would stay. The conditions Rosenholtz cites are:
>
> - Lack of opportunity for professional growth.
> - Inadequate preparation time.
> - Conflict with, or lack of approval from principals and other administrators.
> - Failure to deal effectively with student misbehavior.

Rosenholtz points out that teacher turnover is highest in urban schools where these factors converge. Although low salaries are not overlooked, teachers leaving the field stress the importance of these other factors over the impact of low salary.

An important implication of these findings is that changes in these conditions for teaching can result in greater teacher satisfaction and higher retention rates. Unfortunately the most important implication is that student outcomes will be improved only when teacher efficacy is increased; and that, after all, is the bottom line.

Much of the above discussion is predicated on the view that teachers' needs can be met by increasing the likelihood for professional accomplishment. It is also equally true that teachers acutely feel the disjuncture between professional expertise and any formal reward system. The psychic reward of professional accomplishment and the extrinsic rewards of money, status, and influence are all important (Levine, 1984, p. 10).

In spite of the problems described above, teaching has in the past been able to attract a substantial number of talented people to its ranks. For the most part, this talent pool consisted of white women, minorities, and upwardly mobile white men who came into teaching from blue collar families and often on the G.I. bill. For reasons that are now well understood, the traditional supply of such people is diminishing and all indications are that it will diminish further. In the past, teaching did not need to provide internal career options, because those in teaching had, or perceived that they had, few career options outside of teaching. This is no longer the case.

IMPLICIT AND EXPLICIT AIMS OF CAREER LADDERS

The problems listed above are inherent in the teaching occupation as it is now structured. Failure to address these problems is likely to have devastating effects on the future of public education in America. Implicitly, the career ladder movement is aimed at addressing these problems in a comprehensive way. Unfortunately, what is implicit is sometimes not explicit. Furthermore, what becomes explicit sometimes distracts attention from that which is implicit.

For example, implicit in the purpose of a career ladder is an improvement in the career earnings of teachers. Explicitly, the purpose often becomes to get underpaid teachers an annual raise as rapidly as possible; thus, the concept of a "fast track" option which is so common in many career ladder programs. Implicitly, the career ladder movement is aimed toward motivating ordinary teachers to give extraordinary performances over a long period of time. Explicitly, some career ladder programs seem to be more concerned with simply identifying and rewarding teachers who are already outstanding and thus a career ladder becomes a surrogate for merit pay.

It is my view that unless that which is implicit in the career ladder movement is made explicit, it is likely that the concept of career ladder will be abandoned as a viable means of reforming the teaching occupation. Furthermore, it seems likely that in abandoning the career ladder movement, policy makers are likely to come to the view that the problems listed above are intractable. Should this occur, not only will career ladders go out with a whimper, but so might public education as we now know it.

FUTURE DIRECTIONS

There are, of course, no easy solutions to the problems and dilemmas that are now being confronted by the career ladder movement. Declaring a moratorium is not the answer and neither is abandonment. Rather, what is needed is a thoughtful redirection of energy so that the energy expended on the career ladder movement becomes more focused on the implicit problems to which the career ladder program needs to be addressed. It is with the hope of contributing to this redirection that I have written this chapter. In the space that remains, my intent is to provide the reader with a framework for (a) analyzing existing career ladder programs, and (b) designing or developing new career ladder programs. This framework is built around a set of evaluative questions and responses.

I believe that the reader will agree that one of the reasons that the career ladder movement is presently under threat is that many of the more prominent programs, especially those designed and implemented at the state level, fail to meet the standards implicit in the questions presented below.

Career Stages

One of the most important evaluation questions that should be put to a career ladder design is: Is the structure designed in such a way that new and/or increased rewards become available to persons over the course of their occupational lives? More specifically, is it possible to gain all rewards in the occupation relatively early or are some rewards reserved and made available only relatively late in the course of the career?

Having reviewed most statewide career ladders in the nation, I can say with considerable confidence that few of these programs address the issue of teaching being a truncated, front-loaded career. For the most part, career ladders are designed so that an individual can gain access to all monetary and status rewards available within the first 12 years of teaching. Once an individual has gained access to these rewards, the only motivating force is fear of losing what one has rather than the prospect of gaining more.

It is typical, for example, to design the career ladder in such a way that a teacher can gain access to the first rung on the ladder within three to four years after entry. Once one has gained access, a single sum (usually $1,000–$2,000) is added to the present salary schedule. After an additional two- to four-year period, individuals who choose to do so and who can qualify can advance further on the career ladder where they will receive an additional salary supplement and sometimes the prospect of extended employment. In almost all cases, a highly motivated, highly competent beginning teacher can anticipate reaching the top of the salary schedule and the career structure in 12 years, thus leaving them with 20–30 years with little to look forward to except not losing what they have.

Fundamentally, such a design simply raises the top of the salary schedule for some teachers. It also makes it possible to give modest raises that might not otherwise have been politically possible to persons near the bottom. However, the basic salary structure remains intact. The only difference between the salaries of top-paid teachers after 12–14 years is where they have arrived on the career ladder. Such a structure is not strikingly different from the present situation in which those with a bachelor's degree are paid less than those with a Ph.D. The point here is perhaps subtle, but it is not trivial.

Under the present circumstances a person who enters teaching with a baccalaureate degree and who chooses to aggressively pursue a master's degree and Ph.D. degree can attain all of the economic and status rewards possible in the structure by the time he or she is 34–36 years of age. Most career ladder designs do not change this condition. There is, however, one important change. Theoretically, at least, the differential rewards passed out to teachers during the first 12 years will be based on performance in the school house rather than the university lecture hall. If, in fact, the quality of performance in the early years can be connected to advancement on the career ladder, it does appear likely that the design of the typical career ladder would serve as a motivating force for outstanding performance among young teachers. However, the typical career ladder program provides few positive incentives for mid-career teachers.

Rewards for Outstanding Performance

A second evaluative question that should be considered regarding career ladders is: Does the design of the career ladder provide increased rewards (money, status, responsibility) for individuals who provide high quality performance over a long period of time or is the design more attuned to providing rewards to persons who give heroic performances in some relatively short period of time?

Few who have designed career ladders have fully thought through the difference between rewarding heroic performance at some point in time and rewarding good or outstanding performance over a long period of time. For example, implicitly and explicitly, most state career ladders are designed to advance teachers who are rated as outstanding as classroom performers and to retain teachers who are less outstanding at lower levels. Furthermore, such advancement often is accompanied by the expectation that outstanding teachers will be removed from the classroom at least on a part-time basis. This leads to the charge that one of the functions of a career ladder is to take the best teachers out of the classroom. In effect, heroes are rewarded by taking them from the battle zone. The tendency to remove heroes is, however, not the most important problem here.

More important is the fact that most career ladder programs implicitly fail to honor commitment coupled with solid performance and tend to overemphasize the honor of stellar performance regardless of commitment. And, as Peter Drucker (1974) has observed, organizations that depend on heroes for quality are likely to fail, for organizational quality depends on the ability of the organization to inspire nearly all to perform in outstanding ways and to reward them for doing so.

By returning to the salary issue discussed earlier, it is possible to get a clearer understanding of what is meant by this critique. As the typical career ladder salary structure is designed, a highly successful beginning teacher can anticipate making 8%–10% more during the first 10 years of his/her career than could have been had the career ladder not been in place. During the second 10 years of the career, he or she will make from 15%–25% more (assuming he/she arrives at the top of the career structure in the earliest possible time). During the next 10 years and every subsequent 10 years, no more will be earned than during the previous 10 years except for the cost of living. Thus, long-term performance, even of stellar quality, is not honored; but heroic performance may be honored, especially by young teachers.

The fact that career ladders are new phenomena in American public education coupled with the fact that veteran teachers are presently able to gain substantial improvements in their salary by moving into the career structure tends to conceal the fact that in the long run the typical career ladder does no more to reward long-term performance of outstanding quality than does the present salary structure. Indeed, about the only thing the typical career ladder program does is to put more into the salary structure and to make access to the top of the structure more difficult, more limited, and hopefully, more performance based. I have no quarrel with the idea that salary, performance, and career opportunities should be linked one to the other. I also acknowledge that present career ladder programs do hold promise of reinforcing this linkage early in the teaching career. My concern is that this linkage and the motivational power that it implies becomes weak in later stages of the career. Thus, the problem of motivating and sustaining solid performance over a long period of time is not addressed.

One of the most difficult problems in thinking through the design of a career ladder is making a distinction between annual salary and career earnings. Discussions that center around beginning teachers' salaries and average teachers' salaries, though important, tend to conceal as much as is revealed. Properly conceived, careers have cumulative benefits. Careerism suggests a preference for deferred gratification. Indeed, some of the most attractive careers (e.g., medicine) require considerable up front investment on the part of the individual with little short-term reward and can do so precisely because the prospect of long-term rewards is so great. Perhaps a specific illustration is in order here.

At the time that I was serving as Special Assistant to the Superintendent in Charlotte, NC, and we were considering what became known as the Charlotte-Mecklenburg Teacher Career Development Program, I conducted a relatively systematic study of the career earnings in various occupations and compared these to the potential career earnings of teachers in Charlotte at that time. One of the more interesting comparisons was between a career officer in the military and a long-term (i.e., career teacher) in Charlotte. At that time, a beginning teacher in Charlotte and a beginning second lieutenant in the army had a roughly equivalent salary (approximately $14,000). Given the salary structure that existed at that time, I calculated that a young teacher coming into Charlotte who got a master's degree within three years of entry and a Ph.D. within seven years of entry (obviously a fast track person) would make approximately $625,000 over a 30-year career. The young military officer who I assumed to be marginal at best (i.e., received promotions at the latest possible time without being relieved from duty and who arrived at the rank of lieutenant colonel in his/her 27th year) would make approximately $950,000 over a 30-year career. Thus, beginning at the same point, the cumulative effect of a career oriented salary structure was that the military officer averaged better than $18,000 more per year than his/her peer in teaching.

Generally speaking, most career ladders are more oriented toward enhancing the annual salary of teachers than toward enhancing the career earnings of teachers. In a community where the average teacher's salary is $24,000 and the top teacher's salary is $30,000, increasing the pay of the top teacher by $5,000 gives the immediate impression of great progress. However, in the same community, where the average salary of a 50-year-old college graduate is $45,000–$50,000, a salary of $35,000 for a teacher with 25 years of experience can be discouraging. The point here is again perhaps subtle, but it is also important.

Properly conceived, career ladders are not intended to provide salary increases for all who enter the job. Career ladders are, or should be, designed to provide increasing rewards to persons who by commitment and performance demonstrate that they are willing and able to pursue the job as a career. Indeed, career ladders should be designed to provide support, nurturance, and sources of motivation to career oriented persons, not to persons who decide to teach, even if the quality of performance is outstanding, for some relatively short period of time. Career ladders should be designed to inspire high quality performance; but career ladders should also be designed to foster long-term commitment from those who perform with quality.

Attention to short-term salary increases (which is needed) will relieve short-term pressures, but it is only when one focuses on the issue of career earnings and future prospects that one is able to design salary structures and career structures that will inspire long-term performance of the highest quality. Put differently, until performance and length of service are combined, and until high quality performance as opposed to minimum competence is viewed as a prerequisite to the continuing opportunity to perform, there is little likelihood that economically feasible and politically viable career structures can be invented in education or any other field.

Immediate Gains or Long-Term Rewards

A third question about career ladders is: Does the salary structure associated with the career structure substantially increase the career earnings of teachers or is the salary structure designed in a way that provides some immediate salary gains with only modest impact on long-term career earnings?

Are the salary structure and the career structure distinguishable one from the other? More specifically, can individuals continue to make salary gains based on performance and longevity even if they do not choose to advance on the career structure, or are salary advancement and career advancement synonymous?

A major problem that typifies many existing career ladder programs is the tendency to make the linkage between salary opportunities and career opportunities so tight as to make it virtually impossible to use these two structures (i.e., the salary structure and career structure) as independent sources of motivation for teachers. As indicated earlier, in the typical career ladder structure, longevity pay continues for the first 10–14 years. This pay can be supplemented by advancing on the career structure. Thus, a teacher who had arrived at career level II after 10 years of experience would make more than a teacher who remained at career level I. However, in the typical career structure, teachers at level II with 15 years of experience would make as much as equally competent career level I teachers with 20–25 years of experience. Indeed, after 12–14 years of experience the only way one can earn a raise (beyond cost of living) is to move up the career ladder and those who arrive at the top of the career ladder early have no prospects at all for a raise. However, most career ladder programs provide individuals who do advance from one career level to another with additional career opportunities (e.g., the opportunity to serve as a mentor or peer evaluator, the opportunity to serve as a leader in curriculum development) and supplemental salary opportunities (e.g., summer employment).

Such a structure has a number of inherent problems if the intent is to provide maximum motivation for sustained high quality performance. First, those who are not motivated by increased career options and/or leadership opportunities, but who might be motivated by a performance based salary structure, really will experience little that is different in the career ladder salary structure than they experience in the traditional salary structure. Performance is linked to salary only through career advancement. Persons who want salary advancement must choose career advancement. This will surely encourage many good career level I teachers to pursue career level II or III even though they really would prefer to carry out the duties of career level I. I do not doubt that one must be an outstanding classroom teacher to be a good mentor, but I do doubt that all outstanding classroom teachers would make good mentors just as I doubt that all outstanding teachers would make good principals.

A second problem is that persons who pursue career options and find themselves dissatisfied with their own performance in their new roles will find it almost impossible to return to the roles they previously occupied without substantial salary loss. Thus, the "Peter principal" is built into many of the existing examples of career ladders.

A final problem is relatively obvious and widely commented on. By assuming that career advancement should serve as a mechanism for sorting out outstanding teachers from those who are less outstanding, one is left with the prospect that the only teachers who will remain at the lower levels of the career ladder after 10–12 years of experience will be mediocre teachers or those who are not motivated by money or career opportunities.

There are a number of ways that these problems could be addressed. For example, the Charlotte-Mecklenburg Career Development Program provides for periodic performance based raises throughout one's career regardless of the level one attains on the career ladder. Indeed, the basic difference between the potential salary of a career level I teacher and a career level III teacher resides in the fact that a career level III teacher has the right to expect year around employment, whereas the career level I teacher does not have such an expectation.

Similarly, in the Charlotte-Mecklenburg Career Development program, the basic difference between a career level I teacher and a career level II teacher is that the career level II teacher has demonstrated competence in carrying out functions in addition to those functions normally associated with being an outstanding classroom performer. For example, a career level II teacher is expected to be competent to and willing to carry out the duties of a peer evaluator if assigned to do so. However, a career level II teacher might be assigned to a regular classroom with no evaluative duties though they could be expected to accept transfers from one school to another if their special talents were called for.

In effect, the CMS program contains a career ladder, a salary ladder, and what some have referred to as a career lattice. More specifically, the Charlotte program has three career levels. There is a monthly salary differential between career levels I and II and between levels II and III. However, most of the salary differential is based on opportunities for extended employment. Furthermore, regardless of one's position on the career ladder, one can anticipate continuous raises based on assessed performance. These raises are not automatic. They can be delayed for a year or more, but when a delay is called for, the delay signifies a crisis and the need for remediation and/or potential personnel action.

The primary advantage to moving up the career ladder in Charlotte other than the opportunities for extended employment resides in the opportunity for career variety. Career level II teachers may become peer evaluators; career level I teachers cannot. Career level III teachers may be called on to provide leadership in research and development activities. Such roles would not be assigned to career level I teachers. The Charlotte plan was explicitly designed to provide teachers with career opportunities and performance based pay opportunities without forcing persons who are satisfied with giving high quality performance in the classroom into roles for which they are not suited or which are not suited to them.

Program Emphasis

A final question that should be asked regarding career ladder designs is: Is the emphasis of the program on identifying and rewarding individuals or is the emphasis on developing, motivating, and maintaining outstanding performers?

Existing models of career ladders have a tendency to give detailed attention to problems of evaluation and only passing attention to problems associated with nurturing and developing outstanding teaching. All one need do is examine many of the state plans and the budgets and staffs associated with those plans to grasp the significance of this critique. For example, one state (Kentucky) is presently beginning a pilot program which calls for the development of an elaborate evaluation system but gives little attention to developing the forms of training and support that would be necessary to develop persons capable of meeting these standards. Early versions of the Tennessee plan were similarly dominated by a heavy emphasis on evaluation and a de-emphasis on training though subsequent revisions have given training a more central role. However, the Tennessee plan and most other state plans tend to be dominated by attention to problems of evaluation and give only limited attention to the problems of training and development.

CONCLUSION

The power of the career ladder concept lies in its potential for encouraging and developing persons rather than identifying and rewarding heroes and heroines. The promise of the career ladder movement is that it has the implicit potential to develop and motivate ordinary people so that they will give the extraordinary performance that our children deserve. Whether this potential will be realized depends in large measure on the degree to which those who design career ladders understand the difference between careers and jobs, salary structures and occupational structures, and the meaning of incentives, motivation, and reward.

REFERENCES

Drucker, P. (1974). *Management: Task, practices, responsibilities.* New York: Harper Row.

Levine, M. (1984, April). *Excellence in education: Some lessons from America's best run companies and schools.* Paper prepared for the Commission for Economic Development.

Lortie, D. C. (1975). *School teacher: A sociological study.* Chicago: The University of Chicago Press.

Schlechty, P. C., & Vance, V. S. (1981). Do academically able teachers leave education? The North Carolina case. *Phi Delta Kappan, 63,* 106–112.

Sizer, T. R. (1984). *Horace's compromise: The dilemma of the American high school.* New York: Houghton Mifflin.

Sykes, G. (1983). Public policy and the problem of teacher quality: The need for screens and magnets. In L. Schulman & G. Sykes (Eds.), *Handbook of teaching and policies* (pp. 97–125). New York: Longman.

Chapter 2

CAREER LADDER PLANS

RUSSELL L. FRENCH

At least 27 states and a number of individual school districts across the United States are currently attempting to implement career ladder programs. These programs vary in many ways; however, most are similar in that they are multidimensional, addressing as many as six facets of educational reform. The six components addressed in most state plans are:

1. Creation of a career ladder
2. Development of a merit or incentive pay structure
3. Development/refinement of a performance evaluation system
4. Restructuring of professional growth and development programs
5. Redefinition of relationships between educator preparation programs and K–12 education programs
6. Reshaping of education governance structures

Several critics of current career ladder development have likened these programs to the differentiated staffing models attempted almost two decades ago. However, examination of the current plans reveals that the majority are more comprehensive than those efforts, and their purposes are usually different.

A characteristic difference is found in primary purpose. Earlier programs attempted to provide incentives and new career opportunities for teachers while improving instruction for learners. However, the primary purpose cited in most contemporary career ladder plans is to identify and reward outstanding educator performance. Rather than move talented teachers into new jobs outside the classroom, today's career ladders are designed to keep them teaching. Career ladders are not **job ladders** as one teacher union has labeled them.

While differences in career ladder plans could be explored in great detail, a more useful discussion for those contemplating the development of a career ladder program focuses on the common components of several programs now in operation. The sections that follow provide discussions for the six components listed above.

THE CAREER LADDER COMPONENT

By definition a career ladder plan results in some sort of career ladder. The key issue in development of the ladder is, "What constitutes its rungs?" If the rungs of the ladder will allow only a few occupants on each rung at a given time, or if climbing the ladder to a higher position requires teacher movement out of the classroom, the ability of the ladder to influence teaching and learning is destroyed. Failure to design a career ladder to match the goals of the effort will result in encouraging climbers to the top where they, and we, will find that the ladder is leaning against the wrong wall.

In Tennessee and several other states (Nebraska, Maine, Wisconsin), teacher certification/licensure provides the framework for the ladder. Each rung of the ladder is, in fact, a certificate of specified length which is gained through performance evaluation and achievement of other criteria such as defined years of experience. Usually, the required performance evaluations can result in certificate renewal (performance evaluated at the same level as was required to gain the certificate originally), certificate advancement (performance evaluated at a defined level above that required for the previous certificate), or certificate loss (performance evaluated at a level below that required to gain the certificate currently held).

In most certification-based plans, the educator who loses a currently held certificate drops back to the certificate at the level below for a specified period of time after which he/she can be reevaluated. The exception(s) to this procedure generally occur with initial (probationary, apprentice) certificates which are often up-or-out certificates. It is assumed that those educators who are in their probationary years must prove their adequacy before being granted a license which will allow them to become a career teacher.

Certification forms the rungs of many state ladder plans because it lends itself to the formation of a career ladder which (a) rewards performance, (b) accommodates any number of educators on any rung at a given time, and (c) provides systematic, orderly treatment of the thousands of educators who comprise the teaching force statewide. Since certification is not controlled by the local education agency, it does not offer a framework upon which a school district can construct a ladder.

Options in Rung Construction

Local school districts (or states which do not choose to build a career ladder on certification) have essentially three options available for **rung** construction: differentiated roles, status, and money (merit pay).

Differentiated Roles

One problem inherent in building a ladder on role differentiation has already been mentioned. A school district can use only so many lead teachers or mentor teachers or curriculum specialists. Unless personnel turnover is great, the rungs of the ladder soon reach their maximum capacity, and a natural quota system results.

A second problem in developing career ladders based on role differentiation has been the fact that the roles identified do tend to take teachers from classrooms or other educators from roles in which they are performing well and move them into new, arbitrarily defined positions. In these new roles, the impact of the individual on the teaching-learning process actually may be lessened, unless the role is temporary (no more than a year in duration). Few persons are interested in climbing to the next rung of the ladder if they will lose that new position after a limited time regardless of performance.

A third problem which creators of role differentiated ladders have found after the fact is that the performance factors which earned the individual his/her move on the ladder are not necessarily the ones necessary to the newly acquired role. For example, a lead teacher must be capable of leading and managing adults, not simply teaching young people well. A mentor teacher must be able to nurture less able teachers. A curriculum specialist must be able to conceptualize his/her discipline and help others to do the same. Unless the skills required for the new rung on the ladder are considered in defining criteria for movement, resulting appointments can be a disaster for the school district and the individual.

Status and Money

If role differentiation is not used in ladder construction, the remaining options are status and financial reward. Status often has been overlooked as an incentive in the educational community. Because teacher unions and some educators have stated that they or their peers should not be singled out for acclaim, we have assumed that all feel that way. Nothing could be further from the truth, as several career ladder programs are now proving. It is not at all difficult to find career ladder participants who flatly state that they want their knowledge and skill to be recognized in their profession and their communities. Special titles, publicity, trophies and other awards may very well offer ladder building materials for educators. However, they may not create enough incentive by themselves to keep outstanding educators in the profession. Status without adequate compensation for outstanding performance may actually lead to better offers outside the schools for the nation's best educators. Almost all current state and local career ladder plans combine a career ladder structure with incentive or merit pay.

Some plans which are being called career ladder plans do not actually embody a career ladder with clearly defined, hierarchical rungs. Rather, they offer educators opportunity for incentives or additional compensation without gaining position on a ladder. These plans will be addressed in the later section on professional growth and development.

THE MERIT/INCENTIVE PAY COMPONENT

It is possible to have a career ladder without merit pay, and it is possible to have a merit pay plan without a career ladder. However, few, if any, of the current career ladder plans lack a merit pay component. In most cases, financial incentives form the centerpiece of the plan.

While compensation amounts for ladder levels vary from plan to plan as do the number of years for which the incumbent is compensated, most planners have heeded researchers' admonitions that merit pay does not provide an incentive if it is not significant in amount, and does not extend for more than one year.

Tennessee's incentive pay plan serves as an example of those currently in existence. In the Tennessee plan, achievement of a Career Level I certificate earns the recipient a $1000 supplement over and above his/her base salary each year for the life of the five-year certificate. This supplement and the Career Level I certificate are based on performance evaluation, thus the supplement can be labeled pay-for-performance.

Career Level II certification is accompanied by a $2000 (per year) performance supplement. In addition, the Career Level II teacher can opt for an extended (11-month) contract. The additional 20 days of work pays an additional $2000.

A Career Level III educator in Tennessee receives a $3000 performance supplement and the right to elect an 11- or 12-month extended contract. Each additional month (20 days) pays $2000. For a Career Level III teacher, the combination of pay-for-performance and extra pay for extra work can produce $7000 per year above base salary.

The Tennessee plan, like many others, has provided significant financial incentives (6 to 40%) above base salary for a minimum of five years (life of a certificate), thereby addressing the problem of small, meaningless incentives for insignificant amounts of time. Further, a major portion of the financial incentive is reward for performance. It is not dependent upon the availability of extra duties or the willingness of the candidate to perform extra duties.

In some incentive pay plans, compensation is not directly related to performance. The Dundee-West Aurora (Illinois) plan has two career paths, one of which offers teachers significant, additional compensation for developing and implementing proposals which will affect teaching and learning in the schools. Although the proposals submitted are screened using predetermined criteria, there are few restrictions on who may submit a proposal. Houston, Texas, and several other school districts have experimented with extra financial incentives for educators who agree to work in especially difficult or hazardous settings. Some school districts are using market-sensitive pay (compensation based on supply and demand) to try to attract individuals to and hold them in fields in which teachers are in short supply (e.g., mathematics and science). However, these financial incentive programs have little to do with career ladders. The two merit or incentive pay structures most often linked with a career ladder have been performance pay and differentiated pay (extra pay for extra work or additional time).

THE PERFORMANCE EVALUATION COMPONENT

Discussion of the performance evaluation component will focus on (a) the development of a performance evaluation system, (b) evaluation instruments and procedures, (c) the use of student performance data, and (d) the selection and training of evaluators.

Development of a Performance Evaluation System

Historically, the evaluation of educators for reward has been credential-based. Credentials such as advanced degrees, completion of additional coursework, and years of experience constituted the criteria for granting tenure and raising pay. If performance entered into the criteria at all, adequacy of performance as perceived by the individual's immediate supervisor was the primary performance criterion.

The performance evaluation movement actually became popular before the career ladder thrust began in 1982–83. Performance evaluation for beginning teachers was shaped in Georgia, Florida, North Carolina, South Carolina, and Virginia in the late 1970s and very early 1980s. Beginning teacher assessment programs focused attention on the individual's ability to behave in classrooms in ways which research has demonstrated to be effective in promoting student achievement. However, the focus of beginning teacher evaluation through classroom observation and other sources of data was still on identification of adequate and inadequate performance.

Since the primary purpose of most of the career ladder programs currently being implemented is to reward educators for outstanding performance, evaluation of performance becomes the major ingredient in any selection process. But, career ladder selection requires an evaluation process quite different from that used to determine the adequacy or inadequacy of performance of beginning teachers. Evaluation for position on the various rungs of a career ladder, the highest of which is labeled "outstanding performer," dictates that (a) the process will discriminate among levels of performance, and that (b) performance evaluated as adequate will be the first or lowest rung on the ladder. By definition and design, career ladder evaluations are meant to identify patterns of performance congruent with whatever number of rungs have been built into the ladder. Obviously, the greater the number of rungs, the more finely the evaluation system must discriminate among levels of performance.

Career ladder evaluations are first of all summative; that is, they result in decisions about licensure, remuneration, and/or employment. The formative (instructional assistance) dimensions of the evaluations, while important, are usually secondary.

Career ladder plans have been controversial within the education profession. At least one concern of those who are potential ladder candidates has been the evaluation component. Since many teachers have experienced little or no performance evaluation, particularly evaluation designed to discriminate among levels of performance, they have questioned the fairness and objectivity of any evaluation system to be used.

Due to the summative nature of the evaluations and their legal implications, the requirement that evaluation systems discriminate among levels of performance, and the skepticism of educators who are potential career ladder candidates, three principles have resulted in most plans now being implemented and formulated:

1. Performance criteria and standards for each ladder level have been designated before evaluation begins
2. Performance criteria have been developed from research on effective teaching and consensus of those to be evaluated
3. Performance criteria, performance standards, and evaluation procedures have been clearly communicated to candidates before evaluation begins

While these principles have long been recognized as essential to effective personnel evaluation, they have often been ignored in day-to-day practice. Career ladder evaluation designers seem to realize that acceptance of the evaluation program as well as legal support for its resultant decisions depends upon the presence of these factors.

Evaluation Instruments and Procedures

Performance evaluation in any setting, including selection for career ladder placement, depends heavily upon observation of the individual's performance by trained observers. However, an analysis of the performance areas typically designated for evaluation reveals that some cannot be validly assessed through observation. Areas for evaluation most often specified in teacher plans, such as those in Tennessee, Georgia, Florida,

Alabama, North Carolina, Kentucky, Virginia, Illinois, and South Carolina, include planning for instruction, teacher evaluation of student progress, classroom management, and basic communication (competence in reading, writing, and oral communication). Of these areas, only instructional delivery, classroom management, and oral communication competency usually can be observed in the classroom. Limited aspects of teacher planning, evaluation of students, and written communication may be observed, if observation occurs very frequently or if the observer happens to be in the classroom at the right time. These limitations dictate that career ladder evaluation systems rely on more than one data source or data gathering procedure.

In addition to direct observation of the career ladder candidate, data sources most commonly used are some sort of structured interview between evaluator(s) and candidate, and analysis of sample materials (lesson plans, tests, memoranda, student diagnostic charts, test and grade results, etc.) contained in a portfolio. Obviously, interview questions and portfolio contents vary with the role and responsibility of the career ladder candidate. The evaluation of administrators, counselors, or librarians can parallel that of teachers in procedure, but not in substance. Even some groups of teachers, such as vocational or special education teachers, use different planning procedures and are required to be competent in areas slightly different from those of general education teachers.

Less used sources of evaluation data are the perceptions of peers (gathered through questionnaires or interviews), the perceptions of students (gathered through questionnaires or interviews), parent perceptions (interviews, questionnaires), and tests of candidate knowledge. However, all of these are used often enough to make them worth mentioning.

Examples of multiple data source usage are many. The Tennessee plan makes use of all of the data sources outlined. Florida's program relies primarily on multiple observations and a test of knowledge. Georgia's plan calls for multiple observation and analysis of a portfolio of materials. Career Path II of the Dundee-West Aurora, Illinois, plan requires multiple observations and peer and supervisor recommendations. Hopewell, Virginia, is piloting a plan which uses a structured interview with the candidate as well as peer and supervisor observations. The Alabama plan requires multiple observations and supervisor assessment of non-observable competencies using whatever means he/she deems appropriate.

Use of Student Performance Data

Legislation underlying a number of career ladder plans calls for the use of student performance data in teacher evaluation (Tennessee, Alabama, Kentucky, Virginia, West Virginia, Florida, Illinois, South Carolina, Arizona). Thus far implementation of this requirement has been slow. Reasons for the hesitancy are (a) the multitude of factors other than educator performance which influences student outcomes, (b) the inadequacy of current student performance data, and (c) the expense of creating student performance data which might be useful in evaluating teachers and other educators.

At present, efforts in the states mentioned focus on (a) broadening public and political perceptions of student performance to include more than cognitive achievement; (b) identifying and refining procedures for relating student outcomes to school (faculty, administration, and support staff) performance; and (c) identifying evaluation procedures which validly link student performance to the performance of individual educators. Inclusion of appropriate student performance indicators in career ladder evaluations is, at this writing, several years away.

Selection and Training of Evaluators

Three basic patterns of evaluator selection can be found in contemporary career ladder plans. Some plans (Kentucky, North Carolina, Florida) require that all aspects of the evaluation be conducted by the candidate's immediate supervisor or bona fide designee. Others (Alabama, Georgia, Illinois, Virginia) allow for the use of evaluator teams composed of the immediate supervisor plus one or more peers or others (e.g., higher education representative, central office representative). A third pattern, used to date only in Tennessee, requires that all evaluators or data collectors be the candidate's peers rather than supervisors. Tennessee legislation even goes so far as to mandate that the three peer evaluators on an evaluation team be Career Level III educators from school districts other than the candidate's own.

The use of peers as data collectors and/or evaluators has been recommended several times in the history of American education by several different critics. However, the career ladder movement of the 1980s marks the first time the concept has been widely implemented.

The length and depth of training for career ladder evaluators varies greatly from one plan to another, although critics and evaluation specialists agree that the ultimate validity and reliability of evaluation results can be traced to evaluator training programs. Since it is difficult to find and fund training time for either educational administrators or teachers, many of the current plans limit training time to two to five days with little or no monitoring and follow-up by trainers. These training programs may be sufficient if (a) the evaluation instruments to be used are simple and few in number, and (b) those undergoing training have extensive background in personnel evaluation and data collection before entering the training for the new evaluation system. However, neither of these conditions appears to exist in most places implementing career ladders. Learning to collect data reliably through low inference observations requires 15 to 20 hours for most people. Interview and portfolio analysis training must be no less rigorous to meet the requirements of summative evaluation. Educational administrators in most states readily admit that they have little previous training for performance evaluation, and most teachers selected as data collectors have none.

The Tennessee Career Ladder Program provides one of the most unique training situations. Since the evaluation teams are composed entirely of peers, and the legislation mandating the program allows for those who are selected as evaluators to be under contract to the state for a year, evaluators can be freed from all responsibilities in their local school systems for that period of time. This procedure provides adequate evaluator training time. Since evaluators collect data from six sources (observations, interviews, written materials, questionnaire administrations to supervisors, candidate peers, and students), three to four weeks of training is required to ensure evaluator reliability and consistency. The Tennessee plan also allows for regular reliability checks of evaluators during the year and appropriate retraining sessions.

THE PROFESSIONAL DEVELOPMENT COMPONENT

As stated previously, most contemporary career ladder plans place great emphasis on professional development. Indeed, some follow the lead of corporations of excellence in stressing career development for the individual. Responsibility for the continuing development of the individual is shared by the individual and the school district or state.

This section will discuss (a) the relationship of performance evaluation to professional development, (b) career development, and (c) other incentive programs.

Relationship of Performance Evaluation to Professional Development

Contemporary career ladder programs link professional development closely with performance evaluation. Advanced degrees, advanced coursework, and evidence of non-required professional development activity are often criteria for career ladder advancement. Certification-based ladders typically require a prescribed amount of advanced coursework before a certificate can be renewed or a new one earned. However, these are not the most important linkages between the evaluation process and the professional development program.

Career ladder evaluation procedures usually require specific feedback to candidates about strengths and weaknesses identified. The feedback comes in two forms: (a) information provided at one or more points during the evaluation process, and (b) information provided at the conclusion of the process.

In-process feedback may be provided by post-observation conferences (a procedure borrowed from the clinical supervision model) or periodic summary conferences which inform the candidate of patterns of data generated from all sources to that point in the evaluation process. The Tennessee plan and several pilot programs in Virginia (e.g., Hopewell and Danville) provide examples of the former procedure. The Alabama plan exemplifies the latter approach.

In almost all of the plans now being implemented, end-of-process feedback is detailed and focused on data gathered about specific skills or competencies. The Tennessee program may provide the clearest example of this approach. Each Tennessee candidate, whether teacher or administrator, who completes evaluation, receives a multiple-page computer printout which details his/her score for each competency area and each behavioral indicator within the competency area by instrument. In addition, a member of the evaluation team trained to interpret the data conducts a summary conference with the candidate and assists him/her in developing a professional growth plan based on the evaluation data.

Professional growth or improvement planning based on evaluation data is also a feature of the majority of career ladder evaluation programs. Someone, either a data collector/evaluator or the candidate's immediate supervisor, is required to assist the candidate in developing the plan.

The provision to the individual of specific information gained from performance evaluation and the use of these data to plan further professional development activities are undoubtedly the most vital links between the evaluation and professional development components of career ladder programs. They extend the professional development of educators far beyond the traditional, arbitrarily defined inservice program and the staff development program based on an assessment of participant wants and wishes (often mislabeled as needs assessment).

Career Development

The concept of career development is coming to fruition through the development of career ladders. A pattern of development activity is beginning to emerge from those programs now in their second and third years of implementation:

Phase One: Strengths and weaknesses in defined competencies are identified through performance evaluation.

Phase Two: A variety of activities and materials are created by the school district and/or state to assist the individual in competency areas requiring improvement.

Phase Three: Successful career ladder candidates are offered opportunities to engage in professional activities beyond the walls of their classrooms or offices which provide new challenges, personal renewal, and broader perspectives (e.g., peer evaluation, mentorship, program planning).

Phase Four: Successful career ladder candidates take on new roles (evaluation of peers, mentorship, curriculum development, etc.) which require training in new and different skills. The school district, state, and teacher training institutions address these needs.

Phase Five: Successful career ladder candidates assist newer or less successful peers in their own professional development.

Phase Six: All parties are constantly involved in setting short-term and long-term career goals and selecting and developing activities to achieve them.

Since the Tennessee Career Ladder Program has been in implementation longer than most others (1986–87 is the third year of operation), a summary of its career development features provides one example of the progression of activity just described:

1983–84: The Tennessee Instructional Model (TIM), a collection of modules for professional development, was developed by the State Department of Education, local school districts, and representatives of teacher training institutions simultaneously with the development of the Career Ladder Teacher Evaluation System. The modules provided training in the competencies being evaluated in the Career Ladder Program.

1984–85: Career Ladder evaluations began, and more than 22,000 educators completed 40 hours of TIM training through local school districts.

1985–86: A second group of career development modules was developed. These focused on additional teaching skills and new skills needed for new roles (e.g., conferencing, mentorship).

1985–86: More than 100 successful career ladder candidates were called upon by the State to serve as career ladder evaluators. Numerous others took on evaluation responsibilities in local school districts. Most career ladder teachers became mentors of younger teachers. Career ladder teachers planned and implemented extended contract (summer) programs for students and professional development programs for peers.

1985–86: Special one-day mentorship workshops were held statewide for career ladder teachers.

1985–86: Career ladder teachers conducted orientations for peers entering the career ladder program in their school districts.

Other states and school districts are progressing similarly in their professional development components.

Other Incentive Programs

Some incentive programs are driven by professional development. Although some are labeled as career ladder programs, they are not ladder programs in the strictest sense because they usually do not result in the selection of individuals for hierarchical positions of some sort. Most often these incentive programs allow educators who meet a few

minimal criteria (designated years of experience, tenure, recommendation of the immediate supervisor) to apply for grants or funded projects
which will enable them to grow professionally while benefiting students
and the school district in some way.

Career Path I of the Dundee-West Aurora, Illinois, Career Compensation Program provides one example. In this program, a teacher can
apply for any of four types of projects, two of which can be personally
designed and two of which are designed by the school district(s). Funds
provided for salary and other project needs vary with the duration,
complexity, and relative importance of the project.

THE K-12-HIGHER EDUCATION RELATIONSHIP

Career ladder programs are doing much to restructure the relationship between the public schools and programs of educator preparation.
In several states, career ladder legislation has strengthened teacher education entry and exit, and course requirements. In a few cases (such as
Tennessee), new requirements have been imposed on faculty as well as
programs. Tennessee law requires all faculty and administrators who are
engaged in educator preparation to regularly spend time in public
schools. Further, any institution in which 30% or more of the teacher
education graduates during a given year do not pass the National Teacher
Examination at the prescribed level is placed on probation. Should the
failure rate continue a second year, graduates of the institution can no
longer be certificated.

Other changes taking place in the higher education setting because of
the career ladder emphasis include the redesign of undergraduate and
graduate coursework, and cooperation with the public schools in conducting performance evaluations and creating career development
programs. Because performance evaluation of teachers in the schools
focuses on effective teaching behaviors, teacher preparation programs
are being forced to reexamine course content and laboratory activities to
be sure that these behaviors are emphasized. Graduate-level, advanced
programs are turning attention to the skills and knowledge needed by
career ladder teachers engaged in mentorship, evaluation, and other
new roles. In some states, the new legislation requires that higher education personnel assist with career ladder evaluations. In other situations,
law or policy simply allows the inclusion of higher education faculty on
evaluation teams. The development of new content and delivery systems

for professional development programs by school districts and state education agencies has caused higher education institutions to offer expertise and assistance in this area. The career development emphasis has created new interest in teacher induction processes among those charged with teacher preparation. Coursework and certification requirements for administrators who are being forced to take on expanded roles in instructional leadership are being mutually examined by administrator educators, state education agencies and local school districts. Although the higher education institutions were slow to become involved in the career ladder movement, they are now actively participating with the schools in shaping its direction.

THE GOVERNANCE COMPONENT

The governance of and responsibility for implementing career ladder programs has three patterns: (a) state-developed/state-operated, (b) state-developed/locally operated, or (c) locally developed/locally operated. There are pros and cons associated with each pattern.

Few local school districts have the human and monetary resources to establish major incentive or merit pay programs, develop carefully tested performance evaluation systems, or create a quantity of materials and human resources for career development programs. State development of career ladders provides more efficient and probably more effective use of development dollars.

The area of performance evaluation poses certain problems for local school districts other than the stringent development requirements. Local operation of peer evaluation programs is difficult because of relationships among peers within the district and local negotiations. Finding time for intensive training of evaluators, whether administrators or teachers, is difficult, and evaluation activities are usually added responsibilities for those who undertake them in their home districts.

Local operation of a state-developed career ladder program requires statewide training of local evaluators to ensure fairness and consistency for all candidates, a process which involves thousands of people. Maintaining the consistency of evaluation once evaluator training is completed is very difficult and costly.

On the other hand, state development and/or operation of a career ladder program makes it difficult to involve extensively the people who will be subject to the program. Communication problems are greatly magnified when a program is state-developed or operated, and communication requires a massive effort.

Career ladder plans are now in implementation which employ all three patterns of governance identified. Tennessee's program may be the clearest example of a state-developed/state-operated program. Florida and Alabama provide examples of state-developed/locally operated models, and school districts mentioned previously in Virginia (Danville, Hopewell) and Illinois (Dundee-West Aurora) offer examples of locally developed/locally operated programs.

A FOOTNOTE

Obviously, career ladder plans come in a variety of shapes, sizes, and forms. However, the preceding discussion should make clear to all that the plans of the 1980s are multifaceted, and most are quite comprehensive. For all their diversity, they contain many common elements which should be considered by those planning additional programs. The comprehensiveness of these plans also highlights the contributions they are making to the reform of American education.

ADDRESSES FOR CAREER LADDER CONTACTS
IN SELECTED STATES

NATIONWIDE	Lynn Cornett, Southern Regional Education Board, 1340 Spring Street, N.W., Atlanta, GA 30309; (404) 875-9211. Free subscription to the **Career Ladder Clearinghouse Newsletter** is available through this agency.
ALABAMA	Dr. Allen Cleveland, Division of Personnel Services, State of Alabama Department of Education, State Office Building, Montgomery, AL 36130.
FLORIDA	Dr. Garfield Wilson, Florida Department of Education, Tallahassee, FL 32301.
GEORGIA	Dr. Lester Solomon, Director of Teacher Assessment, Georgia Department of Education, Atlanta, GA 30334.
ILLINOIS	**The Dundee-West Aurora Center Compensation Plan:** M. J. Harkins, District 300 Administration Center, Dundee, IL 60118.
KENTUCKY	Dr. Roger Prancratz, Associate Dean, College of Education, Western Kentucky University, Bowling Green, KY 42101.

N. CAROLINA   Dr. Bob Boyd, Assistant Superintendent, Department of Education, Raleigh, NC 27611.

VIRGINIA   (a) Danville, Virginia: Dr. Thomas Truitt, Superintendent, Danville Public Schools, Danville, VA 24541.

(b) Hopewell, Virginia: Dr. Jane McCullen, Director of Instruction, Hopewell Public Schools, Hopewell, VA 23860.

(c) Other Virginia districts: Dr. E. B. Howerton, State Department of Education, P.O. Box 6Q, 14th & Franklin Streets, Richmond, VA 23216.

Section II

IMPLEMENTATION ISSUES

Chapter 3

THE PROCESS OF CHANGE: IMPLEMENTING A CAREER LADDER PROGRAM

ROBERT J. ALFONSO

Despite current widespread support for career ladders, it is unlikely that they can be implemented effectively unless careful attention is given to the process of change. Scholars have long been interested in the study of change. As a result, an extensive body of research and theory is available. This chapter discusses the nature of change processes and some selected research findings that have particular application to the process of establishing career ladders. Their establishment is likely to be more successful and long lasting if some basic principles of change are adhered to. This chapter will discuss (a) the concept of change, (b) characteristics of organizational change, (c) analyzing resistance to change, (d) group norms in the change process, (e) change as a transition process, and (f) change implications for career ladder programs.

THE CONCEPT OF CHANGE

History is the record of change in individuals, societies, organizations, and nations. People and organizations must change if proper adaptation is to be made to changes in circumstances and society. In the latter half of the Twentieth Century there has been an overwhelming sense of urgency about the need for change; a belief that if change is not pursued by formal organizations that they will atrophy, become ineffective, and even cease to exist. Yet, all change is not necessarily beneficial. A decision to change can move an organization either forward or backward. This section will discuss the general concept of change, the meaning of change, and the difficulty of bringing about change in schools.

The Meaning of Change

Despite this deeply held conviction about the need for change, it seldom comes easily. Departing from practices and understandings that are time-honored and forsaking the comfortable for the untried almost always leads to some degree of insecurity and resistance. Most people prefer some change in their lives and in their work to the alternative of a monotonous, humdrum existence (Watson, 1967, p. 10). Even so, the very first question people ask about a proposed change is what it means for them and how they will be affected by it. Every proposed change is first evaluated quite personally: How will it affect a person's status, income, circle of friends, workload, responsibilities and relationships with others?

Even when the need for a change is clearly documented, it does not lead automatically to rapid adoption. Change almost never comes easily. Change is always threatening in some degree, because it forces people out of certain ways of behaving. Change moves people from the known and familiar to the unknown and new. It may call for new skills, attitudes, and relationships. It is an interruption in the established and predictable flow of human behavior.

Some changes are concerned primarily with the structure and functioning of organizations, while others are focused more directly on the behavior of individuals within organizations. In other instances, such as establishing a career ladder plan, a change is so broad that it affects not only the operating procedures within an organization but also the behavior, attitudes, and well-being of employees. A change that pervasive requires careful orchestration and a deep understanding of organizations and human needs and behavior if it is to be successful. Even changes that are seen as minor or trivial by the change agent are often viewed as substantial by those being affected. Career ladders will affect both individuals and organizations. It is a pervasive change. The implementation of career ladder programs will alter a time-honored and enduring system of recognition and reward and will dramatically change American education.

Whether career ladders are successfully introduced, accepted, and effective will depend very heavily on the skill and understanding with which state and local leadership personnel attempt to bring about change.

The Difficulty of School Reform

Schools are expected to respond to changes in the larger society and consequently are under public pressure to change, and to change quickly. To compound the situation, there are few public organizations as visible as the school. Each new school reform movement brings hopes of problem resolution, innovation, progress, and improved student achievement. For decades, America's school systems have been urged to change. This often happens under the pressure of a series of reform movements and, on other occasions, by influential reformers. The current educational reform movement, of which career ladders is one element, is the most recent in a long series of efforts to reconstruct American education. Most of these attempts have failed. While there have been some notable changes, schools are, on the whole, remarkably impervious to change efforts.

Cuban (1982) stated that American high schools have the unique ability to withstand change efforts, noting that the typical high school has changed little from its prototype of 40 years ago. Despite the massive amounts of money invested in educational change during the reform era of the 1960s, for example, most changes were not long lasting and died when financial support was withdrawn. Most schools were left much as they had been before this heralded curriculum reform movement started.

While this static characteristic of American education has frustrated some noble and needed change attempts, it also has served some positive ends. It has protected the schools from pressure groups, from self-serving but well supported change agents, and has kept it from moving too quickly and too far in response to each new educational reform.

It is also true that many attempts to change schools have failed because they lacked an effective change strategy, were inadequately supported, had their benefits oversold, and had no mechanism for maintaining and sustaining the change after it had been introduced. The current reform movement to establish career ladders could become, in historical perspective, just one more in a series of flawed and failed reform efforts; or it could be a major element of genuine educational reform.

It appears, however, that public concern—legitimate concern—is so widespread that real change can take place. Career ladder proposals are particularly interesting because they attempt to change long established traditions. Moreover, much of the impetus for career ladders has come from outside the educational establishment itself. Researchers point out that pressure for change frequently comes from forces external to organizations and that initiation of change within the organization is actually an adaptive response to strong external pressures.

Even when there is national consensus that change is needed and when there is some agreement on directions, change will not necessarily come readily. Resistance to change may be open or covert. Change also can be resisted through apathy, a condition that Willower and Jones (1963) found could be easily misinterpreted as acceptance.

Smith (1982) pointed out that what is defined as significant change depends on the perspective of those involved and whether they are affected by the change, introducing it, interested observers, or outside observers or historians. Persons to be directly affected and those trying to produce the change may have a short-range perspective and see actual change. The outside observer may see that little has changed and wonder why a proposal has stirred up so much interest or opposition.

This difference in perspective may explain in part the reaction of many teachers who view career ladders as a major restructuring of the profession and the reaction of observers, politicians and critics of the school who view career ladders as merely a good idea whose time has come. Such outside observers are startled to find opposition to what to them is a natural development.

Change efforts are perceived in a variety of ways as a result of the differing nature of school systems and the variety of forces at work within individuals. Without a doubt, the change forces that support the introduction of career ladders are substantial and strong, but they will have different meanings for different teachers and they will be more readily accepted in some school systems than others. They will also have to overcome obstacles that have thwarted other educational reform movements. The successful introduction and implementation of career ladders, however, will depend largely on decision makers using available knowledge about change processes and the development of careful and systematic change strategies.

CHARACTERISTICS OF ORGANIZATIONAL CHANGE

From the rich reservoir of research on change, a number of findings reoccur. These research conclusions are so well established that, in effect, they become basic principles for organizational change.

An understanding of some of the basic characteristics and principles of effective change is an important forerunner to any attempt to establish career ladders. Certain findings reoccur so often in research that they can be described as recognized principles of organizational change. This section discusses the need for participation in decision making, general strategies and approaches to the change process, and force field analysis.

Participation in Decision Making

Most compelling of all research findings on change is the need for people to be involved in the making of decisions that will affect them. This is a basic principle. In spite of the fact that many research studies have clearly demonstrated that change is more readily accepted when people participate in making decisions, this principle is repeatedly ignored. As a result, changes which might be achieved with relative ease are made difficult and are sometimes defeated because those to be affected are excluded from the process of discussion and decision making.

When people in an organization contribute to decision making and to the process of change, these new directions become their own. They help frame them, understand the reasons, and have a commitment to the process. When such participation does not take place, then change is brought about by selling and pressure, or through the force of law and policy enactments. The importance of involving people or their representatives in the process of determining changes is well documented. It is also a basic principle of life in a democratic society. It is, unfortunately, a principle that is often cited but often ignored, or practiced in transparently inauthentic ways. This principle calls for genuine participation in the development of career ladders.

General Strategies of Change

Bennis, Benne, and Chin (1961) distinguished between the idea of nonintervention (i.e., a laissez-faire approach to change) and the contrary idea of radical intervention (change brought about as a result of conflict). The alternative to either approach is **planned change**, in which process and social technology are used to solve the problems of an organization. To provide direction for change efforts, clear-cut goals must exist. For the efforts to be successful, they must be related to clearly understood and accepted organizational goals.

Rogers (1962) identified the five stages in a change process as: awareness, interest, evaluation, trial, and adoption. He also recognized that these five steps could lead to a decision to reject rather than to adopt a change. Other researchers have identified somewhat similar steps in the change process. What is important is that each researcher emphasized planned, systematic change, which moves sequentially from problem identification to adoption of the change. The intervening steps are necessary if people are to make the proposed change their own and feel that they have any part in the change process.

Preference for a particular change strategy depends largely on whether one sees the organization as people processes, technical processes, or processes centered around things and materials (Chin, 1967). Chin also suggested the following about change strategy:

> Strategies of change is interpreted as including, but not limited to, dissemination and provisions for utilization of pertinent information regarding all aspects of the proposed plan; ways of identifying and dealing with internal and external (environmental) constraints as well as facilitating influences; ways of identifying potential opposition, conflicts and tensions and of resolving them advantageously; appropriate means of helping individuals, organizations and agencies to effect needed changes in their perspectives; and procedures (guidelines) for implementing proposed change. (p. 40)

Change does not just happen—it is directed by an active person or persons. Chin and Benne (1961) identified three general strategies for bringing about change in human systems: (a) **empirical-rational**, (b) **normative-reeducative**, and (c) **power-coercive** strategies. The empirical-rational strategy operates on the assumption that most people are rational and that they will follow the strategy, if their self-interest is revealed to them. Consequently, if it can be shown that a proposed change is in line with the self-interests of a person or an organization, the change will be adopted because it can be rationally justified and because it serves self-interests.

The normative-reeducative change strategy recognizes that people are rational and intelligent, but it argues that real change will occur only if people's orientations to former behaviors and commitments are altered. This means that there must be a change in attitudes, values, skills and relationships, and not merely the presentation of knowledge or information as a rationale for changing practices. Simply put, sociocultural norms must undergo change.

The power-coercive strategy involves the application of power in some form and often has the force of legitimacy or authority. This strategy may require that the force of law or administrative policy be brought to bear. Sometimes, however, power-coercive strategies do not use so much authoritative or legitimate power as they do the massing of coercive power or public opinion to support a change, even if it does not have any legal or policy basis. Intensive pressure has often been brought upon school boards through power-coercive approaches, and, in recent decades, teachers associations have increasingly used such approaches effectively.

In his survey of organizational change, Greiner (1965) found that there are seven approaches to change in frequent use:

1. The decree approach—when a person or group in authority orders a change to be made
2. The replacement approach—when a new person is brought in, or at least someone is removed from his/her position
3. The structural approach—when there is reorganization of required relationships in the organization by changing the role and job definitions, the contracts, and organizational variables
4. The group decision approach—when members of the organization or group decide on a plan and elect to do it together
5. The data discussion approach—when data about the organization and its functioning are brought to the members for review (the feedback procedure)
6. The group problem-solving approach—when internal groups diagnose and collect relevant data about the problem
7. The T-group approach—wherein the emphasis is upon the nature of the relationship of the organizational and interpersonal environment, the quality of trust, openness, power balance, and other such factors (p. 42)

Force Field Analysis

One of the most enduring and helpful explanations of the change process is generally known as **force field analysis** (Lewin, 1961), also known as quasi-stationary equilibrium theory. Lewin argued that there are driving and restraining forces that keep an individual's behavior in a relatively stable condition, as displayed in Figure 1. Given this balanced condition, human and organizational behavior proceeds at a rather steady state until the strength of either the driving or restraining forces are altered. Other researchers have investigated force field analysis and have found it to be a very useful tool for analyzing organizations and for bringing about change.

Figure 1. Force field in equilibrium.

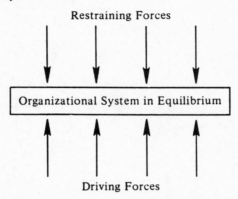

From: Owens, Robert G. *Organizational Behavior in Education*, 2nd ed. (Englewood Cliffs: Prentice-Hall, Inc., 1981), p. 260. Used by permission.

While most people desire change in their lives, this normal desire is often held back for a number of reasons, including a lack of skill, the need for more training, fear of failure, and uncertainty of consequences and whether approval will be received from others. On the other hand, there are factors which make a person wish to change, including the drive for success and recognition, the need for more money, the desire to do well, respond to social pressures, and the desire for new experiences.

In order to bring about change, either the strength of the driving forces needs to be increased, the strength of the restraining forces decreased, or both.

An imbalance of restraining and driving forces will cause an organization to move from a state of equilibrium to a state of change. After the change, equilibrium is reestablished as shown in Figure 2. This process is also referred to as that of unfreezing, moving and refreezing. The refreezing step is important in that it firmly establishes new behaviors. Without refreezing, individuals and organizations can revert to earlier behavior.

Failure to address refreezing probably explains why so many desirable change efforts do not succeed. Many change efforts depend upon increasing the strength of driving forces rather than decreasing the strength of restraining forces. As a result, when the original pressure for a change

Figure 2. Imbalance of force field causes organizational change until a new equilibrium is reached.

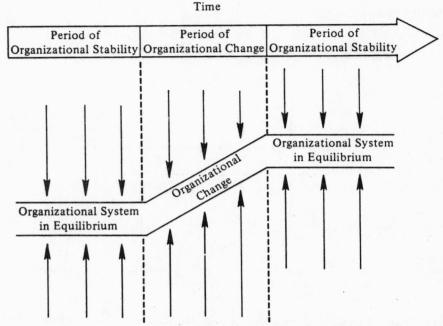

From: Owens, Robert G. *Organizational Behavior in Education,* 2nd ed. (Englewood Cliffs: Prentice-Hall, Inc., 1981), p. 260. Used by permission.

decreases over a period of time, restraining forces may push an organization back to its original level.

ANALYZING RESISTANCE TO CHANGE

The desire for change is normal. If individuals and large groups of individuals (organizations) resist change, an analysis of the reasons for resistance is possible. There is not a human predisposition against change. On the contrary, most people prefer some alteration in their work and responsibilities as compared to an unchanging environment. While there is some satisfaction in the knowledge and repetition of tasks, there is also great satisfaction to be derived from new experiences.

It should be anticipated that an attempt to develop career ladders will meet with some resistance. While some teachers may embrace the new approach enthusiastically, others will resist the change. Their resistance may be based on a variety of reasons, some valid and some invalid, but all very real for the persons resisting. This section discusses resistance to change, the need to identify reasons why a change might be resisted, and the recognition that it is the consequences of a change, rather than the change itself, that sometimes cause resistance.

Identifying Reasons for Resistance

Theorists argue that if a change effort is resisted, there are reasons and these reasons can be identified. The reasons may be in the nature of the change, the nature of the change agent, or may be for reasons not directly related to the change or change agent. The influence of group norms, about which more shall be said later, is an extremely powerful but often overlooked factor in organizational change. If change is resisted, driving force pressures to change can be increased. Another way would be to analyze reasons for the resistance and respond to them.

People resist change when what is proposed is a threat to existing practice. The most certain way to generate resistance to a change is to suggest that what is being done now is useless and needs to be discarded. On the contrary, a change is much more likely to be accepted if it can build on existing practice rather than threaten it. No sensitive, committed person wants to hear that all he or she has been doing is wrong. In fact, it is probably incorrect to say so. Some change agents mistakenly believe that they must first convince a group of the inadequacy of their current practices so that change can take place. A more effective way to overcome resistance would be to indicate how a change relates to current practice, builds on its strengths, and makes people and their organization more effective.

Some people resist change because of a feeling of hopelessness. Watson (1967) pointed out that they feel lost, enmeshed in a system that they can do nothing about. He referred to the illusion of **impotence,** in which people believe that their involvement can really be of no use. As a result, such persons resist the opportunity to contribute or to accept change. They are found in every organization. Their attitude is that "this place will never be any better, nothing I can do will make any difference."

Zander (1961) identified six factors related to resistance to change:

1. The nature of the change is not made clear.
2. There is confusion when people see different meanings in a proposed change.

3. People are caught between strong forces; some driving forces asking them to change and other restraining forces discouraging change.
4. People are pressured to change while themselves having no say in the change.
5. The change is based on personal grounds rather than impersonal ones.
6. The proposed change ignores group norms and existing customs. (p. 544)

Zander further suggested that resistance can be prevented to the degree that the changer helps the changees develop (a) their own understanding of the need for the change, (b) an explicit awareness of how they feel about it, and (c) plans for what can be done about those feelings.

While some changes are rejected because they are viewed to be not worth the trouble, other change efforts run into difficulty because they are too complex. The cost of an innovation (Forsdale, 1964; Mort & Cornell, 1941) also affects the success of change efforts. Costs may include money, time and energy. The greater the cost and complexity, the longer it takes for a change to occur. These obstacles can be overcome in part if changes can be made divisible; that is, if they can be made incrementally rather than all at once. If change agents adopt an all-or-nothing attitude, they may threaten the adoption of valuable but complex changes. Complex changes take longer to bring about and they require built-in implementation supports. Wayland (1964) also found that the more routine a change, the more quickly it could be adopted. Changes requiring continued creativity are much more difficult to institutionalize.

Identifying Organizational Consequences

Change is often resisted because of consequences not directly related to the purpose of the change. It may unbalance the system, bringing about different salaries, status, procedures, methods, and rewards. Starbuck (1965) and Hollingshead (1949) pointed out that changes are frequently a threat to vested interests and status of individuals or groups and therefore may meet stiff resistance.

Changes are frequently resisted not because of the change itself but because of the social consequences of the change, resulting in status disequilibration (Morison, 1961). When people attempting to bring about change in organizations meet with resistance, they frequently continue to promote or sell the change itself believing that it is resisted because people do not understand it. In fact, the change may be understood very well and merit may be seen in it, but is resisted because of the social consequences of the change. This research finding contains some particularly intriguing implications for implementing career ladders, in that differential salaries and recognition may create new forms of status for teachers, alter existing and long-standing professional and personal relationships, and threaten what have been stabilizing cultural forces.

Powell and Posner (1980) expressed two cautions related to analyzing and overcoming resistance to change. They note that the literature on change gives major attention to methods for dealing with negative responses to change and overcoming of employees' natural resistance to it. While resistance is frequently present, they point out that the capability of employees to actively desire and feel a readiness for change is seldom considered. Secondly, they caution against an **anticipation** of resistance to change that may in fact lead to the **development** of resistance that might not otherwise have occurred. Anticipating resistance can be a self-fulfilling prophecy.

These observations by Powell and Posner are particularly interesting in respect to career ladders. While there undoubtedly will be some resistance, many teachers are fully ready to embrace this new concept. It is foolhardy to assume that there will be no resistance, but it would be equally unwise to presume more resistance than actually exists.

GROUP NORMS AND THE CHANGE PROCESS

One of the most fascinating areas of research on change processes has to do with the nature and impact of group norms. This area of research is rich with implications for the establishment of career ladders, a change that will require rethinking if not an abandonment of some long established forms of behavior in schools. This section will discuss the meaning of group membership, group cultural norms, cultural adaptation, and the usefulness of group norms.

The Meaning of Group Membership

Membership in a group provides support and safety in a complex world. Groups teach us what to think, and how to behave in an acceptable manner. In a complex society, membership in a group is almost essential to human survival. Those who shun group membership are often referred to as **isolates, loners,** or still worse, **troublemakers.** For most people, group membership is essential.

Groups such as fraternal orders, neighborhood groups, and church groups each have certain values or needs that bind them as a group. Formal organizations can be viewed the same way. Values can be held so uniformly, for example, that an entire faculty in a school may be seen as a group with its unique norms and expectations. In other cases, there may be several subgroups within a school, each with its own unwritten rules of behavior and values that may conflict with those of other groups in the organization.

To be a member of a group exacts a price. To be a "good" group member, one must adopt the values and beliefs of the group as one's own, although there are some degrees of freedom. The strongest members of the group are granted the greatest amount of flexibility and freedom; the weakest members of the group are those under the greatest obligation to conform. Groups exert pressures on their members, because the person who behaves in a different way from that approved by the group becomes a threat to group solidarity and achievement (Festinger, Schacter, & Back, 1950).

Group Cultural Norms

We can find in schools an example of Schein's (1984) definition of organizational culture. He said, "to make something 'cultural' is this 'taken for granted' quality, which makes the underlying assumptions virtually undiscussable" (p. 10). Culture is important; it serves the function of stabilizing both external and internal environments for an organization. It would not be beneficial to any organization if every generation of new members could introduce new perceptions, language, assumptions and behavior. New members do bring ideas and influence, but the culture of an organization is an important and necessary stabilizing force. The fact that it sometimes works against the introduction of a change does not diminish its importance.

The "strength" or "weakness" of a culture can be defined in terms of stability of group membership, length and intensity of shared experiences, and a group's history of success in coping with difficult problems (Schein, 1984). In schools with particular characteristics (stability, older faculty, successful battles with administration), the "strong" culture of that school may work against the establishment of career ladders. In contrast, if a school has had much turnover among faculty, has not faced difficult issues, and lacks stability, they may not have enough shared experience for the entire group to have a sharply defined culture. As a result, establishment of career ladders may be easier in such a situation. It should be noted, however, that there are commonly shared values and assumptions among all teachers, regardless of locale, stability, or length of service.

The more cohesive a group is, the more difficult it is to bring about change. In organizations that are long established, group norms are often firmly entrenched and provide formidable obstacles to change. Norms therefore become standards. Researchers have found that change is much easier to bring about in younger organizations in which members have been together for shorter periods of time, or in older organizations in which there has been a considerable turnover of personnel.

Even new members of an organization are instructed in what is expected behavior. If they accept the values of a dominant group they are granted "membership." If they do not, they may always be on the fringe of the group.

Older teachers, for example, communicate what is expected to new teachers (Willower & Jones, 1963). New teachers are often cautioned about being too innovative. Those who are too ambitious and cooperative, or not ambitious enough, are often informed of what is appropriate behavior. Migra (1976) found this process at work even during a student teaching experience and demonstrated a shift in the values of student teachers as a result of the influences of regular teachers and their group norms. To be a teacher, the student teachers learned, was to adhere to certain kinds of established values. The culture of the school altered values they had developed during their teacher education program. This phenomenon is not unique to schools and is found across all organizations.

Established groups create their own particular "culture." Schein (1985) pointed out that culture solves problems for groups or organizations by influencing the ways in which group members perceive, think and feel about their environment and give meaning to it. These commonly shared assumptions reduce the anxiety that would result from not knowing how to categorize and respond to one's environment. Schein stated that "culture gives a group its character, and that character serves for the group the function that character and defense mechanisms serve for the individual . . . once an organization has evolved a mature culture because it has had a long and rich history, that culture creates the patterns of perception, thought, and feeling of every new generation in the organization" (p. 313). Such shared assumptions characterize the culture of schools, yet the career ladders program requires changing beliefs that are so deeply rooted throughout generations of teachers that they are taken for granted.

Group norms are neither necessarily good nor bad. They merely exist. They can work in support of a change effort or they can work against it, but the existence of groups and their value systems should not be ignored. Membership is so important that frequently a person is unable to express an opinion on an issue until he or she ascertains what position is held by the group. Individual opinion is often held captive to group opinion. Change efforts have frequently failed because they focused on changing individual behavior, rather than changing group behavior.

Cultural Adaptation

Sahlins (1981) and Smith (1982) cautioned that changes do not always go in the direction that the motivated person wants them to go. Change agents have miscalculated the efforts of their actions or were unaware of other forces acting simultaneously. This kind of misreading most often occurs when members of one cultural unit attempt to change the values, behavior or assumptions of another cultural unit. The result may be new behavior that neither group intends, resulting in a revision of cultural paradigms.

This analysis has direct application to career ladders, in which members of a cultural group outside the school (e.g., a governor and state legislature) are attempting to change the values and behavior of the teaching profession. It is a particularly good example of what Smith means by perspective and Sahlins describes as cultural miscalculation. Changes frequently have unanticipated consequences. If new behaviors are established as a response to career ladders, new interpretations of the culture of the school may someday be needed in order to understand what is going on.

Sahlins (1982) stated the case clearly for cultural adaptation to a changed environment, noting that what kind of cultures will survive in a given environment cannot be predicted but that cultures do not stand idly by waiting for their environment to act on them: "Genetic experiments may be blind, but experiments on human social systems are not. The members of a group themselves worry about their survival, analyze their environments, make the best prediction they can about what it will take to survive, and then attempt to create a culture that will have survival potential" (p. 310). The teaching profession is currently going through such culture adaptation, creating a new culture that will enable them to be safe and secure in a changed environment.

The Usefulness of Group Norms

While change efforts have an extremely difficult time if they run counter to the established norms of cohesive groups, group norms can also be used to support change. When a cohesive group commits itself to a particular change and decides it is desirable, new supporting group norms become an important ally in the change effort. Also, if the decision is made by the group, it is more likely that a change will diffuse quickly and become permanent. If a change effort succeeds in changing group norms, a new force field will be established and it will facilitate the change process. New norms will demand adherence to a new code of behavior if former group members wish to remain as group members.

Until a group commits itself to a change, however, individual members will resist any change that has the potential for placing them in conflict with the group. In seeking to bring about change in long established groups, key members of a group, those whose influence is greatest and who are granted special prerogatives, should be sought out and utilized. The power of such persons' group prestige can provide invaluable support for a change effort.

Frequently, change agents seek out individuals in an organization who are anxious to follow their lead and adopt a change. When these persons are without group membership and without prestige, however, the early adoption of a change may only decrease the likelihood that others in an organization will follow. As difficult as it may be to change the norms of a group, in the long run, this may be a more successful approach than to seek change through individual responses.

CHANGE AS A TRANSITION PROCESS

In this section, change is viewed as a transition process, the moving of an organization from where it is to where a change agent wishes it to be. Discussed in this section are the need for planning for the transition and the managing of the decision or change process.

It is important to recognize that organizations do not move quickly from an existing state of operation to the new state that is desired. One way of viewing a major change is as a **transition** (Beckhard & Harris, 1977). Between the time of initiating a change and the time that it is complete and fixed in an organization there is an intervening transition stage. It is this transition stage that is so important, because it determines not just what the future state of an organization will be, but its quality. Beckhard and Harris suggested that one of the first and most important steps in managing the transition is to develop and communicate a clear image of the future. Future state is what would ideally exist after the change. If people are uncertain about the future state of the organization, resistance and confusion may develop. When images of the future are not clear, rumors arise and people create their own expectations of the future; they may act on these rather than on the actual characteristics of the change effort. Nadler (1981) stated that "it is important to communicate information to those involved in the change, including what the future state will look like, how the transition will come about, why the change is being implemented, and how individuals will be affected by the change" (p. 202).

Planning for Transition

Planning for the transition state seems particularly important when establishing career ladders, and it is absolutely essential that this stage be managed well. It may well be that in preliminary attempts to establish career ladders, too much attention has been given to the future state and not enough to the transition state. It should also be anticipated that when group norms are strong, as they are in schools, that the transition state needs to be particularly well planned and of considerable duration. In addition to the transition state being the **process** implementing change, it enables people to "let go" of what has been and prepare themselves for the future.

Nadler (1981) further suggested the following organizational arrangements for managing change:

1. **A transition manager.** Someone should be designated as the manager of the organization for the transition state. This person may be a member of management, a chief executive, or someone else. Frequently it is difficult for one person to manage the current state, prepare to manage the future state, and simultaneously manage the transition. This transition manager should have the power and authority needed to make the transition happen and should be appropriately linked to the steady-state managers, particularly the future-state manager.

2. **Resources for the transition.** Major transitions involve potentially large risks for organizations. Therefore, they are worth doing well, and it is worth providing the needed resources to make them happen effectively. Resources such as personnel, money, training, consultation, and so on, need to be provided for the transition manager.

3. **Transition plan.** To manage an effective movement from one state to another, and to measure and control performance, a plan is needed with benchmarks, standards of performance, and similar features. Implicit in such a plan is a specification of the responsibilities of key individuals and groups.

4. **Transition management structures.** Frequently, it is difficult for a hierarchy to manage the process of changing itself. As a result, it may be necessary to develop other structures or use other devices outside the regular organizational structure during the transition-management period. Special task forces, pilot projects, experimental units, etc., need to be designed and employed for this period. (pp. 203–204)

The management of transition also requires a feedback mechanism to obtain information on the effectiveness of the transition, including data on areas which require additional attention or action. Feedback mechanisms are useful during the transition state because normal communication networks sometimes break down.

Managing the Change Process

In a review of the literature on change, Howes and Quinn (1978) identified 12 guidelines that managers of change can use. They organized these guidelines into two phases, as shown in Figure 3. The first guidelines have to do with creating an adequate orientation environment, and the second have to do with creating the support networks for the implementation of a change effort.

Figure 3. A framework for guiding the process of implementation.

A. *Phase 1: Set Up an Adequate Orientation Environment.*
  1. Set aside enough time for an adequate introduction to the change.
      a. Identify what will be changed.
      b. Plan workshops, meetings, and in-service seminars.
  2. Make the relative advantage of the change easily visible.
      a. Package it so that it is easily understood, easily referenced, and easily related to performance.
  3. Show organization members (users) that their efforts will be supported.
      a. Identify, obtain, and confirm availability of support services and resources.
  4. Show members it will be easy to institutionalize the change and that it will be relatively nonthreatening afterward.
      a. Clarify the expectations of each member during and after implementation.
  5. Show that immediate superiors accept and support the change.
  6. Clearly identify the roles and relationships of all who will be involved in the change process.

B. *Phase 2: Set Up Adequate Support Networks for the Implementation Effort.*
  1. Produce and make supportive services available.
  2. Set up formal training programs to develop members' roles.
      a. Provide in-service training, continuing workshops, seminars, etc.
  3. Encourage and reward the use of horizontal and vertical communication channels.
  4. Relax standard operating procedures in affected (changing) units.
  5. Integrate change agents, managers, and members.
      a. Provide frequent and individual contact.
  6. Make sure members feel adequately involved.
      a. Establish problem-solving meetings and shared decision-making norms.

Figure 3. A framework for guiding the process of implementation, from Howes and Quinn, "Implementing Change: From research to a prescriptive framework." *Group and Organization Studies.* March, 1978, 3(1) p. 73. By permission.

A basic assumption of the 12 guidelines provided by Howes and Quinn is that people's desire for change can be influenced if the proper environment or **marketing strategies** are employed. In phase two, the six steps are activities that need to be undertaken in order to facilitate and provide support for the change effort. As noted earlier, many potentially valuable change efforts are abandoned for lack of systematic strategy and support services.

People need to feel some degree of stability and security during change efforts. The unknown always creates a certain amount of anxiety, and a change that is imposed on individuals or organizations reduces their sense of autonomy and self-control. Nadler (1981) pointed out that most management systems are designed to run organizations that are already in place, rather than to manage transitions. Heads of organizations overlook the need for a transition stage when they become preoccupied with the future state and believe that all that is necessary is to design a newer organizational arrangement for the future. Change is not simply a matter of moving from one point to another.

All organizations have political systems composed of different individuals, groups, and coalitions. A natural feature of formal organizations is that the people all compete for power and influence. During a transition, the dynamics of political power may become even more intense since a transition allows for new coalitions and new power groups to emerge or gain additional influence. The greater the uncertainty created by change, the greater the likelihood that political activity will take place.

Research Conclusions

The literature on change is extensive and one encounters different points of view about essential elements and procedures. It should be emphasized again, however, that the most consistent finding in all research on change is the need for participation of those to be affected. It reduces resistance, creates a feeling of ownership, and motivates people to want to make the change work. If people participate in the change effort, they also have the opportunity to communicate about it, to ask questions, and to verify perceptions.

While there is no question that participation enhances the effectiveness of a change effort, it also has some costs. It involves relinquishing some control, taking an additional amount of time, and possibly creating conflict between competing groups.

A person's participation in a change effort should be determined by the change itself, the motivation for the change, the likelihood of its broad acceptance, political realities, and the amount of time available.

There is still much that is not understood about change, but there is an abundance of research and experience to provide guidance for those charged with bringing about major changes in schools. Information about why organizations work the way they do and why people respond as they do to proposed changes has been presented. The next section of this chapter will discuss some of the particular implications of research for implementation of career ladder programs.

CHANGE IMPLICATIONS FOR CAREER LADDER PROGRAMS

Even the brief review this chapter provides on research on change processes provides ample evidence of the need for the establishment of career ladders to proceed systematically, sensitively, and in recognition of what is known about the change process. In the research summarized above, a number of implications for career ladder programs become apparent. This section discusses a number of those implications by looking at career ladder characteristics with respect to what is known about the change process, utilizing force field analysis, selecting a change strategy, dealing with resistance to career ladders, and the climate for change.

Career ladder proposals pose some particularly interesting problems in the light of what is known about change. While interest in them is widespread and their growth in a short period of time has been remarkable, their introduction has also been met with resistance, misunderstanding and, in some cases, apathy. The career ladder proposals are also being promoted by forces external to the school itself. In some states the influence has been largely political or governmental, as in the state of Tennessee where Governor Lamar Alexander is the chief and most visible supporter.

This is not to suggest that teachers, local school administrators, and boards of education do not desire some change, but it should be recognized that the major impetus for the career ladder program has originated outside the traditional school mechanisms for change. On the other hand, this is not the first time that widespread societal pressure has attempted to change schools and their structure. The Sputnik era of the 1950s and the curriculum reform era of the 1960s are also examples of times when there was widespread public discontent with the schools and a desire to bring about rapid change.

Career Ladder Characteristics

Establishing career ladders requires significant changes in school systems. It is important, therefore, to recognize how certain aspects of career ladder plans relate to what is known about the change process.

The list that follows identifies certain characteristics of career ladders as they relate to principles of change discussed earlier in this chapter. These characteristics may pose some particular problems in implementation of career ladders.

1. Career ladders are being proposed by strong external forces.
2. They also are being opposed by strong internal and external forces.
3. They challenge existing group norms and standards.
4. They threaten existing age-status relationships.
5. They propose new requirements and levels of achievement.
6. They represent possible advantage to other teachers in the organization.
7. They represent a threat to existing practice.
8. They represent a reasonably complex change.
9. Their implementation would require considerable time and effort.
10. They represent a threat to existing cohesive groups.
11. They would change the existing system of recognition and reward.
12. They would enhance the success and status of some teachers.
13. They would create the fear of failure and loss of status for some teachers.
14. They are primarily directed at entrenched faculty in organizations in which there has been little turnover.
15. They challenge some long held values inherent in the egalitarian nature of the teaching profession.

While these characteristics of career ladders and change do not apply uniformly to individuals or school districts, they represent some general issues that are worth considering. As pointed out earlier in this chapter, each faculty member will first evaluate the career ladder in terms of what it means for him or her. Despite what has been said about the strength of group norms, perceptions about career ladders and their benefits for each person will vary. Teachers and groups of teachers will need to continue to be motivated to perform their normal tasks despite considerable upheaval in the organization during the time that career ladders are being implemented. They must face being told that familiar tasks and structures are no longer applicable.

The list above identified certain characteristics or consequences of career ladders that may pose some implementation problems. Many of these same characteristics may also become positive elements for some teachers: the drive for success, the desire to be recognized for excellence, the need for higher income or status, a liking for challenge, or a general conviction that career ladders will be good for education and for the profession.

However, those who plan to implement career ladder programs need to be primarily concerned about recognizing and overcoming resistance to change. It is important to listen to those who resist change, for often they communicate things that are important. To treat all resistance as uninformed obstinacy is to deny some important information about the organization and its members that would be beneficial in bringing about change.

Given the fact that the majority of career ladder programs have received strong impetus from outside the school itself, many teachers and administrators may feel that they have had too little say and that the change is being thrust upon them. In truth, the national ground swell for some form of merit pay or career ladder is substantial.

For most teachers, a career ladder conflicts directly with what they have subscribed to and defended throughout their professional careers. While some teachers and administrators have long favored some type of merit system, the traditional system of incremental salary adjustments without reference to performance has been generally accepted and defended.

For other teachers, such a dramatic change can be seen as coming too late in their careers. With only a few years left before retirement, some teachers may not want to adapt to such a major change, which may include visible evaluation and possible threats to status. If the career ladder plan is voluntary, this will pose less of a problem. But when plans call for mandatory participation, the change will become still more threatening. Risks may be seen as too great and the benefits too few.

The "graying" of the teaching profession and the issue of age and longevity may be major factors in the implementation of career ladders in some school districts. Younger employees may see the world as rewarding boldness and risk taking. As employees age, they often become more concerned with security, self, health, and satisfaction of personal needs. School leaders should expect that there will be some differences in perception and acceptance of career ladders as related to the average age of a group of faculty.

There is public clamor for changes in schools along with strong external and internal pressures for career ladders. At the same time, teachers must wrestle with the weight of tradition and values. Therefore, teachers are caught between strong opposing forces, some urging them to change and others urging them not to.

To presume that career ladders can be introduced easily and without controversy and stress is naive. Even relatively minor changes can generate stiff resistance, but a career ladder program is not a minor change. It truly is a significant change. A state or a local school district contemplating a career ladder should assume that there will be some resistance and misunderstanding. All change is to some degree threatening, but a career ladder challenges some beliefs that are almost sacred within the education profession.

What all of this suggests is that implementation of a career ladder must be done intelligently, sensitively, systematically, and in recognition of what is known about change processes and people's reaction to change.

Utilizing Force Field Analysis

While there are strong forces which encourage teachers to respond positively to a career ladder proposal, there are other strong forces which may cause them to resist. Force field analysis (see Figures 1 and 2) is a uniquely appropriate way to assess the driving and restraining forces concerning career ladders. Educators are aware of public pressure and are sensitive to the support that career ladders have received from people in high places. Yet, they also know that skepticism remains concerning their benefits. The profession itself remains rather divided, and the organized teaching profession at state and national levels has wavered between opposition to the concept and cautious support. Some of the concerns of the profession are addressed in the two chapters in this book on teacher association support.

In addition to strong internal and external forces that either support or oppose career ladders, individual teachers have their own concerns about how this change will affect them: Will I be successful? Will it cost me friendship with colleagues? Is it worth the effort? Is it too late in the game for me to become involved? At the same time, teachers have a desire to be viewed as professionals, be responsive, and be thought well of by superiors and peers. They also see that the potential financial and status awards may be significant.

The implementation of a career ladder program is likely to be more successful if the force fields are analyzed and if deliberate attention is given to increasing the strength of legitimate driving forces as well as reducing the strength of those forces that may cause teachers to resist.

Selection of a Change Strategy

In the light of the strength of external forces and the public clamor to do something to fix problems in education and the teaching profession, it might be tempting to resort to a power-coercive change strategy or, even worse, to believe that no change strategy at all was needed—that is, the call for a career ladder is so compelling that no change strategy need be devised. Generally, a normative-reeducative strategy would appear to be most plausible. Educators are trained to deal with evidence, to weigh facts, and to reach conclusions. They try to encourage such thought processes and thinking skills in students. Such a change process requires time, but it is this process that is more likely to gain support of educators rather than, for example, a power-coercive strategy or over-reliance on persuasion.

The normative-reeducative strategy would lead to new ways of thinking, to heightened aspirations, and, ultimately, to a change in the expectations and norms of groups. For a career ladder plan to be effective, it must have the support of teachers; they must believe that it is not only good for the school system but good for them. This reorientation would not take place through the exercise of power. Power-coercive strategies may bring compliance, but they do not generate commitment.

The need for teacher groups to be full participants in discussions concerning the enactment of career ladders and the identification of their particular characteristics is validated by decades of research findings on change. Participation is an essential component of the normative-reeducative process.

The nature and extent of participation will be affected by local and state conditions as well as by the strength and amount of agreement or disagreement among various political forces. To ignore the necessity of participation is to proceed with a change effort at great peril. Obviously, when strong internal and external forces all support a career ladder plan, implementation is easier and the need for participation less critical; but it is still needed. Regardless of whether educators support the concept of a career ladder, a plan will not become their own unless they have made some contribution to the development and feel some sense of ownership.

The work of Howes and Quinn (1978) concerning two phases of a change effort (see Figure 3) is particularly applicable to the introduction of a career ladder plan. The first phase involves setting up an adequate orientation environment. This is when the change is introduced, a reorientation of teachers takes place, issues are clarified, and support for a career ladder is gained. It is a process of educating, clarifying, and altering of group expectations. Phase two involves designing specific training programs, relaxing of existing procedures, arranging for problem solving sessions and workshops, and creating new relationships between teachers and others in a school system.

All change research points to the need for a systematic and sequential change process, moving from awareness or introduction of a change to the final point at which it is fully accepted and institutionalized.

It is particularly important to manage the transition period. This is a delicate time span when teachers leave what is familiar and comfortable and take the first steps into a new system of evaluation, recognition, and reward. They may need some time to mourn what has passed. It is characteristic of human beings that we mourn for the "good old days," even when the good old days are better in memory than they were in reality.

Dealing With Resistance to Career Ladders

The existence of a successful career ladder plan in another school district or another state is not sufficient evidence to guarantee its local adoption. If teachers and administrators can observe a career plan at work in a nearby system that is similar to their own, however, it may help convince them that it will work in their own system. Historically, programs in highly innovative school districts have seldom been replicated. The observation that "it is a fine idea but it won't work here" is often an effective way of resisting change. Such a reaction doesn't condemn the idea; it just rejects it as being inappropriate for a particular situation. As career ladders become adopted throughout the country, uncertainty about them will decrease. Their introduction will be easier as evidence accumulates to show that they not only are working but are also gaining support from teachers as well as the public.

Even desirable changes, however, are resisted for reasons that sometimes have nothing to do with the quality or nature of the change itself. This also can be anticipated with career ladders. Some teachers may conclude that the proposed plan is too complex and too demanding, and that qualifying for advancement up the steps of the career ladder may require more time and effort than the rewards and opportunities that are provided justify. Others may fear that attaining a special status will alienate them from colleagues.

Research noted earlier in this chapter pointed out that changes are often resisted because they create an imbalance in the social system. It should be anticipated that the system may in fact become unbalanced. When some teachers choose to pursue career ladder opportunities and some colleagues do not (or pursue them unsuccessfully), collegial relationships may be strained. Cohesive groups may find themselves divided. The fragile network of human communication that keeps schools operating effectively may be damaged. Some time may be needed before new relationships and informal communication networks are established.

A sensitive administrator or change agent will recognize the need for support for all educators during the change process. This includes supporting not only those who are able to respond to the new opportunities, but also those who for deeply held personal reasons find it difficult to do so.

Climate for Change

Lastly, change agents should not be surprised when the introduction of a career ladder plan receives mixed reviews. Even the most carefully developed plan, supported by a systematic strategy and enjoying extensive internal and external support, may run into all sorts of unexpected problems. It can be anticipated that there will almost always be some resistance to a change. In districts where relationships between school boards, administrators, and teacher organizations are already strained, a career ladder proposal may run into particular difficulty. Certainly, an assessment of existing conditions should be made to determine whether they support the introduction of a change as dramatic as a career ladder. To attempt to bring about (or even impose) a substantial change in the face of existing difficulties would be risky at best. Conditions must be right in order to support a major change. Part of the process of change is to establish a proper climate. Where there is wide interest in a career ladder plan, there exists an opportunity for states, school districts, administrators and teachers to collaborate on something truly important.

This new development, with all of its complexities and uncertainties, also addresses the normal desire of all educators to do well and be recognized for excellent performance. When developed sensitively and with regard to what is known about the change process, teachers, administrators, and board members may find a new spirit of cooperation in working on a program that responds to issues which have long been of concern to all. Change is threatening, but a desirable change successfully carried out is also richly satisfying.

RECOMMENDATIONS FOR IMPLEMENTING CAREER LADDERS

Following is a list of recommendations about implementing career ladders. These recommendations are derived from an extensive amount of research based information on the theory and process of change. From that reservoir of information a number of findings seem to have particular applicability to the implementation of career ladders. These appear below as a set of recommendations, but they are not a set of laws.

Persons responsible for implementing career ladders should find these recommendations useful, but they must be interpreted and applied in recognition of the particular situation, including the design of the change, the history of the organization, and the readiness to accept career ladders. A careful consideration and use of these recommendations, however, will greatly increase the likelihood that career ladders will be implemented successfully. Change seldom comes easily and, as noted earlier, career ladders signal a dramatic change in long established traditions in American education. Fortunately, many decades of research on change processes have provided us with valuable information and guidelines to make change processes more successful.

Career ladders are a bold new venture. It is important that their future not be threatened by failure to address adequately the process of implementation. There is much that we still do not know about the mysteries of change, but there is much that we do know. Those responsible for implementing career ladders should act on the basis of the best research based information available.

Recommendations

1. Involve teachers and teacher groups from the earliest stages of discussion.
2. Create linkage between the goals and objectives of the school and the career ladder program.
3. Recognize that the role of teachers in the change process will vary from one state and district to another, depending upon the origin of and source of power in support of a plan.
4. Design a plan which allows for movement through the various stages of change from awareness to adoption.
5. Provide an opportunity for people to see/study a program at work in a system similar to and nearby their own.
6. Establish a liaison and seek commitment from key leadership personnel in teacher groups.
7. Decide what the focus of the change strategy will be (i.e., on individuals or on structure).
8. Develop an appropriate, systematic, and comprehensive change strategy.
9. Make certain there is a clear commitment from administrators and the board of education and make the commitment visible.
10. Allow for sufficient time—a transition state—to create understanding, and to deal with problem-solving, acceptance, and implementation.
11. Provide a mechanism for obtaining feedback on the progress and acceptance of implementation.
12. Establish a formal link between external change agents or consultants and the school organization.
13. Understand the relationship and comparative strengths of forces supporting career ladders and forces opposing it.
14. Analyze and deal deliberately with potential resistance and barriers to change early in the progress.
15. Identify and use those forces that support the concept of career ladders.
16. The person responsible for implementation should have prestige and acceptance in the eyes of teachers.
17. Seek leadership and acceptance of career ladders from individuals with group membership and esteem.

18. Recognize the presence and influence of group norms and the ways in which group ladders may challenge them.

19. Listen both to the supporters and the resisters; they each have important information to communicate.

20. Provide for revision and reconsideration if experience should indicate that a change in plans would be desirable.

21. Build in new kinds of experiences (e.g., professional travel, leadership responsibilities) that interest participants.

22. Recognize that some teachers, for reasons of age or other personality factors, may find career ladders unattractive if not unacceptable.

23. Incorporate some existing procedures into the new program, thereby building on practices already familiar and accepted.

24. Cease continuing to "sell" the need for the career ladder when the time for implementation has arrived.

25. Emphasize individual achievement and growth via career ladders, rather than competition between individuals.

26. Employ normative-reeducative and persuasive change strategies where time permits; use facilitative strategies when a problem is recognized and there is general agreement that career ladders are desirable.

27. Power coercive change strategies may need to be used when time is short and/or commitment is low; but such a strategy is unlikely to increase commitment.

REFERENCES

Beckhard, R., & Harris, R. (1977). *Organizational transitions*. Reading, MA: Addison-Wesley.

Bennis, W. (1961). A typology of change processes. In W. Bennis, K. Benne, & R. Chin (Eds.), *The planning of change*. New York: Holt, Rinehart and Winston.

Bennis, W., Benne, K., & Chin, R. (Eds.). (1961). *The planning of change*. New York: Holt, Rinehart and Winston.

Chin, R. (1967). Basic strategies and procedures in effecting change. In E. L. Morphet and C. O. Ryan (Eds.), *Planning and effecting needed changes in education* (p. 40). Denver: Publishers Press.

Chin, R., & Benne, K. D. (1961). General strategies for effecting change in human systems. In W. Bennis, K. Benne, & R. Chin (Eds.), *The planning of change* (pp. 22–45). New York: Holt, Rinehart and Winston.

Cuban, L. (1982). Persistent instruction: The high school curriculum, 1900–1980. *Phi Delta Kappan, 64*, 113–118.

Festinger, L., Schacter, S., & Back, K. (1950). *Social pressures in information groups*. New York: Harper and Brothers.

Forsdale, L. (1964). 8mm motion pictures in education: Incipient innovation. In M. Miles

(Ed.), *Innovation in education* (pp. 203–230). New York: Teachers College Press, Columbia University.

Greiner, L. (1965). *Organizational change and development.* Doctoral dissertation, Harvard University.

Hollingshead, A. (1949). *Elmstown's youth.* New York: John Wiley.

Howes, N. J., & Quinn, R. (1978). Implementing change: From research to a prescriptive framework. *Group and Organization Studies, 3*(1), 71–84.

Lewin, K. (1961). Quasi-stationary social equilibrium and the problem of permanent change. In W. Bennis, K. Benne, & R. Chin (Eds.), *The planning of change* (pp. 235–236). New York: Holt, Rinehart and Winston.

Migra, E. (1976). *The transition from theory into practice: A microethnography of student teaching as a cultural experience.* Doctoral dissertation, Kent State University.

Morison, E. E. (1961). A case study of innovation. In W. Bennis, K. Benne, & R. Chin (Eds.), *The planning of change* (pp. 592–605). New York: Holt, Rinehart and Winston.

Mort, P. R., & Cornell, F. G. (1941). *American schools in transition.* New York: Bureau of Publications, Teachers College, Columbia University.

Nadler, D. (1981). Managing organizational change: An integrative perspective. *The Journal of Applied Behavioral Science, 17*(1), 191–211.

Powell, G. N., & Posner, B. Z. (1980). Managing change: Attitudes, targets, problems, and strategies. *Group and organization studies, 5*(3), 310–323.

Rogers, E. M. (1962). *Diffusion of innovations.* New York: Free Press.

Sahlins, M. (1981). *Historical metaphors and mythical realities.* Ann Arbor: University of Michigan Press.

Schein, E. (1984). Coming to a new awareness of organizational culture. *Sloan Management Review, 25*(2), 3–16.

Schein, E. (1985). *Organizational culture and leadership.* San Francisco: Jossey-Bass.

Smith, M. (1982). The process of sociocultural continuity. *Current anthropology, 23*(2), 127–142.

Starbuck, W. H. (1965). Organizational growth and development. In J. G. March (Ed.), *Handbook of organizations.* Chicago: Rand McNally.

Watson, G. (1967). Resistance to change. *Concepts for social change.* Washington, DC: Cooperative Project for Educational Development, National Training Laboratories, National Education Association.

Wayland, S. R. (1964). Structural features of American education as basic factors in innovation. In M. Miles (Ed.), *Innovation in education* (pp. 203–230). New York: Teachers College Press.

Willower, D. J., & Jones, R. G. (1963). When public control becomes an institutional theme. *Phi Delta Kappan, 45,* 107–109.

Willower, D. J., & Jones, R. G. (1963, December). Barriers to change in educational organizations. *Theory into practice, 2,* 257–263.

Zander, A. (1961). Resistance to change—its analysis and prevention. In W. Bennis, K. Benne, & R. Chin (Eds.), *The planning of change.* New York: Holt, Rinehart and Winston.

Chapter 4

DECIDING ON CAREER LADDER FEATURES

FENWICK W. ENGLISH

Just as a prospective car buyer knows only too well, the basic automobile is merely the beginning point for determining what extras will be included. Each extra or option has a cost. So too, there are options and features with teacher career ladders. Each has a cost and will result in major and minor differences in implementation and administration once adopted.

Career ladders should be solutions to problems. As such a career ladder should be considered to attract and retain the right people in the classroom. One definition of the "right" people is that they are **qualified** (they can do the job) and they are **certified** (they are officially licensed to do that job).

This chapter will deal with issues of market sensitivity and career ladders, types of differentiated employed on career ladders, the dilemma of school structure and how it reinforces teacher homogeneity, fast tracking and the use of quotas, career ladder policies and dealing with the implications of career ladders on the administrative/supervisory roles in school systems.

THE FIRST CRITICAL CAREER LADDER FEATURE: MARKET SENSITIVITY

Most school systems are not really serious that they want the "best" people. To be able to get the services of the best people, a system must have comparable best salaries and working conditions. If a school district desires the best teachers in the USA, they should have the best salary schedule in the USA, or they are not serious about getting the actual best.

The data indicate that at least in the area of math and science, that approximately 30% of these teachers in the nation are neither certified nor qualified (Toch, 1983). How can the teaching profession get the best people when it can't get the right ones? This is an unaddressed issue with teacher career ladders. Will career ladders really solve problems with supply and demand?

Organizations pay people for only two reasons: **to get** the right people (attract them) and **to keep** the right people (to retain them). There are no other reasons in a competitive marketplace that organizations pay people any more or less than necessary to satisfy these two critical labor requirements. And as with most other occupations and professions, organizations and society do not pay a dime more than they must to secure the level of services needed.

While it is argued that teacher career ladders will be able to attract and retain the necessary marketplace skills for the classrooms in the future (Cornett & Weeks, 1985), the facts that are before us belie the claim. For example, if a person with a B.A. in physics can earn $27,500 as a starting salary in an industrial position, and a teacher of physics can earn only $18,500, how will a career ladder enable school systems to compete any better than before in this kind of market (Cresap, McCormick, & Paget, 1984)?

If an $18,500 starting salary is very adequate for driver education teachers, do we want to make a career ladder in driver education just to show it can be done? Why?

In this situation the starting salary of $18,500 may be able to attract good driver education teachers. With physics teachers it is inadequate and noncompetitive. If a school system is unable to attract the right people (let alone the best ones) it has a **recruitment problem**. However, let us suppose that while the same system can attract driver education teachers, it can't keep them. Turnover occurs about the fifth to seventh year with some regularity (Schlechty, 1985). In this case the system has a **retention problem**. It means that the schools can get the right people but they can't keep them.

Since it can easily be shown that the same market forces in teaching do not affect the entire occupation in the same way (Akin, 1984), a career ladder that is not market sensitive by area or subject discipline will simply exaggerate the same market forces at work in whatever time frame it is implemented.

So perhaps the very first issue to be faced as a major feature of any career ladder plan is whether or not it is to be **market sensitive**. A market sensitive career ladder will not treat all curricular subject areas alike, nor will it offer the same financial/career based incentives. Indeed, for true market sensitivity to exist, there may only be career ladders in scarce fields and none in fields of adequate supply or oversupply.

A non-market sensitive career ladder would make these assumptions about the teaching cadre:

1. All fields of teaching are of equal worth and difficulty.
2. All fields of teaching will be subject to the **same** general responses and terms despite the fact that salaries are not adequate to attract a good pool of candidates in some teaching fields such as chemistry and physics.
3. To be competitive in fields of scarce supply, entry level salaries would have to be competitive there first, or the idea would not enable teaching to really attract competent people in these areas (and doom the ability of the career ladder to secure competent teachers in these areas).
4. Some teaching fields in which current salary conditions are adequate to attract a good supply of candidates (for example, physical education) would be **overpaid** in terms of what the dollar can purchase in the market.

A non-market sensitive career ladder holds on to the "myth of the unitary profession," a term coined by Lieberman (1960, p. 86) in his provocative book, **The Future of Public Education.**

It seems highly unlikely that starting salaries of teachers generally will be competitive with the most rigorous and demanding of the curricular subjects, notably the mathematical and physical sciences, in a marketplace moving to a high tech society at breakneck speed. That kind of quantum leap in salaries for all teachers is simply beyond the ability of state budget-makers and legislators to sell or fund.

If a career ladder plan is not market sensitive to the most demanding roles within the teaching cadre that must be filled, then a career ladder will not solve an entry problem for the teaching profession in these same areas. That means that after the implementation of a career ladder, there will still be a shortage of qualified and certified math and science teachers.

Now suppose the career ladder becomes competitive at the entry level for math and science teachers. However, current salary conditions are not capable of retaining these same teachers because they can earn more at quicker time intervals in the private sector. How will a career ladder compensate for these discrepancies in school systems?

As long as all teachers are considered interchangeable when compared to market demands, a career ladder will not be able to support enough math and science teachers to retain them in adequate numbers. Imagine a four-tiered career ladder in which over 50% of the Master Teachers were either in math or science. That is the way it might have to be in order to compensate for the loss of such persons in the future. Such a ratio would not be salable to the remainder of the staff pushing for entry to these upper level jobs.

If the chances for a physical education teacher, an art teacher, or an English teacher were too greatly diminished from access to becoming a Master Teacher in a career ladder, the concept would not be politically viable very long. Yet these are the market conditions facing the teaching profession. Without a career ladder being market sensitive, it is highly unlikely that much will change in the teacher labor force in the future.

A market sensitive career ladder would make these assumptions about the teaching cadre:

1. Teaching is really a field of diverse constituencies centered around curricular subjects.
2. Some teaching fields are more nearly representative of parallel jobs in the private sector than others.
3. Those areas in which teaching curricular expertise can be directly translated into corollary roles in the private sector are going to be of interest to teachers, particularly if salaries are better there.
4. Some teachers are going to be motivated by salaries, especially those who have knowledge of significantly higher salaries in jobs which are corollary and competitive to those they hold in schools.
5. Teachers will be motivated to remain in teaching if salaries in teaching are not substantially different than those they could earn elsewhere at the level in which they are currently performing (salary and other job conditions) or might be earning at some point in the future.
6. Teachers **will change jobs** because of significantly greater salaries and other job related benefits being available in the private sector.

Despite the fact that most teachers understand that curricular differentiation is the only basis for their current job differentiation in schools, their unions will negate such differences in order to treat all the same and believing that homogeneity of the ranks will lead to the highest average salaries for all (English, 1972).

CLASSROOM VS. NON-CLASSROOM DIFFERENTIATED CAREER LADDER

Ask yourself, after having implemented your concept of a career ladder, will it be possible to walk down the corridors of the school and peer into the classrooms and after a while **know** if one is looking at a Master Teacher, Senior Teacher, or the like? If the answer is "no" because there are none to be observed **in the classroom**, then the model of the career ladder is **nonfunctionally differentiated** as it pertains to actual classroom duties.

What this means is that the real role differentiation probably occurs with extra duties before or after the school day, or in the summer months. The non-classroom differentiated career ladder assumes that whatever constitutes classroom teaching as a core is the same for all teachers, no matter what their job title might say otherwise (English & Sharpes, 1972, pp. 74–133).

This would mean that if a Master Teacher was working next door to a Senior Teacher, one could not observe functional differences between what they did. Both would be expected to lecture, work with small groups, read stories, design bulletin boards, correct papers, and work with students one to one. Now if the differences were qualitative (i.e., the Master Teacher did these tasks **better** than the Senior Teacher), the career ladder would still be nonfunctionally different. It would, however, be qualitatively different with the **same functions**.

One of the major differences between career ladders today and differentiated staffing tried 20 years ago is that in the past trial with the idea, the concept of changing the structure of schools was felt to be necessary along with teaching roles (Rand & English, 1968). This led to innovations such as flexible scheduling which freed teaching talents from the lock step school organization. Today, organizational change does not appear to have the same priority. It is assumed that no major changes must occur within schools even if roles are going to be altered or teachers paid differently. An assumption of the uniformity of teaching roles within schools means that teachers will all be used the same whether or not they have equal or different abilities. The salary schedule shows the difference, not in what teachers really DO in classrooms.

A **non-classroom differentiated career ladder** means that the focus for the difference between the roles is not the differences between learners but on additional tasks for teachers. That is the essence of a bureaucratic form of career ladder, similar in many respects to the administrative career ladder (English, 1984–1985).

The medical career ladder is centered on the difference of tasks and their level of specialization (as between doctors and nurses) and between maladies and parts of the body (as a cancer specialist or a heart specialist). Functional differences between medical personnel are observable in what medical personnel do. A **functional career ladder** is much to be preferred over one that is not. The differences between teachers are not visible to them in the type of organizational structure in which they typically function. Teachers are often at a loss to explain salary differentials on any other criteria besides "favoritism" when they **cannot observe** the actual job differences between themselves.

However, while extra day job responsibilities are visible they do nothing to reward the extraordinarily competent classroom teacher who wants no such responsibilities. Changes **within** school structures facilitate this dilemma to: (a) permit teachers to observe one another at work, and (b) utilize teaching talent differently **within** the school. This brings us to the issue of school structure.

SCHOOL STRUCTURE AS A DEVICE
TO REINFORCE TEACHER HOMOGENEITY

The school structure of today which is manifested in self-contained classrooms, hallways and lockers reflects the idea that teachers are a homogeneous mass. Differences between them are not functional. Rather they are a reflection of the age of the student (9th or 10th grade) and curricular subject specialization (math, history, science) (Dreeben, 1973).

The idea of **teacher homogeneity** is strongly reinforced in the bricks and mortar of most school buildings, the salary schedules that pay teachers, and the methods of assigning teacher work loads. It has only been fairly recently that teacher union contracts called for a recognition of the differences in students as one way of calculating a correct teacher/pupil ratio (e.g., where learning disabled students are counted as something more than a full-time student, FTE).

Teacher career ladders that do not propose changes in school structure are limited in just what a career means on a career ladder. Without actual differentiation in what teachers do in classrooms, acquiring a new title means more of the same or more in summer months. A career ladder without real differentiation in duty is little more than warmed-over merit pay. In addition, other issues are raised. Why would it recognize and pay that talent differently and not **use it differently?**

Therefore one of the early critical decisions with career ladders will have to relate to whether or not changes in the school structure and scheduling are anticipated in order to use teacher talent differently once it has been identified.

This early dilemma was highlighted in the first career ladder effort in 1965 in Temple City, California (Dayton & Jones, 1973). The Temple City model was widely discussed and published in the late 1960's in a variety of professional journals and books (Caldwell, 1973; Stover, 1972). The Temple City model was a four-level teacher hierarchy where the major basis of differentiation was extra work tasks both within and outside of the school day and school year. The first two roles were Associate Teacher and Staff Teacher. The second two were Senior Teacher and Master Teacher (Rand, 1972).

Early in the implementation period Temple City teachers reported a loss of morale, especially sharp among teachers below Senior Teacher who had thought they were of Senior or Master Teacher caliber (English, 1970). Tennessee teachers have reported the same sense of loss in that State's career ladder plan (**Education Week**, 1985).

Without observable differences in the functions teachers really do which are directly linked to the rungs of a career ladder, schools will find it hard to maintain status differentials between teachers with salary differences over time. In fact, Temple City had to abolish the bottom two rungs on its famed four-tiered career ladder (Associate Teacher and Staff Teacher) because of the lack of functional differences between the two roles.

SCREENING PROCESSES AND SELECTION ISSUES

Career Ladders at work in Tennessee and elsewhere pay teachers more money after they have attained senior rank. The salary is based on some differentiation of work load and an extended work year in some cases. However, in order to qualify for the advanced status on the ladder, teachers have to demonstrate their superiority as teachers by taking an objective exam, being observed by trained specialists and attaining a high mark, and submitting a portfolio of materials in support of their application (Tennessee, 1984).

This procedure stands in contrast to the selection process for advancement on the administrative career ladder. Suppose that a district is screening a principal. Candidates are screened on paper for the characteristics desired and then interviewed. From the interview, a decision is made. Normally, it is an accepted fact that in the final four or five persons, almost any one of the candidates **could** do the job. What the screening process does is to find "the goodness of fit." This means that the district is looking for the best "match" between the talents and personality characteristics of the potential administrator and the job requirements.

The screening process for teachers on a career ladder appears to be aimed at a more discriminating level of analysis. Presumably, all teachers who could qualify to be Senior Teachers or Master Teachers via the selection process will or should be so recognized. However, there is a good bit of evidence that the actual numbers will be determined more by budgetary constraints than by the real pool of qualified people. What this means is that the number of advanced ranks for teachers is limited, not by some determination of the real number in existence, but by the capability of the budget to support some arbitrary number. Thus, procedures have to be manipulated to coincide with the budgetary constraints present in most plans.

Once again, consider promotion within the administrative career ladder. The number of positions is fixed by virtue of job responsibilities. A school needs only one principal. Several people within a school or a school district **may be** qualified to be a principal, but only one **can be** a principal. While there may be some hurt feelings from those not selected, the number is fixed by responsibility, not by some arbitrary budget projection. Here, the administrative career ladder demonstrates the advantage of functional differentiation between roles as opposed to arbitrary differences which are imposed by financial fiat.

FAST TRACKING AND THE USE OF QUOTAS

Fast tracking refers to the concept of being able to match salary advancement with growth on the job in a more immediate and sensitive relationship than the standard salary schedule permits. On the latter, it is not possible for most teachers to reach the top of a salary schedule based on experience and degrees sooner than 15 years. On the other hand, a fast tracked individual would theoretically be able to reach the maximum salary step in 5 to 10 years.

If career ladders are to provide incentives for teachers to grow more rapidly on the job than the standard salary schedule permits, then career ladders must be sensitive to teacher growth and result in more rapid movement than would otherwise be possible. Some career ladders have a minimum amount of time that is required to be served on one rung before advancement to the next is possible. That time may be as little as 18 months. However, requiring teachers to be at a rung for more than two years prior to being eligible for the next rung is more an indication of seniority or time served than sensitivity to growth and improved job/classroom performance.

If fast tracking is used as a device to promote merit pay, then it must be decided whether a teacher could "backtrack" as well as "fast track." If a teacher's performance fell off noticeably, is it going to be possible to go backward as well as forward? This raises another issue related to a career ladder. Is a Senior Teacher **always** a Senior Teacher? Does advancement mean never going back **for any reason?**

Movement of some teachers down the career ladder would open up opportunities for others to move up. If there is not movement on the career ladder **both** up and down, it will be hard to sustain the argument that the ladder serves as an incentive for teachers at the bottom of the ladder if there is not room for anyone else at the top. Advancement to the top may be limited because of a lack of positions available or a lack of funds to support more teachers at the upper levels.

Indeed, it appears in many career ladder plans that the only time it can be argued that the creation of senior teaching positions can really motivate staff is initially when all slots are open for competition. After placement, the number of open positions is the determinant factor in the capability of a career ladder to motivate teachers to consider advancement.

It is interesting to note that in the private sector where accounting firms and law firms practice fast tracking on career ladders, there is a kind of forced movement of people out at the senior levels in order to create room at the top for movement from the bottom by the fast trackers. For example, in the accounting firm in which the author was previously a partner, a mandatory retirement age of 55 as well as an expanding business base created a kind of permanent shuffle for a percentage of top level positions every year.

Now consider the case of many universities where an open or tacit personnel policy fixes the number of full professors with tenure at somewhere around 30% of the total faculty. What is the result? One is that younger non-tenured faculty are in a state of constant flux and movement. The options are not attractive for younger faculty: Either they face a sort of permanent role on the bottom rung of the academic career ladder or get out and move to another institution. Many school districts limit the number of years of teaching experience they will count for salary purposes for teachers transferring into the district. This results in reduced flexibility for public school teachers to move to another school district without a sacrifice in salary.

But what about the impact on morale? What happens in an institution in which there is a constant shuffling of lower-ended people searching for openings at the top for advancement? Does the imposition of such a system stimulate their growth? Does it motivate performance? An innovator would be hard pressed to make a case for the academic career ladder or any other kind in which movement at the top is not possible.

The use of quotas is another feature of a career ladder. If the career ladder is used to stimulate the growth of only a small percentage of superior teachers, limited by definition to 5% of the total teaching force, 95% of the teaching cadre will be locked out of the capability of the career ladder to stimulate their professional advancement, no matter how competent they become. The use of a quota simply makes it more obvious that the career ladder is not really a tool to stimulate teacher growth so much as it is a tool to divide the teaching cadre into quartiles and maintain a permanent inferior status for well over the majority of the staff.

From what is known about quotas on excellence which are imposed in career ladder models, the loss of morale of those left in the lower ranks affects their commitment prior to the installation of the career ladder plan. This is particularly true when all senior slots have been filled and any extra effort will not result in advancement. In this case, rewarding 5% of the teachers may mean lifting the ceiling for a small percentage and lowering the floor for the other 95% of the staff. The overall impact of the career ladder with quotas is to **reduce,** not expand, the productivity of the teacher workforce. Nobody thinks about it that way or wants it to happen, but it has happened and will continue to be a reality in quota driven career ladder models (English, 1970).

If one were to drop quotas, then one must be prepared to find out how many Master Teachers there really are out there prior to putting a career ladder into effect. It portends murky budgeting practices and makes finding the money somewhat of a mystery since the amount is pure conjecture until the process is completed. Asking teachers to go through an elaborate screening process and assuring them that a slot is really going to be available means that some sort of number (whether a quota or not) is used in financial planning. Therefore, most states seem to have used some sort of number which acts like a quota.

THE "UP OR OUT" APPROACH TO CREATING MOVEMENT ON THE CAREER LADDER

One option which may be chosen to create some teacher movement in the career ladder is to adopt an "up or out" policy. This means that a teacher is either working to become a Master Teacher (or whatever the top title is named) or is encouraged to leave the system. The school district is saying that it does not want any permanent teachers at other or lower levels. It wants only Master Teachers. Some accounting and law firms have adopted a similar stance. In these circumstances either one is aiming to become a partner or one should leave the firm.

The result is that there is a loss each year at all levels of people who become discouraged and are encouraged by others in the organization to quit. This in turn provides openings for others to move up. The "up or out" philosophy can work **unless** there is a shortage of people in the pipeline. What that means is that with a steady stream of recruits coming into a school system, it is a reasonable idea to make hard and fast rules about what is necessary to become a Master Teacher. However, with the dawn of the national teacher shortage, such a strategy seems impossible to adopt, especially with areas of very scarce supply like chemistry, physics, computers, bilingual education, and others (Darling-Hammond, 1984).

If a system does not opt for the "up or out" approach to career ladders they are almost forced by circumstances to adopt some form of protection for those who have been in the system a long time. The reality is that some teachers with long seniority will not be Senior Teachers. Few plans for career ladders simply remove teachers if they are not qualified to be Senior Teachers. Rather, some form of protection is adopted, most often in the guise of "grandfathering."

Grandfathering means that a teacher's salary and fringe benefits are preserved as the district moves from one model of staffing to another. Grandfathering is not only a politically necessary maneuver to adopt a different staffing model, it is also humanitarian. Nonetheless, the cost of grandfathering can be substantial over an extended time period. Grandfathered teachers are, in essence, locked in place but are usually given whatever across the board increases all other persons receive. In some cases they may be afforded the opportunity to proceed along the older salary schedule, and thus their salaries actually increase.

Another working assumption of many career ladder plans is the "two-thirds" "one-third" ratio. What this means is that at some future time point, two-thirds of the actual staff will be at the bottom two career ladder rungs, and one-third at the top. This means that the existing staff is redistributed via attrition, new hiring practices with salary ceilings, so that total costs are generally balanced for all teachers if there were no career ladder. Costs can then be controlled much more closely than is now the case. The ratio system is displayed in Figure 1.

Figure 1. Distribution of the teaching staff in a four-tiered career ladder after grandfathering expires.

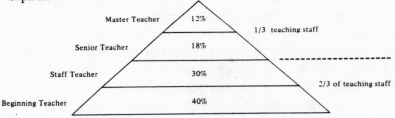

The division of the teaching cadre into quartiles (with a four-tiered model) is expensive (French, 1985). In the Tennessee Career Ladder Plan, to make it palatable to enough teachers over the objections of their own unions, all teachers had to receive an approximate 2% across the board increase. In addition, those who made it into the top two ranks would stand to gain more. Tennessee also allowed some flexibility with the Senior Teacher on the eleventh month extra work period. Some Senior Teachers were allowed to work only ten months who desired the eleventh month off.

THE REWARD VS. PROMOTE DICHOTOMY WITH CAREER LADDERS

Establishing a career ladder is intended to attract many non-teachers through incentives of a stronger nature than now exist in the profession. While many fail to recognize that strong collaborative nature of teaching as an incentive (Sergiovanni, 1985), the argument is not won on this basis.

Rather it will be argued that a career ladder will recognize some forms of a teacher's contribution and thereby constitute a reward. However, a career ladder can only promote or stimulate performance under the following conditions:

1. When a teacher's performance is motivated by external advancement promises or expectations (when much of the evidence indicates it is internal). (Lortie, 1975)
2. When there are positions available and open for the teacher to aspire to or the reasonable opportunity of being available in the immediate future.
3. When additional duties and/or a longer work year are desired as a reward along with the additional compensation.
4. When the remainder of the teaching cadre is supportive of the additional ranks or is at least neutral towards them and not antagonistic. (Murphy, 1985)

But the administrator or teacher planner should also realize that if incentives are going to be offered they must not only be aimed at improving individual performance and group performance but **at the same time** enable the school system to attract and retain the exact people such districts are not now able to attract and retain.

What we may have are two **separate** problems. The first is the perceived lack of career opportunities in teaching for all teachers. The second is the lack of the teaching profession to attract and retain specific talent in some curricular areas, with or without a career ladder. By mixing the two together with the same solution, exaggerated promises are made concerning what career ladders can or cannot do to improve the teaching profession.

Career ladders appear to work in other occupations for reasons which may not apply to teaching. For example, it is doubtful that large numbers of school districts or states will realistically adopt an "up or out" approach for teachers to become top rated on a career ladder. This is particularly true if the career ladder is based on extra responsibilities and duties rather than on a differentiated classroom division of labor than exists in most schools today.

So far career ladders do not show the capability of solving the forth-coming teacher shortage, nor will they resolve the historic shortcoming of the teaching profession to attract and retain qualified and certified personnel in every curriculum area for which schools are responsible. They appear to have been a political ploy to convince reluctant legisla-tors that more money in teacher salaries may provide something different. So career ladders will have been the strategy for upgrading teacher salaries one more time.

Whether our political system can stand a long-range solution to a complex and nagging problem is doubtful. The next wave of elected officials will be as impatient as the last. Without flexibility within the schools to use talent differently, and without any aspect of market sensitivity, the promise of career ladders to actually upgrade what is going on in the nation's classrooms is small indeed.

While many options and features are possible with the development of a career ladder plan, these two, in-school role flexibility and external market sensitivity, are the two most crucial to be considered.

CONSIDERATION OF THE IMPACT ON THE ADMINISTRATIVE CAREER LADDER

Almost immediately any thought of extending the role of the class-room teacher by creating super teaching roles runs amok with the admin-istrative career ladder. Are Master Teachers within a career ladder plan more powerful than principals? Are Master Teachers merely supervisors who teach or who may work an additional month?

The relationship of the career ladder to the administrative/supervisory roles has not been well thought-out in most of the efforts to date. Either the problem is ignored, or it is assumed not to have much impact (Eve & Peck, 1972).

Yet these administrative/supervisory roles evolved from the role of teacher historically and broke away from it. The current definition of classroom teacher is the cornerstone of all other roles in the organization. Like throwing a rock into a pond, a change in the role of teacher has a ripple effect on all others. The closer roles to that of the teacher will receive the more profound impact.

For example, if Master Teachers are to serve as mentor classroom teachers, what are principals supposed to do that is different? Are principals still required in the same capacity as before? That people in these older roles view the new roles with less than enthusiasm can be expected. These new teacher roles often do not have the same allegiances to the administrative agenda of organizational control. Master Teachers may be viewed as super teachers, with exceptional skills as teachers leading other teachers. They may not have the same responsibility for the overall running of a school building, or for construction of the curriculum, or for continuity across buildings or between programs.

A career ladder for teachers portends a severe disruption of administrative and supervisory functions as they have been traditionally defined in most school systems. Therefore, one of the early decisions for those considering establishing career ladders will have to deal with what should be done with the older administrative/supervisory career ladder already in existence. If one is allowed to replace the other, we have merely substituted one administrative/supervisory ladder with another with different titles. If the two coexist side by side, what functions overlap and are duplicated and what functions are left undone? (See the chapter on roles of teachers and administrators.)

A thorough rethinking of the organizational structure will most likely have to be considered, especially as it pertains to the work year and to salary. If teachers in a career ladder are not to be administrators but teachers are, will the functions teachers perform be rewarded in the same manner as those in the administrative hierarchy? For instance, is a Senior Teacher on the third step of a career ladder the salaried equivalent of a school principal?

If the answer is "no" to this question, how can a career ladder exist if it does not compete for talent that would otherwise go to the administrative career ladder? If extended teacher roles in a career ladder are always below the salary that administrators and supervisors are paid, then the administrative career ladder will still dominate as the most important one in terms of power, prestige, and money.

If, on the other hand, teachers are paid similar amounts as to those in the administrative career ladder, how much more will this add to the overall costs of the teaching career ladder? Will the administrators and supervisors demand higher wages in order to maintain the dominance of their power and prestige in the school system or state?

In models implemented thus far, these questions have not been adequately considered. In some cases, administrators and supervisors are offered a chance to become Master Principals or Master Supervisors through merit pay or management by objectives with no actual change in role or job responsibilities (Gentry, Pellicer, & Stevenson, 1985, pp. 19–20). This approach simply ignores the question of differentiating between administrative and supervisory functions and teaching functions.

From the Temple City experiment in the sixties to the Tennessee plan of the eighties, career ladders have tried to elevate the role of the classroom teacher within the concept of a teacher's hierarchy. To date, the results have been disappointing. Charters (1973, p. 40) found no evidence the administrative career ladder or authority had been altered. Garms and Guttenberg (1970) also found scant evidence that any real change had occurred even in models like Temple City that tried hard to change the traditional role of the school administrator.

Too many of the implementors of the eighties display a shocking naivete about the rigidities of organizational structure in stifling the intended salutary effects of a career ladder in schools built on the standardization of teaching (English, Clark, French, Rauth, & Schlechty, 1985, pp. 8–9).

Too many of the advocates of career ladders are ignorant of what was tried and learned in the sixties and seventies with differentiated staffing (English, 1984–1985). In fact a pamphlet written by the Association of Teacher Educators published in 1985 cites not one reference prior to 1979. It is as though an entire body of literature had been lost in the archives and was instead developed in toto exclusively in the eighties (ATE, 1985).

The fact that the career ladder's historical precedent was the early Lancastrian School introduced in the U.S. in the early 1800's (Meyer, 1965) is all but ignored by modern proponents. The fact that the early pilot role for Master Teacher in Temple City was a pronounced failure has likewise been ignored and all the reasons for it (English, 1984–1985).

It seems most likely that we shall learn on a grander and more costly scale the same lessons as were learned a lot more cheaply 20 years ago. The archives and libraries are full of testimony and data about differentiated staffing. Very few of the reformers and innovators appear to have the least inclination to do their homework. When Temple City finally gave up its career ladder that was one thing. When Tennessee faces the same dilemma, that will be quite another. The parallels are already disturbingly similar (Olson, 1986, pp. 1–24).

RECOMMENDATIONS CONCERNING CAREER LADDER FEATURES

The following recommendations are made from the perspective of someone who has worked with career ladders in California, Arizona and Florida under three varying approaches and ideas of what a career ladder should do.

1. Market Sensitivity
   A. Before market sensitivity can become a reality, all teacher salaries must be substantially raised, otherwise the "reach" for the necessary salary scales for scarce positions is too large to afford. Actual market sensitivity becomes uneconomical and not feasible politically.
   B. Career ladders should be market sensitive or they will not solve the problem of attraction to the profession.
   C. The market sensitivity of career ladders should be comparable to what people with certain skills and knowledges can command in areas where the school district must compete for human talent. If the district must compete statewide, the salary must be competitive statewide. If only local alternatives are available for the same human talent the district requires, then the career ladder must be only locally market sensitive.
   D. Market sensitivity must be an element in the upper levels of a career ladder in order to retain human talent that could go elsewhere.
   E. Market sensitivity does not have to be a universal element for all positions in a career ladder, only those for which the district is in short supply. To do otherwise would be to overpay (on market conditions) some areas needlessly.
2. Type of Differentiation Employed on a Career Ladder
   A. Whatever type of differentiation is employed to separate teaching roles in a career ladder should be observable to everyone.
   B. Part of the differentiation should pertain to actual classroom

teaching responsibilities and expertise. This should also be observable.

   C. Functional differentiation should not remove teachers from classrooms, thus relocating teaching talent away from students.

3. Altering School Structure in a Career Ladder

   A. Unless school structure is altered, actual role differentiation among and between teachers is quite limited during the school day.

   B. Part of altering school structure to accommodate varying levels of expertise and responsibilities must be to change and improve the decision making channels of schools which now are the exclusive domain of administrators.

4. Screening Processes with Career Ladders

   A. Screening processes may combine elements of meritorious performance in the classroom prior to advancement being possible on the career ladder. Certain elements will necessarily be subjectively assessed.

   B. Once on a position with a career ladder, provisions should be made for moving down as well as up or staying on the same rung. The position should be continually "earned" in this respect. This is the only way a position on the ladder can provide continual incentive to perform. Otherwise, one year's performance guarantees a person a position for life. At this point, the career ladder is nonperformance based.

5. Fast Tracking and the Use of Quotas

   A. Fast tracking ought to be possible within a career ladder in order to provide the best use of incentives for advancement as teachers perform.

   B. No more than two years should be required to stay on any one rung of a career ladder before being considered for advancement.

   C. Fast tracking should pertain to initial placement in order for the career ladder to be market sensitive to attract teachers.

   D. Quotas should only be used in budgetary planning and be based on optimistic estimates. The availability for advancement should be open for all teachers.

6. Creating Movement on the Career Ladder

   A. Unless movement is possible within the career ladder, the only time it may appeal to teachers is for initial placement. If all slots are filled after that, there can be no motivation for growth/advancement unless there is movement.

B. Movement should be created on a career ladder by fast tracking and backtracking.

C. Great caution should be used in accepting the "up or out" dictum for a career ladder, especially if the overall ladder is not market sensitive and there is a general teacher shortage. It is probably not possible for every teacher to be a "Master Teacher."

D. Flexibility in work months and work day should be part of a career ladder.

7. Reward vs. Promote with Career Ladders

A. Career ladders should be designed to retain the incentives that already exist in teaching for teachers.

B. Both features of a career ladder must be anticipated, i.e., its initial capability to attract teaching talent and its ability to retain that same talent.

C. Unless career ladders are competitive in the marketplace at the college level, they will solve only retention problems now facing the profession.

8. Administrative Issues Concerning Career Ladders

A. One need not feel compelled to design a career ladder for administrators since there already is one in existence.

B. Any move towards establishing "Master Principals" as the case for "Master Teachers" without substantial role modification is merely merit pay or a form of MBO (management by objectives). These can be implemented **without** career ladders.

C. A career ladder will impact the existing administrative/supervisory structure by creating "dual" positions of authority in schools. New relationships will have to be anticipated and planned, rather than allowed to occur and become disruptive.

D. Actual career ladder positions must be competitive salary-wise with comparable administrative positions or the teacher career ladder is **NOT** a viable alternative for teachers to remain teachers and be advanced. Some position with the teacher career ladder should be comparable to the principalship. The top position should be within reach of the superintendency. My thought is at least within 10% of the superintendent's salary.

E. If career ladders don't solve teacher shortage problems (attraction) and the loss of talent from teaching (retention) they aren't worth the administrative time to put them in or keep them.

REFERENCES

Akin, J. (1984). *Teacher supply/demand 1984.* Manhattan, KS: Association for School, College and University Staffing.

Association of Teacher Educators. (1985). *Developing career ladders in teaching.* Reston, VA, 25 pp.

Caldwell, B. G. (1973). *Differentiated staffing: The key to effective school organization.* New York: Center for Applied Research in Education, 274 pp.

Charters, W. W., Jr. (1973). *Measuring the implementation of differentiated staffing.* OR: Center for the Advanced Study of Educational Administration.

Cornett, L., & Weeks, K. (1985, July). Career ladder plans: Trends and emerging issues. *Career Ladder Clearinghouse.* Atlanta, GA: Southern Regional Education Board.

Cresap, McCormick, & Paget. (1984). *Teacher incentives.* Reston, VA: National Association of Elementary School Principals, pp. 19–20.

Darling-Hammond, L. (1984). *Beyond the commission reports: The coming crisis in teaching.* Santa Monica: The Rand Corporation.

Dayton, C., & Jones, B. G. (1973). *Brief overview of the differentiated staffing project in the Temple City Unified School District, 1966–73.* Unpublished report, American Institutes for Research, Palo Alto, CA, 20 pp.

Dreeben, R. (1973). The school as a workplace. In R. W. Travers (Ed.), *Second handbook of research on teaching* (pp. 450–473). Chicago: Rand McNally and Company.

English, F. W. (1970). Field testing a differentiated teaching staff. In J. L. Olivero & E. G. Buffie (Eds.), *Educational manpower.* Bloomington, IN: Indiana University Press.

English, F. W. (1972). AFT/NEA reaction to staff differentiation. *The Educational Forum, 36*(2), 193–197.

English, F. W., & Sharpes, D. (1972). *Strategies for differentiated staffing.* Berkeley: McCutchan Publishing Corporation.

English, F. W. (1983–1984). Merit pay: Reflections on education's lemon tree. *Educational Leadership, 41*(4), 72–79.

English, F. W. (1984–1985). We need the ghostbusters! A response to Jerome Freiberg. *Educational Leadership, 42*(4), 22–25.

English, F. W., Clark, D., French, R., Rauth, M., & Schlechty, P. (1985). *Incentives for excellence in America's schools.* Alexandria, VA: Association for Supervision and Curriculum Development.

Eve, A. W., & Peck, R. H. (1972). Differentiated administrative staffing. In J. A. Cooper (Ed.), *Differentiated staffing* (pp. 91–102). Philadelphia: W. B. Saunders.

French, R. (1985). Dispelling the myths about Tennessee's career ladder program. *Educational Leadership, 42*(4), 9–15.

Garms, W. I., & Guttenberg, R. (1970). *The sources and nature of resistance to incentive systems in education.* New York: Teachers College.

Gentry, J., Pellicer, L., & Stevenson, D. (1985, September). How to set up an incentive system for administrators. *AASA School Administrator,* pp. 19–20.

Lieberman, M. (1960). *The future of public education.* Chicago: University of Chicago Press.

Lortie, D. C. (1975). *School teacher.* Chicago: University of Chicago Press.

Meyer, A. E. (1965). *An educational history of the western world.* New York: McGraw-Hill.

Murphy, M. (1985). *Teacher career ladders in Britain: A study of their structure and impact.* Salt Lake City, UT: University Council for Educational Administration.

Olson, L. (1986). Pioneering state teacher-incentive plans in Florida, Tennessee, still under attack. *Education Week,* 5(18), 1–24.

Rand, M. J., & English, F. W. (1968). Towards a differentiated teaching staff. *Phi Delta Kappan, 49,* 264–268.

Rand, M. J. (1972). A case for differentiated staffing. In J. A. Cooper (Ed.), *Differentiated staffing* (pp. 45–53). Philadelphia: W. B. Saunders.

Schlechty, P. (1985). Remarks to author and reinforced in an undated handout xeroxed which was entitled, Charlotte-Mecklenburg schools career development program.

Stover, M. (1972). Temple City differentiated staffing project. In A. J. Fiorino (Ed.), *Differentiated staffing: A flexible instructional organization* (pp. 41–71). New York: Harper and Row.

Sergiovanni, T. (1985). Teacher career ladders: Myths and realities in implementation. *Teacher Education and Practice, 21*(1), 5–13.

Tennessee Department of Education. (1984). *Teacher orientation manual career ladder plan.* Nashville, TN.

Tennessee teachers critical of career ladder, poll reveals. (1985, September 4). *Education Week,* p. 2.

Toch, T. (1983, July 27). 200,000 reasons for concern: A profile of those who teach science. *Education Week,* p. 10.

Chapter 5

ROLES OF TEACHERS AND ADMINISTRATORS

Judith C. Christensen

INTRODUCTION

The education system in the United States has a problem keeping good teachers in the classroom. In the last two or three years the problem has been brought to the attention of the public through reports issued by many sources from the White House to local school boards. The attention has caused great activity in political and educational arenas.

The problem is not new but has been complicated by societal changes and demographic changes across the United States. New career options for women, relatively lower pay for teaching careers and new expectations for schools to provide for the wide variety of children's needs are some of the issues that contribute to the problem of attracting and retaining the best people to teach in our schools.

Another problem is the relative "flatness" of a career in teaching. Lortie (1975) refers to a teacher's career as being unstaged. He stresses that "staged careers produce cycles of effort, attainment and renewed ambition" (p. 85).

John Gardner, former Secretary of Health, Education and Welfare under President Lyndon B. Johnson, said, "The teaching profession is one of the few in which the time of a superb professional with 20 or 30 years of experience is used in just about the same way as the day he first walked into the classroom" (National School Public Relations Association, 1970).

This lack of differentiation between teachers has contributed to many teachers leaving the profession. Their needs for more salary, varied job responsibilities, status and/or recognition were not satisfied in education and they sought other professions where they were rewarded in ways not available to teachers.

In an effort to make teaching a more desirable career, the career ladder model has been explored by many states. The notion of a career ladder⁻ for teachers is not new. While the basic model has been in existence for at least 20 years, reasons for implementing career ladders have changed from a need for instructional change and innovation to a means for providing career options and increased accountability and pay for teachers. The term career ladder initially was used in the literature to describe team teaching models which provided career alternatives for teachers. Later the term was used to describe differentiated staffing.

This chapter will examine the roles and responsibilities of teachers and administrators by examining an historical review of the origins of career ladders in team teaching and differentiated staffing models. Then, a composite of current career ladder models will be explored followed by a discussion of how administrative and supervisory roles will be changed when career ladders for teachers are established. The chapter will end with a set of recommendations for roles of teachers and administrators.

TEAM TEACHING MODELS

Teachers have been working together formally and informally for years. John Goodlad, according to York (1971), pinpointed the beginning of the formal team teaching design:

> ...at a meeting held in 1955 in the office of the Ford Foundation for the purpose of discussing teacher education in a new frame of reference. Goodlad stated that: we were concerned with finding ways to differentiate rewards for teaching so that outstanding teachers would not find it financially necessary to moonlight or to enter administration during mid-career; to assure self renewal for the overburdened teachers in the elementary schools' self-contained classroom; and to induct neophytes meaningfully into teaching. (p. 13)

Shaplin (1964, p. 2) traced the growth of team teaching in the United States from 1954 to 1964 when over 1500 teachers were involved in the model. Many pilot projects involved universities and school districts. Some of the widely publicized programs involved Harvard University and the Lexington, Massachusetts schools; the University of Wisconsin and the Wisconsin Improvement program with numerous school systems across the state; and in California, the Claremont Graduate School and several surrounding school districts.

As with any innovation, the variety of team teaching plans in operation was diverse. Shaplin (1964) gave the following definition of team teaching:

> Team teaching is a type of instructional organization, involving teaching personnel and the students assigned to them, in which two or more teachers are given responsibility, working together, for all or a significant part of the instruction of the same group of students. (p. 15)

When team teaching models are operationalized, the roles and responsibilities of personnel throughout the school are changed. A hierarchical team organization provides a career pattern in teaching and can be relatively simple, such as having an experienced teacher serve as a leader for several beginning teachers, or it can be more complex involving levels of teacher expertise and nonprofessional personnel.

The organizational structure of the Lexington, Massachusetts Team Teaching program displayed in Figure 1 is an example of a fairly complex hierarchical organization (Bair & Woodward, 1964, p. 68).

Figure 1. Organizational Structure for the Lexington (MA) Team Teaching Program

A TEACHING TEAM

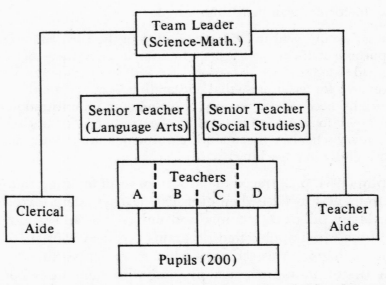

The following section suggests a variety of activities for personnel within a hierarchical model.

Roles and Background of Team Teaching Personnel

The literature on team teaching is replete with suggested duties for people on a team (Chamberlin, 1969; Shaplin & Olds, 1964; York, 1971). Bair and Woodward (1964) provided a comprehensive discussion of roles of school personnel involved in a team teaching program. Responsibilities, criteria for selection, and monetary compensation are discussed in each of the following sections for (a) team leader, (b) senior teacher, (c) teacher, and (d) principal.

Team Leader

Responsibilities:

1. Teaches approximately two-thirds of the time
2. Serves as a member of the administrative cabinet and the instructional cabinet for the school and helps interpret cabinet decisions and plans to the team
3. Serves as chair for most meetings of the team, in which he/she places special emphasis on the planning, teaching, and evaluating cycle
4. Initiates and coordinates daily and longer-interval schedules for teachers and pupils within the team
5. Serves as a coordinator and supervisory agent in his/her field of specialization as materials of instruction, lesson plans, and/or units are developed or taught; develops and strengthens this special competence
6. Supervises instructional practices of the team members including lesson plans, teaching techniques, evaluation techniques, and reporting practices
7. Helps plan and evaluate grouping practices and individual progress to improve learning rate of pupils
8. Studies, evaluates, and recommends to the principal what the team needs and reports progress in terms of personnel, curriculum, materials of instruction, and pupil supplies
9. Plans and coordinates parent meetings to interpret the work of the school, team, and pupils
10. Has all the duties and responsibilities of senior teachers
11. Coordinates curriculum revision with the team
12. Plans and helps with orientation procedures for the team

Position Criteria:

1. Education beyond a master's degree with emphasis on curriculum, instruction, supervision, human relationships and educational sociology
2. Experience as a teacher and a senior teacher in a team teaching situation
3. Ability to coordinate, administer, and supervise activities of a team

Compensation:

1. $1,000 above teacher scale (Bair & Woodward, 1964, pp. 69–72)

Senior Teacher

Responsibilities:

1. Has all the duties, functions, and responsibilities of a teacher
2. Serves as a member of the instructional cabinet for the school and helps interpret its decisions and plans to the team
3. Serves as a coordinator and supervisory agent in his/her field of specialization as materials of instruction, lesson plans, and units are developed or taught; develops and strengthens this special competence
4. Plans and conducts team meetings concerned with his/her area of specialization
5. Coordinates daily and longer-interval schedules relating to his/her field of specialization for the team
6. Helps develop and evaluate grouping practices and individual progress of youngsters within his/her special field
7. Studies, evaluates, and recommends to the team leader and to the instructional cabinet ways of improving his team's operation
8. Works with the team leader in planning, supervising, and coordinating the team's activities as time and ability permit

Position Criteria:

1. Experience as a teacher on team
2. Educational training beyond a master's degree in curriculum, instruction, supervision, human relations, educational sociology, and/or his/her content field

3. Skill in identifying student needs, organizing groups, identifying better teaching techniques
4. Skill in supervising and training less experienced team members

Compensation:

1. $500 above the salary scale for a teacher with this level of education and experience (Bair & Woodward, 1964, pp. 72–73)

Teacher

Responsibilities:

1. Teaches most subjects to pupils with differing needs in groups of varying sizes in many types and sizes of rooms
2. Serves as a member of the teaching team
3. Shares in cooperative planning and subsequent evaluation of units and lessons
4. Studies unique needs of pupils in the team to aid in planning better learning opportunities for each
5. Keeps parents informed through conferences and written comments as well as through participation in meetings with parents
6. Cooperates with team leaders, senior teachers, and other teachers in the planning, teaching, and evaluating cycle

Position Criteria:

1. Willingness to cooperate fully on a continuous basis with other team members
2. Willingness to plan and evaluate jointly the major objectives to be taught
3. Willingness to let their work be judged by fellow teachers

Compensation:

1. Teacher's salary scale appropriate to experience and background (Bair & Woodward, 1964, p. 74)

The position descriptions for teachers listed here are typical of many lists found in the literature. Changes in the typical teaching role affect the role of the principal and many central office staff positions. The following description shows how the responsibilities of the school principal could change. There will be further discussion of the school principal and central office positions in the section on differentiated staffing.

Principal

Responsibilities:

1. Manages and coordinates the school
2. Serves as an active member of the superintendent's cabinet
3. Serves as chair of the school's administrative cabinet and coordinates the efforts of the team leaders in developing administrative policies and making administrative decisions
4. Serves as chair of the school's instructional cabinet and coordinates the efforts of the team leaders and senior teachers in the development and implementation of the school's instructional program
5. Develops programs for the improvement of the supervisory techniques of the team leaders and senior teachers and instructs the teachers of teachers in the process of teaching and learning
6. Develops, in cooperation with the superintendent's office and his/her leadership personnel, an orientation program for professional and noncertified members of the staff, pupils, parents, and citizens
7. Works with parents to keep them informed and to seek their assistance in carrying out the aims of the school
8. Keeps the superintendent's office informed of the progress of the school
9. Shares ideas with the profession through speaking and writing
10. Informs the administrative officers of the needs of the school for supplies, equipment, space, and personnel to enable the staff to continuously work for improved instruction
11. Develops and administers annual budgets to provide for Item 10 above

Position Criteria:

1. Education beyond master's degree; perhaps a doctorate
2. Considerable experience as a teacher including being a team leader in a team teaching school
3. Training in educational administration, group dynamics, supervision, curriculum and educational sociology
4. Ability to work with teachers, team leaders, and university personnel in a leadership role
5. Initiate and create new techniques of operation in school

6. Must be flexible
7. Be able to evaluate programs (Bair & Woodward, 1964, pp. 67–68)

When a team teaching model is in place, administrative responsibilities will be redistributed throughout the school and at the district level as well. Teachers and principals assume decision-making power once reserved for the central office personnel. These changes are even more evident in the differentiated staffing models which will be examined in the following section.

DIFFERENTIATED STAFFING PLANS

Differentiated staffing models grew out of, or were a refinement of, the team teaching models of the 1960's. The following definition by Scobey and Fiorino (1973) captures the significant goals and unique components of a number of differentiated staffing models:

> Differentiated staffing is a planned operational model for staff utilization. It takes advantage of the differences in teaching specialties, experiences, talents and ambitions, compensating of them in differentiated levels of assigned instructional responsibilities, time and salary. (p. 6)

Dwight Allen (National School Public Relations Association, 1970) whose differentiated staffing plan was used as the basis of the Temple City, California, Model, gave the following as possible benefits of differentiated staffing for education:

1. When positions are identified delineating what needs to be done and are assigned on the basis of competence, there will be a basis of salary differentiation on which school boards, administrators, and teachers can agree.
2. Good teachers, who deserve as much money as administrators, will be able to afford a career in classroom teaching.
3. There will be a place for those teachers for whom no amount of money can make up for the lack of job satisfaction.
4. There will be a place for talented teachers who want only limited professional responsibility (e.g., the teaching housewife).
5. Teachers will be able to take postgraduate courses to make themselves more competent in their specific jobs instead of taking courses on an indiscriminate units-equal-dollars basis.
6. Longevity, with all its educationally crippling effects, would cease to be a criterion for promotion.

7. Inservice teacher training could be an internal program aimed at solving problems at hand rather than problems perceived by someone once or twice removed from the school's student population.
8. Evaluation could be based on real knowledge from intimate contact and cooperation between teaching professionals.
9. Many existing problems in negotiating salaries and existing differences between professional teachers and administrators should disappear in a staff wherein status derives from performance and competence.
10. Young talent would be encouraged to grow.
11. The school would regain some control over apportioning dollars now committed to perpetuating the median rise in salary costs brought about by tenure, longevity, and automatic promotion practices (pp. 4–5).

Allen also identified three conditions which are essential to a differentiated staffing structure:

1. A minimum of three differentiated staff teaching levels, each having a different salary range
2. A maximum salary at the top teaching category that is at least double the maximum at the lowest
3. Substantial direct teaching responsibility for all teachers at all salary levels, including those in the top brackets (p. 5–6)

These conditions led to considerable criticism in the 1970's, especially from leaders in teachers' organizations who felt the plans called for merit pay rather than pay based on differences in responsibility. Similar criticisms have been expressed about current career ladder plans.

The Temple City Differentiated Staffing Plan

Models of differentiated staffing varied greatly from one district to the next and even within districts. The Temple City, California plan was one of the earliest and most widely publicized and studied differentiated staffing models put into operation. The Temple City Differentiated Staffing Plan used during 1969–1971 is displayed in Figure 2 (Cooper, 1972, p. 51). Responsibilities and/or extended contract options were built into the model at each of the levels.

Figure 2. Temple City Differentiated Staffing Plan, 1969–1971

			Nontenure
		Nontenure	**MASTER TEACHER** Doctorate or equivalent
	Tenure	**SENIOR TEACHER** M.A. or equivalent	
Tenure	**STAFF TEACHER** B.A. and Calif. Credential		
ASSOCIATE TEACHER B.A. or Intern			
100% teaching responsibilities	100% teaching responsibilities	60% staff teaching responsibilities	40% staff teaching responsibilities
10 months $6,500-$9,000	10 months $7,500-$11,000	10-11 months $14,500-$17,500	12 months $15,646-$25,000

Teacher Roles in the Temple City Model

Boutwell (1972) described the duties of the teacher in the differentiated teaching model:

Associate Teacher

1. Beginning, least experienced teacher
2. In classroom 100% of time
3. Participates in inservice training and skill development
4. Works closely with other teachers to improve skills and suggests program improvements

Staff Teacher

1. Full-time classroom teacher
2. Capable of working with small, medium or large groups of students
3. Knowledgeable about trends, materials and practices within his/her field

4. Able to prepare materials, guides and implement these within the curriculum
5. Serves on committees, involvement in decisions about curriculum and instruction

Senior Teacher

1. Demonstrates superior teaching abilities and has capabilities needed for leadership
2. Teaches about 60% of time
3. Forty percent (40%) of time is devoted to leadership functions such as demonstration teaching, development of exemplary materials, coordi-nating paraprofessionals and student teachers, guiding implementation of innovations in curriculum and teaching, facilitating change
4. Helps select and evaluate faculty and paraprofessionals
5. Is aware of research in his/her content area and is able to translate these to others
6. Assists in identifying district-wide objectives and developing curriculum

Master Teacher

1. Demonstrates superior teaching ability
2. Combines teaching ability with research and leadership abilities
3. Responsible for training Senior Teachers
4. District-wide responsibilities in defined curricular areas
5. Knowledgeable about research trends and practices in these curricular areas
6. Able to relate research findings to others
7. Has research skills in experimental design and evaluation design
8. Uses his/her classroom to develop exemplary lessons for inservice program use (p. 21)

Administrative Roles in the Temple City Model

As more decision-making authority is distributed among teachers, the role of the principal becomes that of a "manager and orchestrator of the school plant and program." Boutwell (1972) outlined some general responsibilities of the principal as:

1. Coordinates school schedule and use of facilities
2. Deploys resources
3. Provides expertise in the areas of group dynamics, learning and human relations
4. Provides expertise in identifying problems and proposing solutions
5. Coordinates work of academic experts (senior and master teachers)
6. Teaches
7. Acts as a catalyst and a leader (p. 22)

The differentiated responsibilities listed above affected the administrative design in the district. The organizational structure of two school systems with and without differentiated staffing are displayed in Figure 3 (English, 1970, p. 197).

Figure 3. Organizational Structure of School Systems With and Without Differentiated Staffing

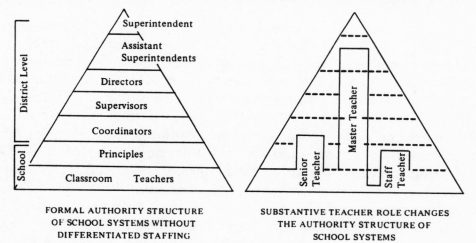

FORMAL AUTHORITY STRUCTURE
OF SCHOOL SYSTEMS WITHOUT
DIFFERENTIATED STAFFING

SUBSTANTIVE TEACHER ROLE CHANGES
THE AUTHORITY STRUCTURE OF
SCHOOL SYSTEMS

The pyramid on the left side of Figure 3 represents a district with a typical hierarchical organizational structure. The pyramid on the right side of the figure indicates responsibilities that might be assumed by various people in a differentiated teaching plan.

Outcomes of the Temple City Model

English (1970) outlined the following possible outcomes of the Temple City differentiated staffing model:

The effect of such differentiation is to elevate the teacher from a base of classroom teaching to a position of status and influence within the authority structure, while at the same time changing the structure itself. Some of the traditional roles of the organization are considerably reduced or eliminated. When role interrelationships are readjusted and redefined, organizational structure is changed. If the adjustment can capitalize upon the desire and competence of teachers for greater autonomy and influence in the organization, and advance the cause of professionalization, it will be accepted and adopted by the teaching profession as a whole. If teacher roles can remain as the foci of the differentiation and the instructional roles expanded vertically, the weight of the organization can become more responsive to the teacher and to the individual needs of the students. Greater utilization of the combination of human resources can be attained, thus creating a vehicle to apportion varying amounts of teacher expertise to the diversity of diagnosed student performances. A more flexible and sensitive staffing pattern is an integral component of the "unequal" school. (pp. 197–198)

District-level organizational structure also is influenced by a differentiated staffing system. Changes can occur both in the roles of the personnel and in the number of positions. As more decisions are made by teachers who assume roles as senior or master teachers, there is less need for a heavily staffed central office. Funds are redistributed to implement the differentiated staffing models, and the remaining, smaller, central office staff is responsible for coordinating and facilitating the decisions made by curriculum committees and leaders within the schools.

The Temple City differentiated staffing model described above is only one of many which were implemented during the 1970's. Other plans including those from the Mesa, Arizona, and the Cherry Creek, Colorado, school districts and Wisconsin Research and Development Center are described by Scobey and Fiorino (1973) and the National School Public Relations Association (1970).

As forerunners of the recent career ladder movement, it is not surprising to see so many commonalities between models for team teaching and differentiated staffing and models of current career ladder plans. The next section will examine roles of teachers and administrators in some of the career ladder plans of the 1980's.

CAREER LADDER MODELS

The name and basic design of career ladders have been known to educators for years as evidenced by an article in **American Education** entitled "Building a Career Ladder" (Connors, 1969). Politicians have helped rediscover the idea in an effort to stem the "rising tide of mediocrity" in American education. Tennessee's Governor Lamar Alexander announced a plan called the Better Schools Program in January 1983. The plan included a career ladder program which, according to English (1984–1985), is the Temple City differentiated staffing model. Alexander's bold move to mandate a career ladder focused renewed attention to the idea by people in legislatures, education departments and school districts.

The career ladder concept was seen as a way to (a) make teaching a more attractive profession, (b) provide alternative roles for teachers without forcing them to leave the classroom, (c) retain good teachers in the profession, (d) provide monetary incentives and (e) create levels of expertise toward which teachers can strive. The idea caught on fast. By January, 1985, 38 states were considering or had implemented some initiative involving career ladders or merit pay (Staff, 1985). A Career Ladder Clearinghouse was established by the Southern Governors' Association and the Southern Legislative Conference. This clearinghouse provides current information on plans and issues throughout the United States " . . . so that state legislatures and boards of education would have pertinent information prior to and during the 1985 legislative sessions when many career ladder discussions were pending" (Cornett & Weeks, 1985, p. 1).

The following sections will present two current career ladder models and a discussion of teachers' roles within each.

The Association of Teacher Educators Career Ladder Model

The Association of Teacher Educators (1985) presented a model of a career ladder after carefully reviewing existing models from across the United States. The model includes the steps of teacher, associate teacher, senior teacher and master teacher. A description of each step in the model and illustrations of teacher's roles at each step in the model follow.

Teachers

Teachers are responsible only for instructing students, with no additional professional responsibilities.

Associate Teachers

Associate teachers are responsible for instructing students and additional professional responsibilities. The additional duties enable an associate teacher to be an independent contributor to a school and professional goals. An associate teacher is not involved in planning and organizing these other duties; that is done by those higher on the career ladder. Rather, he or she performs them when called on, based on needs in the school and the district. An associate teacher spends most of his or her time instructing students. When extra duties require an associate teacher to be away from instruction, a substitute teacher or another full-time teacher hired for this purpose takes charge of the associate teacher's students. Associate teachers choose from the following list of additional duties:

1. Supervise student teachers
2. Work with other preservice teachers
3. Serve as a mentor for first-step teachers in their own building
4. Teach new curriculum on an experimental basis
5. Continue their own professional development through graduate courses, staff development programs and other means
6. Participate in the evaluation of first-step teachers in other buildings

Most of these duties do not take the associate teachers away from students.

Senior Teachers

Senior teachers are responsible for instructing students and additional professional responsibilities, which include those identified for associate teachers plus other choices. These duties enable the senior teacher to assume more responsibility for the continuing education of others through the planning and the coordination of inservice education programs. Because senior teachers are usually involved in a number of additional duties, they spend more time away from students than associate teachers do. Senior teachers choose from the following list of additional duties plus those listed for associate teachers:

1. Help first- and second-stage teachers
2. Help guide first- and second-stage teachers during their "year of transition"
3. Teach in staff development programs
4. Help reassigned teachers (those recently assigned to a different school or grade level)
5. Serve on textbook selection committees
6. Teach during summer school with appropriate pay
7. Prepare and evaluate instructional materials
8. Serve on curriculum development committees
9. Serve as a mentor for second-stage teachers in their own building
10. Participate in the evaluation of second-stage teachers in other buildings

Master Teachers

Master teachers are responsible for instructing students and additional professional responsibilities, including those identified for associate and senior teachers. These additional tasks enable the master teacher to assume more responsibility for planning and organizing (a) curriculum, (b) preservice and inservice teacher education, (c) the evaluation of teachers at early stages of the career ladder, (d) instructional materials, (e) textbook selection, (f) research projects, and (g) other efforts that shape the direction of the school program and teaching as a profession.

Master teachers are instructional leaders and may choose to spend up to half of their time on duties other than instructing students.

Master teachers choose duties from the following options plus those listed for associate and senior teachers:

1. Help teachers at all levels in their teaching
2. Serve as a mentor for third-stage teachers in their own building
3. Coordinate staff development programs
4. Coordinate faculty involvement in curriculum development
5. Coordinate and participate in the professional development and evaluation of first-, second-, and third-stage teachers during their year of transition

6. Coordinate and participate in the evaluation of first-, second-, and third-stage teachers in other buildings
7. Coordinate and participate in the evaluation of other master teachers
8. Coordinate the development and evaluation of new instructional materials
9. Conduct demonstration lessons for others while working in their own classrooms with their own students
10. Coordinate the assignment of student teachers or other preservice teachers to cooperating teachers
11. Conduct research
12. Coordinate textbook selection committees
13. Serve as department chair, grade level chair or team leader (pp. 13–18)

The McDonnell Career Ladder Model

A career ladder model which includes several unique features has been proposed by McDonnell (1985). The model is similar to one approved by the Wisconsin Task Force on Teaching and Teacher Education for the Department of Public Instruction (1984). McDonnell's (1985, p. 230) career ladder is displayed in Figure 4.

The unique features in the McDonnell model are the undergraduate liberal arts degree, the fifth year program and the options at the top of the ladder. In this model, the Professional Teacher position is considered "home base" on the career ladder. Individuals work up to this level and may remain here for the remainder of their career. Some may choose to move up to the Career Teacher or Teacher Specialist step. If desired, they may move back to the Professional Teacher step from either of the other two. Teacher Specialists in this plan:

1. Will have demonstrated at least three years of successful teaching
2. Will spend at least 50% of their time in classroom teaching
3. Will be selected upon performance assessment and district needs in specialty areas
4. Will have a post-baccalaureate degree or other type of training and experience in a specialty area
5. Will be employed on an extended contract to work with teacher, students or on curriculum development
6. Will be paid on a salary scale different than other teachers

Figure 4. McDonnell's Career Ladder Model

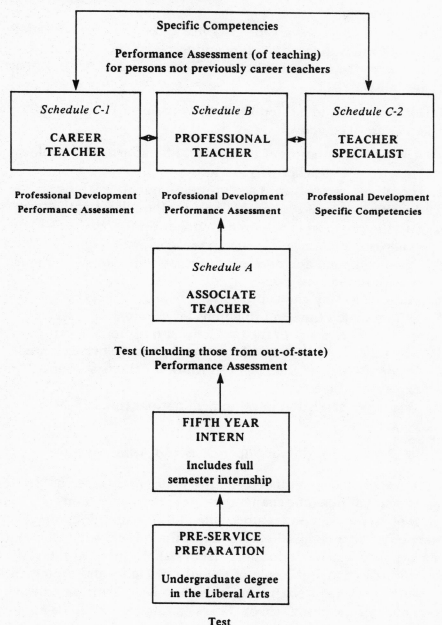

The Career Teacher is the other alternative at the top of the career ladder. Teachers electing to move to this step are superlative teachers who want to spend the majority of their time in the classroom. These teachers would:

1. Be assessed on criteria established to determine the outstanding teachers
2. Serve as model teachers for inservice and preservice education
3. Try out innovative curriculum and teaching strategies
4. Be on an 11-month contract and the same salary scale as teacher specialists

McDonnell (1985) identified the following benefits of the career ladder model described above:

1. A beneficial mixture of academics, liberal arts, and professional knowledge in teacher preparations
2. Incentives, rewards, and recognition for good teaching
3. An internal status system obtainable without leaving the classroom
4. Specific career alternatives dependent on the teacher's life-style, expertise, interests, and stage in the teaching cycle
5. Encouragement for administrators and specialists to return or remain in the classroom
6. More autonomy and control in the hands of teachers
7. Differentiated time and functions for differentiated salary
8. Avoidance of many of the problems of traditional merit pay
9. Allowance for more capable teachers to engage in specialized roles
10. Differentiation of the responsibilities for the first year and more experienced teachers
11. Various research and development options (pp. 247–248)

Modified Roles for Supervisors and Administrators

Team teaching, differentiated staffing plans, and career ladders have many commonalities. The changing role of the teacher is one of the most obvious of these common features. One of the assumptions about career ladders noted in a comprehensive list in the career ladder monograph (Association of Teacher Educators, 1985) stated, "altering the system of schooling will change the role of school principals and their relationships with teachers. Recognizing this may be a critical factor in the success of any innovation" (p. 6). This same statement can be applied to curriculum supervisors and other administration at the school and district levels.

Shared decision making will be the norm in any of the models. As teachers acquire more authority and status, they will also take on increased responsibilities in a variety of areas once reserved for administrators and supervisors. For many years teacher's organizations have been working for more member involvement in curriculum decisions, staff development, textbook selection, and instructional development. The career ladder plans provide a structured framework to implement shared decision making while increasing teachers' status and authority at the same time. For a fuller discussion, see the chapter on decision management by Carl Glickman.

As teachers assume more responsibility, principals and supervisors will take on roles of facilitators and coordinators. It is likely that the number of central office supervisory staff will diminish and funds will be distributed to teachers at higher levels of the career ladder who assume different responsibilities. It will be important to have someone to coordinate efforts of teachers with the school and across the district. This will be the primary function of the building principal and district supervisors.

RECOMMENDATIONS

The goal of schooling is to provide the best possible education for the most students. Research has repeatedly shown that the teacher is one of the most important variables in the process. In an effort to provide good teachers who can implement curriculum and provide excellent learning experiences for students, new structural organizations have been explored for many years. The past 30 years have witnessed numerous changes in society and schools. Team teaching, differentiated staffing and career ladders are three plans which have been tried as alternative models to meet the changing needs of students, teachers and schools.

This chapter has explored each of the models to find alternative roles for teachers, and, in turn, to identify how new roles for teachers will influence other roles within a school system. Experiences from the past and present have shown us that change takes place slowly within schools and in people's minds. The traditional roles of teachers and administrators are deeply embedded in the school structure and one change will cause a ripple effect on roles throughout a system. The following recommendations combine what we have learned from past experience and what should be considered to make teaching an attractive career in the future.

1. Career ladder plans must provide for variety in a teacher's career and increased status, recognition and authority.
2. Career ladder plans should provide a gradual induction into the profession and opportunities for continual advancement.
3. There should not be a quota system on any steps on the career ladder.
4. Movement on a career ladder should be up or down to take a teacher's life changes into consideration.
5. Careful evaluation procedures should be part of any changes on the career ladder. There should be multiple information sources for evaluation including observation, parent and student opinions, self-evaluation.
6. Regular evaluation should be for everyone on the career ladder.
7. There should be a transition year prior to any move on the career ladder.
8. There should be at least four levels on the career ladder.
   8.1 Level one is the beginning level. Teachers at this level will be responsible for teaching and personal professional development. They will participate on school committees and, after one or two years, on district-level committees. They will remain at this level at least three years. The third year will be a transition year to prepare for level two.
   8.2 Level two teachers will assume the same responsibilities as level one teachers and will be able to add to their options. They can serve on any school or district committees, supervise student teachers, serve as a team leader or serve as mentors for level one teachers. This is the level where teachers from outside the district will enter if they have at least three years of experience. Teachers will remain at level two for at least two years.
   8.3 Level three is a level where teachers can choose to remain for their entire career or they can come back to it at anytime. At this level a teacher's primary responsibility is teaching but he/she will select from any of the options for level two teachers. These people will serve as mentors and model teachers. They can choose to work extended contracts, to be involved in curriculum development, summer school teaching, special summer programs, help with staff development offerings, help level two teachers with their transition year or test and evalu-

ate curriculum materials and techniques. Teachers should remain at this level at least three years.

8.4 Level four teachers will have two options. They can choose to remain in the classroom full-time and assume responsibilities directly involved with instruction and helping others with instruction or they can choose to teach at least 50% of the time with released time to assume other responsibilities.

Those who choose the classroom options will be expected to model exceptional teaching techniques, work with other teachers to help transmit their expertise, become involved in classroom research, evaluate new techniques and materials, and choose any of the options available to level three teachers.

Teachers who choose the released-time option will be involved in leading work on curriculum development, staff development, classroom research, school-university collaboration, parent communication, sharing content expertise and choosing any of the options available for level three teachers. Level four teachers will have the option of 11-month contracts. To stay at level four, teachers will be evaluated yearly on performance goals they set with their supervisors. The level four part-time teaching option positions will be competitive based on specified needs of the school and district.

9. Teachers at level four will be the most likely to change the roles of principals and curriculum supervisors. Principals will develop a team of administrators and responsibilities will be shared. The principal will need skills in communication and organization to coordinate the efforts of several people on his/her staff.

10. District level personnel will also need organization and communication skills to make optimum use of the teachers' expertise. Their skills will be needed to coordinate activities throughout the district.

11. Funding of positions will change as teachers assume responsibilities once reserved for administrators.

REFERENCES

Association of Teacher Educators. (1985). *Developing career ladders in teaching*. Reston, VA: Author.

Bair, M., & Woodward, R. G. (1964). *Team teaching in action*. Boston: Houghton Mifflin.

Boutwell, C. E. (1972, August). Differentiated staffing as a component in a systematic change process. *Educational Technology, 12,* 20–21.

Chamberlin, L. J. (1969). *Team teaching: Organization and administration.* Columbus, OH: Charles E. Merrill.

Connors, J. (1969, February). Building a career ladder. *American Education, 5,* 15–17.

Cooper, J. M. (1972, January). Differentiated staffing: Some questions and answers. *The National Elementary School Principal, 51*(4), 49–54.

Cornett, L., & Weeks, K. (1985, July). Career ladder plans: Trends and emerging issues—1985. *Career ladder clearinghouse.* Atlanta, GA: Southern Regional Education Board.

English, F. (1970). Field testing a differentiated teaching staff. In J. L. Olivero & E. G. Buffie (Eds.), *Educational manpower: From aides to differentiated staff patterns—bold new venture* (pp. 189–225). Bloomington, IN: Bloomington Indiana University Press.

English, F. W. (1984–1985, December–January). We need the ghostbusters! A response to Jerome Freiberg. *Educational Leadership, 42*(4), 22–27.

Lortie, D. C. (1975). *Schoolteacher: A sociological study.* Chicago: University of Chicago Press.

McDonnell, J. H. (1985). A career ladder and career alternatives for teachers. In P. J. Burke & R. G. Heideman (Eds.), *Career-long teacher education* (pp. 223–249). Springfield, IL: Charles C Thomas.

National School Public Relations Association. (1970). *Differentiated staffing in schools* (Stock No. 411-12754). Washington, DC: Author.

Scobey, M. M., & Fiorino, A. J. (Eds.). *Differentiated staffing.* Washington, DC: Association for Supervision and Curriculum Development.

Shaplin, J. T. (1964). Description and definition of team teaching. In J. T. Shaplin & H. F. Olds, Jr. (Eds.), *Team teaching* (pp. 1–23). New York: Harper & Row.

Wisconsin Department of Public Instruction. (1984, January). *Final report of the state superintendent's task force on teaching and teacher education* (Bulletin No. 4250). Madison, WI: Department of Public Instruction.

Staff. (1985, February 6). Changing course—a 50-state survey of reform measures. *Education Week,* pp. 11–30.

York, L. J. (1971). *The roles of the professional and para-professional in team teaching: Module II.* Dallas: Leslie Press.

Chapter 6

DECISION MAKING IN SCHOOLS

CARL D. GLICKMAN AND LANCE V. WRIGHT

The advent of career ladders in education has profound implications for the work and learning of all individuals within a school. Not only will it change the status, recognition, and advancement of individual teachers, but it will affect and change roles and expectations of all teachers, administrators, and school personnel. The ultimate purpose for career ladders is improvement of instruction for students. The use of senior and master teachers to focus and direct energy on instructional improvement beyond the four walls of a single classroom provides, at last, the opportunity for a school staff to take on the true characteristic of a profession. That characteristic is the responsibility for making decisions about how to better perform one's collective job.

This chapter will describe in regard to decision making in schools: (a) implications of effective schools research, (b) responsibilities and role descriptions, (c) preparation of senior and master teachers, (d) planning organizational changes within individual schools to support the new decision making roles of master/senior teachers, and (e) preparation of administrators to support such changes. The chapter will conclude with specific recommendations about decision making responsibilities of career ladder teachers to improve schoolwide instruction.

IMPLICATIONS OF EFFECTIVE SCHOOLS RESEARCH

The evidence is rather clear that the professionalization of the teaching role is characteristic of our most successful schools. Wilbur Brookover's study on improving schools, as contrasted with declining schools, found that improving schools were distinguished by less satisfaction on the part of teachers with their instruction (Brookover, Beady, Flood, Schweiter, & Wisenbaker, 1979). The Fifteen-Thousand Hours study (Rutter, Maughan,

Mortimore, Ouston, & Smith, 1979) of 12 inner-city London High Schools reported that:

> ... the teachers in the schools which were more successful ... were much less likely to report that they had absolute freedom in planning their course. (p. 112)
>
> It was striking, however, that in the less successful schools teachers were often left completely alone to plan what to teach with little guidance or supervision from their senior colleagues and little coordination with other teachers to ensure a coherent course from year to year. (p. 136)

In **A Study of Schooling,** John Goodlad (1984) reported that of the 13 triples (a triple consists of an elementary, middle, and high school that pass the same students on to each other), the greatest predictor of school success was goal congruence between teachers, administrators, students, and parents. Effective schools were perceived as work places that provided autonomy as well as involvement in educational decisions.

Judith Little (1982) found in her study of six urban, desegregated schools (three elementary and three secondary) that the two high success schools differed from the rest in that:

> ... teachers engage in frequent, continuous, and increasingly concrete and precise talk about teaching practice. By such talk, teachers build up a shared language adequate to the complexity of teaching, capable of distinguishing one practice and its virtues from another, and capable of integrating large bodies of practice into distinct and sensible perspectives on the business of teaching. (p. 331)

All of the major research studies on effective schools have noted an organizational phenomenon of **collective action, agreed on purpose, and belief in attainment** (Pratzner, 1984). On the other hand, every major research study on ineffective schools has noted an absence of such purpose.

The simple point is that successful schools do not happen by accident. People in the schools are working actively to professionalize teaching by bringing teachers together to discuss, debate, and to decide upon common directions for instructional improvement. In successful schools, teachers work in common with each other, complementing and reinforcing each other's work. The prevailing characteristic of less-than-effective schools is a situation where teachers go their own way, close their doors to each other, and often teach in ways that contradict and cancel each other's efforts.

The work environment of teachers has been characterized by isolation, fragmentation, and individualism (for elaboration see Dreeban, 1973; Glickman, 1985; Goodlad, 1984; and Jackson, 1968). Most teachers rarely receive any feedback on their classroom work other than a once-a-year checklist evaluation. Most teachers have never observed or been observed by their peers (Blankenship & Irvine, 1985). Rarely do teachers engage in instructional improvement discussions. DeSanctis and Blumberg (1979) recorded the mode length of **professional** discussion during a typical school day as less than two minutes. Faculty meetings are used usually to inform and direct teachers, not for involving teachers in decision making. Such a bleak portrayal of the lack of teacher involvement in school-wide decisions is not intended to describe an everlasting condition. There are some schools such as those found by Brookover et al. (1979), Rutter et al. (1979), Goodlad (1984), and Little (1982), which have turned this state of affairs around and are succeeding.

Opportunities

A tremendous opportunity for turning schools into credible and forceful organizations is available by the careful use of career ladders. Master teachers have the credibility and openness to engage their peers in decision making that many administrators do not. They do not have the "baggage" of management and authority that often stifle teacher debate and candid expression. They are closest to the source of the problems to be focused on (instruction of students) and closest to those who instruct. They potentially are tremendous catalysts for making the school a professional and responsible decision making organization.

Cautions

Without careful role descriptions, planning, training, and phasing in of decision making responsibilities for senior and master teachers, the opportunity to improve schools could be lost. If so, then another layer of stifling administrative bureaucracy will be laid over schools and the catalyst for instructional school-wide improvement will remain dormant.

RESPONSIBILITIES AND ROLE DESCRIPTIONS

Teachers who advance within a career ladder should be given graduated responsibilities for coordinating and leading school groups. Since part of the criteria for career advancement is knowledge of and proficiency in using effective instruction, persons with such expertise should be given responsibilities for sharing their knowledge with groups that are formed to make team, grade level, departmental, or school-wide decisions about instruction.

The domain of decision making about instruction includes assessing and evaluating instructional programs, changing discipline and management procedures, selecting teaching materials, making curriculum revisions, planning inservice for improving teaching skills, and improving direct assistance (observing and providing feedback) to teachers. Matters outside of instruction such as bus scheduling, scheduling lunch duties, collecting attendance records, disciplining students, and evaluating teachers for contract renewal purposes should **not** be included in the domain of instructional decision making and should **not** be the responsibility of teachers advancing in the career ladder.

The role of a teacher advancing through a career ladder should focus on advancing instruction by using groups of teachers in the school to make decisions which will be implemented by all. Other matters not directly related to instruction should be the responsibility of school administrators.

To involve the advancing teacher in organizational matters not directly related to instruction would severely impede that person's work with teachers for instructional improvement. For example, if other teachers saw the master teacher doing the paperwork, scheduling, and assisting in formal evaluations of teachers for contract renewal (in effect, being the right hand of the school principal) then teachers would be less open in group meetings to express their perceptions of existing instructional practices, use of curriculum, or effectiveness of certain programs. If master teachers carried the principal's authority around with them, the candor and conflict of ideas so vital to productive group decision making would be suppressed. Therefore, there is solid rationale for separating the advancing teacher's responsibilities for instructional improvement from noninstructional administrative responsibilities.

Teachers advancing up a career ladder should retain some ongoing teaching presence in classrooms. As teachers move to advanced levels, their responsibilities for teaching a single classroom should be reduced and team, grade level, departmental, or school-wide instructional responsibilities should be increased. However, a teacher should never completely abandon the classroom. Teaching one period a day, conducting several demonstration lessons a week, or substituting for others on a weekly basis would keep the senior or master teacher credible with peers. Other teachers would still see the master teacher as a human being, at times struggling with students in the same ways that they do. Therefore, when it comes time to sit around a table to select and plan new instructional priorities in the school (e.g., increasing inquiry or promoting more cooperative learning), the master teacher's input would be based on knowledge of teaching combined with recent experience in the classroom.

The advancing teacher's responsibilities need to be clearly delineated (a) for decision making concerning instruction, and (b) for keeping the teacher in the classroom. The intent of this careful delineation is to free master teachers of potential role obstacles that would inhibit their effectiveness in working with peer groups. Since the aim of professional decision making in schools is to increase collective instructional effectiveness, a group leader needs to know what people think about issues under discussion. Once decisions are made, these same teachers will be expected to go back into their classrooms and implement the instructional decisions. The intent of the role separation between the administrator and the advancing teacher is not to create antagonism and tension between the two, but rather to enable coordination and distribution of all the important school tasks that need to be done. If the roles are not clearly described, then it is likely that the advancing teacher would become and be perceived to be another school administrator. The advancing teacher would become barricaded in his/her office with discipline referrals, paperwork, and requisition forms while school-wide instructional improvement would continue to be neglected.

PREPARATION

An outstanding classroom teacher is not automatically an outstanding instructional leader. There are three prerequisite domains of preparation for effective group leadership. One domain is **knowledge** about how groups function. A second domain is **interpersonal skills** for working with groups. The third domain is **technical skills** for planning and implementing group decisions.

Knowledge

A leader needs to be able to determine the experience, commitment, and expertise that group members have with a particular instructional problem under consideration. Furthermore, the leader needs to be able to determine the prior level of group work (i.e., How familiar are group members with each other? What norms of group behaviors have been previously established? How have group members worked together in the past? How well do they communicate with each other?). Obviously a newly formed group consisting of unfamiliar members who are inexperienced in group work and limited in their own collective expertise about the instructional topic under consideration will heed a different type of group leadership than a group which possesses great familiarity and expertise, and has a "track record" of previous success.

Besides knowledge about the group as a whole, the leader needs to be able to observe group members' individual behaviors. Benne and Sheats (1948) described a myriad of functional and dysfunctional group member roles. A leader must be aware of voids in functional roles (i.e., lack of information seekers, information givers, opinion seekers, and harmonizers) and be able to delegate or assume those absent roles. A leader also must be aware of dysfunctional roles (i.e., self confessors, aggressors, and dominators) and know when to ignore, deflect, confront, or even change seating arrangements to minimize such behaviors.

Furthermore, successful working of groups is conditioned by a leader knowing and attending to both task and human satisfaction interactions (Bales, 1953). In order for a group to make its decisions in an efficient manner, the leader needs to keep discussions focused, review group progress, propose next steps, and set agendas and time lines. These are all task interactions. However, to be solely task oriented creates a formal atmosphere devoid of the free play of emotion, opinion, and ideas so important to creative decision making. People tend to avoid meetings when there is an absence of humor, encouragement, or personal recognition. For the group to accomplish its task productively and wisely and still have the willingness of members to work together in the future, the group leader needs to provide verbal praise, levity, and nonverbal assurances. By being conscious of both the task and human satisfaction interactions of successful groups, the leader will know when to emphasize one set of interactions over the other.

Interpersonal Skills

The second prerequisite of group leadership is knowledge of interpersonal skills so that a leader can acquire and use a repertoire of approaches with various groups. There are at least four distinct approaches: (a) laissez-faire, (b) non-directive, (c) collaborative, and (d) directive.

The leader can take a **laissez-faire** approach with a group and let the group meet and make decisions on their own. The leader can take a **non-directive** approach and act as a facilitator of the group process by asking questions that lead the group through the steps of problem solving (i.e., identifying the problems, proposing alternate actions, considering consequences, setting priorities, agreeing to actions, and evaluating actions). In a non-directive approach, the leader facilitates the process but stays away from influencing the decision. In a **collaborative** approach, the leader acts as both a facilitator of group process and also as an active group member with the same rights and responsibilities as any other member to contribute and influence the final decision. Another approach that can be taken is a **directive** one whereby the leader lays out the procedures for the group, identifies the group's task, proposes alternatives for the group and asks the group to select from among those choices.

Group leadership approaches run the spectrum from allowing the group to operate by itself and determine its own decisions to having the leader prescribe procedures and decisions for the group. A skilled leader will determine an appropriate approach to use based on knowledge about the group and their current level of operation, and then over time will give the group greater responsibility for determining its own process and product (Glickman, 1985, pp. 156–174; Gordon & Glickman, 1984).

Technical Skills

The third prerequisite domain for group leadership is technical skills. This domain includes skills in assessing, planning, decision making rules, and evaluating instruction. The leader needs to be familiar with ways of helping a group collect data about an instructional problem. Written surveys, oral interviews, official records, formal testing, the Delphi technique, and the use of check and ranking lists are all ways to collect information about the scope and nature of an instructional problem before a group proceeds to consider solutions. In Clinton's study of decision making skills (Clinton, Glickman, & Payne, 1982), most instructional leaders lacked the technical skills for collecting information to identify a problem before solving it. Once a group has identified a problem, clarification of the group's decision making rule becomes important. The leader needs to help the group determine whether the decision making rule will be by consensus, majority vote, minority vote, or by a single individual before reaching the final decision (Johnson & Johnson, 1982). If a decision making rule is not known prior to deliberations on a final decision, the leader runs the risk of a "post-hoc" decision making rule being perceived as selected to ensure a particular solution.

Once a decision has been made, the leader needs to use the technical skills of planning in order to monitor group implementation of the decision. If the instructional improvement decision involves actions from numerous persons over an extended period of time, then a plan is usually necessary to indicate what is to be done, by whom, and when. The use of flowcharts, time lines, and management by objective procedures can aid in clarifying and detailing the various activities.

The proof of a group's work is not in their discussions and decisions but rather in their implementation. Whether decision making groups become an established and creditable force for school-wide instructional improvement depends largely on whether decisions are carried out. The senior/master teacher can help other teachers set realistic and feasible plans to ensure such implementation.

The final technical skills are those for evaluating the outcome of the group's decision to implement an instructional change. If the group's decision is made and carried out, then the last question is "did it improve learning for students?" Leaders need to avoid cardiac responses to instructional change when it is said that "we know in our hearts that it is good" (Wolfe, 1969). Instead, group leaders need to establish with the group the data that will be collected, assessed, and evaluated after a certain implementation period. The collected data should be similar to the needs assessment data (surveys, interviews, rating lists, tests, or records) so that the group has comparable pre-post data. Collecting such information, no matter how scarce and informal, gives a group future directions for continuing, revising, or discarding the improvement plan.

ORGANIZATIONAL CHANGES

A school must either reorganize itself or revitalize its existing organizational structure for increased and ongoing group decision making. As teachers advance up the career ladder, their responsibilities for group leadership should increase. For example, a career ladder scheme of teacher, associate teacher, senior teacher, and master teacher might correspond to decision making responsibilities about instruction at these ascending levels: (a) Teachers are responsible for decisions about small groups of students within a classroom, (b) associate teachers are responsible for decisions about the classroom as a whole, (c) senior teachers are responsible for decisions about team of teachers (grade level, department, or ad hoc groups across departments or grades), and (d) master teachers are responsible for decisions about the school as a whole. Advancement up the career ladder should correspond to responsibilities to coordinate and lead groups in a wider sphere of instructional decisions.

A school organization for group decision making should reflect these widening spheres of instructional concerns. Therefore, each school needs a vehicle for each teacher to make decisions about their own classroom, and also a vehicle for teachers to make decisions about instructional issues beyond their own classroom. The need for decision making to promote a collective impact has been described previously as characteristic of a professional and successful school.

An elementary school should have defined groups for deciding upon grade level as well as across-grade-level concerns. Middle schools and high schools should have (a) groups for grade level, team and departmental concerns; and (b) groups for across grade levels, teams, and departmental concerns.

Many schools have organizations that encourage grade level or departmental decision making, usually under the sponsorship of a grade level chairperson or departmental head. What many schools are missing is another organizational structure that makes people think and act on interests larger than their own immediate team or department. Teachers often have allegiance to their own classroom and, at best, to their team or department; but they have little opportunity to participate and act on concerns beyond their own four walls or their own subject area. The installation of career ladders and a corresponding organization for decision making groups in a school could alter the self-interest and protectionism in many of our schools which impedes progress in school-wide instructional improvement.

How might this organization take place? The following is a proposed model for a large school of more than 35 teachers. The model is an adaption of many others and is explained according to the successful implementation by a particular high school (Oglethorpe County High School, 1983). It is meant to be illustrative of the kind of decision making organization that can be created. This model is not meant to be a definitive guide for all schools and systems. The proposed organization for decision making is intended to fulfill the following criteria.

1. Involve all faculty in school-wide instructional decisions.
2. Provide wider spheres of instructional responsibilities for teachers at various levels of the career ladder.
3. Prevent resistant faculty from slowing down the work of those faculty committed to improvement.
4. Provide an ongoing faculty focus and actions directed at school-wide instructional improvement.

Figure 1. ORGANIZATIONAL MODEL FOR SCHOOL–WIDE
          INSTRUCTIONAL DECISION-MAKING

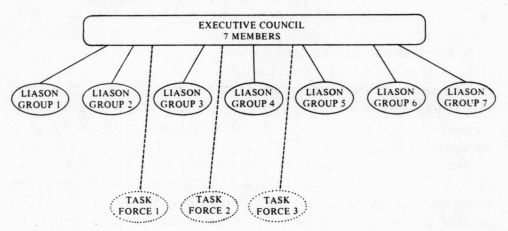

An organization model for school-wide instructional decision making is presented in Figure 1. An **executive council** consists of seven members including five teachers, one master teacher, and the principal. The five teachers could be existing department heads, grade level heads, team leaders, department heads, and union representatives or they could be elected at large from the faculty or formed by a combination of election and appointment. They hold a term of at least three years and then move off the council at staggered times. The master teacher serves as the chairperson of the executive council (if a school has several master teachers they could be co-chairs or rotating chairs). The principal is a member of the committee with the same rights and responsibilities as any other member. The executive council's responsibility is solely for acting on and monitoring school-wide instructional improvement recommendations. The executive council does not involve itself in administrative matters, community relations, school board policies, or personnel matters. They act upon instructional improvement recommendations that they as a faculty have the legal power to carry out. This differentiation between instructional and administrative responsibilities helps avoid problems of delving into matters beyond the school's own control.

Liaison groups are formal groups set up for communication between the faculty and executive council concerning needs, reactions, opinions, and ideas about school-wide instruction. The liaison groups meet formally only two or three times a year, but they are an important link for considering the faculty's ideas and opinions towards certain instructional ideas. In the case of a school with 50 teachers, there could be seven liaison groups consisting of approximately seven faculty members each. An alphabetized list of all faculty names is gathered and each person is assigned a number from one to seven. All one's go to liaison group one, all two's go to liaison group two, and so forth. This assignment procedure ensures that members in each liaison group come from various departments and grade levels. Each liaison group is a smaller composite of the entire school. One executive council member is assigned to each liaison group and serves as the liaison group's representative to the council. The executive council member can (a) call the liaison group together from time to time for a brief meeting to review a specific recommendation under executive council consideration, (b) gather written opinions about a particular proposal, or (c) simply drop by and talk to the various liaison group members. The last groups shown in Figure 1 are the task forces. These are ad hoc task groups that are formed after the executive council has solicited feedback from all the liaison groups about perceived school-wide instructional needs and reviewed any existing data on school-wide instruction. The executive council then targets priority instructional areas for the next one to three years. Such school-wide priorities might be increasing instructional time, coordinating curriculum, teaching higher order thinking, improving school discipline, increasing student attention, improving the quality of student homework, or improving test scores.

Once the needs for improvement have been selected by the executive council, ad hoc task force groups are formed by recruiting volunteers who have an interest and commitment to the particular topic. At least one executive council member serves on each task force, but this person normally does not serve as chair of the task force. The task force meets, reviews their task, selects their own chairperson, schedules meetings, and sets a time line for making a final recommendation for school-wide action to the executive council. Depending on the topic, a task force might meet three times to make a recommendation in three weeks, whereas another task force might meet every other week for five months before making a recommendation. Senior level teachers in a career ladder should be expected to take an active role on at least one task force committee each year.

When the task force is ready to make a recommendation, the chairperson reports to the executive council. The executive council can discuss the recommendation and make an immediate decision or table it until the next meeting. During the interim, the executive council can check with their respective liaison groups for entire faculty input. Any recommendation approved by the executive council will be implemented and monitored by the council. Therefore, if any doubt about faculty receptivity exists, it would be best to garner total faculty input through the liaison groups prior to making a commitment to action.

The purposes for using this suggested model for organizational decision making are to (a) involve all staff, (b) increase the sphere of responsibility for career ladder teachers, and (c) increase the opportunities for cross-fertilization of ideas and unification of school actions. The changing nature of task force committees for solving particular school-wide problems under a permanent, ongoing structure of executive council and liaison groups keeps a focus on school-wide instructional improvement. It is a flexible yet permanent organization for decision making. Such organizing for decision making has been found not only to work in schools but also with successful corporations (Ouchi, 1981; Peters & Waterman, 1982).

Organizing a school for decision making is not new to education. This proposed model and many others emphasizing group decision making about school-wide instructional improvements are adaptations of action research first proposed in the work of Lewin (1948) and Corey (1953). If a structure for instructional decision making already exists in schools in the form of a leadership council, it need not be discarded. Instead it should be revised to incorporate the added responsibilities of career ladder teachers.

For example, some schools have continued the organizational structure formed for self-study and accreditation purposes and used the steering committee as an executive council for implementation of recommended improvements. Small schools (10 to 15 faculty members) have less need for formal liaison groups but the executive council and task force groups still might be appropriate. Small faculties might act as committees of the whole.

The organizational revisions that a school makes should ensure that career ladder teachers have additional group responsibilities and that all teachers have the opportunity to focus on the school as the unit for instructional change.

PREPARATION FOR THE PRINCIPAL

Teachers in career ladders will be expected to take instructional leadership responsibilities in schools where the principal still controls the lever for change. The need to delineate the career ladder role as one of a staff position with teachers, not a line position, was emphasized earlier. The advantage for doing so is that the senior or master teacher has free access to the real world of teaching.

Instructional improvement efforts will be difficult if not impossible without career ladder teachers being supported by the principal. The career ladder teacher's role for instructional leadership can be likened to a jack-in-the box where the principal is the person who can either release the latch and spring the career ladder teacher into action, or keep the latch securely fastened leaving the career ladder hemmed in on all sides. It is necessary, therefore, to identify three specific considerations and preparations necessary for the principal.

First, it is important that school principals appraise their own level of functioning concerning instructional leadership. If they are involved in an ongoing manner with teachers in all the supervisory tasks of direct assistance (e.g., observing and conferencing), inservice, curriculum development, program evaluation, and action research, then they can determine where the senior or master teacher can assume some of this work. Thus, the principals would be freed to concentrate on a particular task or to work with particular teachers. If principals appraise themselves as attending only to some tasks and not others, then they can give the responsibilities of the missing tasks to the career ladder teachers. Finally, if principals assess themselves as not being instructional leaders but rather being more like business managers, plant administrators, or public relations directors, then they should allow the career ladder teacher to assume the major instructional role for the school in all five tasks. Therefore, a first step for principals in determining decision making in the schools is to assess their current supervisory function. Two such formal inventories that principals can use to assess supervision of instruction in their schools have been prepared by Jones (1986) and Rogers (1986).

Second, principals need to be involved in the professional development of career ladder teachers. When teachers assume a higher career stage, principals need to meet with them and review role expectations and responsibilities. Principals can help career ladder teachers determine how gradual the assumption of decision making responsibilities in the school should be and what inservice or internship experiences can be provided during this transition phase. Developing a job target and action plan with specific inservice activities would be one way of focusing on the transition.

Principals also should participate in at least some of the inservice activities designed for career ladder teachers. Principals would benefit by occasionally participating in the prerequisite training for group leadership (knowledge, interpersonal, and technical skills). Equally important, the principal's attendance would lend support and credence to the master teacher's use of the skills. Studies of successful implementation of inservice skills by teachers have shown the importance of the school administrator's active participation in the training (Lawrence, 1974).

Third, principals should go public with discussions, role delineations, action plans, inservice programs, and organizational rearrangements for decision making in the school. Going public means standing with the teachers of the highest career stages in front of the school faculty and explaining the new roles and plans for decision making.

Arthur Blumberg has written about the misunderstanding that exists between people of various positions in a school. The title of his book, **Supervisors and Teachers: A Private Cold War** (Blumberg, 1980), captures the point that a lack of clear and honest communication between teachers and supervisors engenders mistrust and suspicion. Teachers may not believe written reports or descriptions by master teachers concerning changes in professional decision making through councils and ad hoc task forces. In their own minds, teachers might suspect that the principal has a different or hidden plan in mind. When master teachers and principals together explain changes in the organization and their roles with all teachers, teachers will start to sense that this new decision making for instructional improvement is real.

RECOMMENDATIONS FOR DECISION MAKING IN THE SCHOOLS

The purpose of this chapter was to describe the tremendous opportunity that exists for instructional improvement in schools by giving the career ladder teachers increased responsibilities for bringing staff together to make collective decisions. A critical element of successful schools is the professionalization of the work environment of teachers so that they are aware of each other's instruction, are able to talk with each other about instructional concerns, and finally are able to plan and implement coordinated actions. The advancing career teacher has the credibility and expertise as a classroom teacher to engage peers in open problem solving for instructional improvement without the fear of being perceived as a threat by individual teachers. The career ladder teacher typically can gain more access, candor, and exploration of ideas with other teachers than the school principal could. In the spirit of improving school-wide instruction, the following recommendations are made:

1. Responsibilities of career ladder teachers should be related solely to instruction.
    A. Career ladder responsibilities should focus on matters dealing with instructional improvement and **not** on administrative matters. Career ladder teachers should not be responsible for handling discipline referrals, teacher evaluations, or administrative paperwork. Career ladder teachers should **not** be administrative assistants to the principal.
    B. Career ladder teachers should continue to teach but their responsibilities for an individual classroom should lessen as they advance to higher levels. Instructional responsibilities for observing, conferring, and leading groups at the grade, team,

departmental, and school level should increase as they advance to higher levels.

2. Career ladder teachers should be prepared for group leadership. It can't be assumed that outstanding classroom teachers will automatically be outstanding instructional leaders.

   A. Preparation should focus on **knowledge** of groups concerning (a) experience, commitment, and expertise of individual group members; (b) prior level of group norms, cohesion, and communication; (c) functional and dysfunctional group member roles; and (d) task and human satisfaction interactions.

   B. Preparation should focus on leader's **interpersonal skills** including laissez-faire, non-directive, collaborative, and directive approaches that can be chosen according to a group's current level of operation in an effort to stimulate the group to greater collective responsibility.

   C. Preparation should focus on **technical skills** of a group leader for assessing, clarifying decision making rules, planning, and evaluating so that implementation of a group's instructional improvement decisions becomes a reality.

3. Organizational structures of schools should reflect the increased decision making capacity of faculty and the new responsibilities of career ladder teachers.

   A. Each school needs a vehicle for ongoing instructional decisions to be made at classroom, grade level, team/departmental, and school-wide levels. As career ladder teachers advance, their instructional improvement responsibilities should move to higher levels of group decision making (i.e., level one teachers might work with subgroups within the classroom, level two teachers might work with the classroom as a whole, level three teachers might work across classrooms, and level four teachers might work with the school as a whole).

   B. An executive council or steering committee that has the granting authority for school-wide instructional improvement should be a permanent fixture in a school. It should be led by master teachers and consist of representatives from the entire school.

   C. **Ad hoc** task force committees that are formed to recommend ways to improve particular school-wide instructional concerns should be an ongoing part of school improvement and should be open to all who are interested in participating. Senior and/or master teachers should have active roles in the task force groups.

D. All faculty should have the opportunity to convey their thoughts, ideas, and reactions to instructional improvement plans prior to final deliberations by the executive council. This input could be obtained either through formal liaison groups or informal polling of individual teachers.

4. Administrators should be prepared to support schoolwide decision making. The school principal needs to see the advancing career ladder teacher as augmenting and complementing his/her own instructional leadership role rather than competing with it.

A. School principals should appraise their own functioning in terms of instructional leadership in the school and determine where the career ladder teacher can assume responsibilities for previously neglected tasks.

B. School principals should plan with each career ladder teacher concerning yearly role expectations, graduated decision making responsibilities, and needed inservice/internships experiences. The principal also should participate in the training of career ladder teachers concerning group leadership skills.

C. The school principal and senior/master teachers should discuss the new role delineations and plans for school-wide decision making with the entire school faculty so that the staff clearly understands the coordination and responsibility of the senior/master teacher for instructional improvement.

CLOSING THOUGHTS

The intent of educational reforms are to improve learning for students. No reform, including implementing career ladders, is of merit unless something different and better happens for students. Those schools where research has shown better education for students have been marked by professional engagement of staff. The use of career ladder teachers to foster and stimulate decision making in the schools can break the barriers of teacher isolation, invisibility, and stagnation and come closer to the reformers' ideas of an intellectual community of adults working for the betterment of all students (Boyer, 1983; Goodlad, 1984). Instructional improvement is not the province of a single administrator, supervisor, department head, or teacher, but is the province of all. Using career ladder teachers to advance the collective and professional will in a school is a gradual process needing careful role separation, preparation, and planning. Policy makers need to ensure that implementation of the career ladder will support increasing professional decision making by equipping the career ladder teacher with an ongoing organizational structure for making school-wide instructional decisions. Preparing the school administrator to understand and capitalize on the capabilities of career ladder teachers as leaders is an opportunity to make instructional improvement an ongoing school-wide effort.

REFERENCES

Bales, R. F. (1953). The equilibrium problem in small groups. In T. Parsons, R. F. Bales, & E. A. Shils (Eds.), *Working papers in the theory of action* (pp. 111–161). Glencoe, IL: Free Press.

Benne, D. D., & Sheats, P. (1948). Functional roles of group members. *Journal of Social Issues,* 4(2), 41–49.

Blankenship, G., Jr., & Irvine, J. I. (1985). Georgia teachers' perceptions of prescriptive and descriptive observations of teaching by instructional supervisors. *Georgia Educational Leadership,* 1(1), 3–7.

Blumberg, A. (1980). *Supervisors and teachers: A private cold war* (2nd ed.). Berkeley, CA: McCutchan.

Boyer, E. L. (1983). *High school: A report on secondary education in America.* New York: Harper & Row.

Brookover, W., Beady, C., Flood, P., Schweiter, J., & Wisenbaker, J. (1979). *School social systems and students' achievement: Schools can make a difference.* New York: Praeger.

Clinton, B. C., Glickman, C. D., & Payne, D. A. (1982). Identifying supervision problems: A guide to better solutions. *Illinois School Research and Development,* 9(1).

Corey, S. M. (1953). *Action research to improve school practices.* New York: Teachers College Press, Columbia University.

DeSanctis, M., & Blumberg, A. (1979, April). *An exploratory study into the nature of teacher interactions with other adults in the schools.* Paper presented at the annual meeting of the American Educational Research Association, San Francisco, CA.

Dreeben, R. (1973). The school as a workplace. In R. M. Travers (Ed.), *Second handbook of research on teaching* (pp. 450–473). Chicago: Rand McNally.

Glickman, C. D. (1985). *Supervision of instruction: A developmental approach.* Newton, MA: Allyn & Bacon.

Goodlad, J. I. (1984). *A place called school: Prospects for the future.* New York: McGraw-Hill.

Gordon, S. P., & Glickman, C. D. (1984). Applying developmental supervision: Tactical and strategic dimensions. *Thresholds in Education,* 10(2), 24–26.

Jackson, P. W. (1968). *Life in classrooms.* New York: Holt, Rinehart & Winston.

Johnson, D. W., & Johnson, F. P. (1982). *Joining together: Group theory and group skills* (2nd ed). Englewood Cliffs, NJ: Prentice-Hall.

Jones, J. W. (1986). *A data collection system for describing research based instructional improvement practices.* Unpublished manuscript, University of Georgia, Department of Curriculum and Supervision, Athens.

Lawrence, G. (1974). *Patterns of effective in-service education: A state of the art summary of research on materials and procedures for changing teacher behaviors in in-service education.* Tallahassee, FL: Florida State Department of Education. (ERIC Document Reproduction Service No. ED 176 424)

Lewin, K. (1948). *Resolving social conflicts.* New York: Harper and Brothers.

Little, J. W. (1982). Norms of collegiality and experimentation: Workplace conditions of school success. *American Educational Research Journal, 19*(3), 325–340.

Oglethorpe County High School. (1983). *School improvement: Organization, responsibilities, and procedures.* Unpublished manuscript, Oglethorpe, GA.

Ouchi, W. G. (1981). *Theory Z: How American business can meet the Japanese challenge.* Reading, MA: Addison-Wesley.

Peters, T. J., & Waterman, R. H., Jr. (1982). *In search of excellence.* New York: Harper and Row.

Pratzner, F. C. (1984). Quality of school life: Foundations for improvement. *Educational Researcher, 13*(3), 20–25.

Rogers, G. (1986). *Direct supervisory services questionnaire.* Unpublished manuscript, University of Georgia, Department of Curriculum and Supervision, Athens.

Rutter, M., Maughan, B., Mortimore, P., Ouston, J., & Smith, A. (1979). *Fifteen thousand hours: Secondary schools and their effects on children.* Cambridge, MA: Harvard University Press.

Wolfe, R. (1969). A model for curriculum evaluation. *Psychology in the Schools, 6,* 107–108.

Chapter 7

IDENTIFYING AND EVALUATING TEACHERS

Thomas L. McGreal

As a result of the intense debates about educational reform, many states and localities have begun to consider alternatives for evaluating and rewarding teachers. More than 40 merit, master, career ladder, and incentive plans are in operation or under consideration in the United States ("Changing Course," 1985). Among the many difficult problems in designing and implementing these plans, the most difficult of all is the problem of evaluation (Cohn & Natriello, 1984; Johnson, 1984; Jordan & Barkow, 1983). Teachers' acceptance of evaluation procedures will in large measure determine the success or failure of the new career development and compensation plans (Epstein, 1985). Statements like these reflect the general feeling about the crucial nature of effective evaluation procedures in the development of successful teacher career ladder plans.

This chapter will include a discussion of (a) background on evaluation, (b) basic commonalities of effective evaluation plans that could be used in career ladder programs, and (c) recommendations for identifying and evaluating teachers in career ladder plans.

BACKGROUND ON EVALUATION

There seems little need to offer extensive justification for the existence of teacher evaluation. Among educators it is, in fact, one of the few areas in which there is agreement. While there is often some argument at the local level about the espoused versus the "real" purpose of evaluation, educators overall are in accord regarding its general purpose: **to safeguard and improve the quality of instruction received by students** (Bolton, 1973). Bolton listed the following specific functions of teacher evaluation as the means for fulfilling this major purpose:

1. To improve teaching through the identification of ways to change teaching systems, teaching environments, or teaching behaviors.
2. To supply information that would lead to the modification of assignments, such as placement in other positions, promotions, and terminations.
3. To protect students from incompetence, and teachers from unprofessional administrators.
4. To reward superior performance.
5. To validate the school system's teacher selection process.
6. To provide a basis for teachers' career planning and professional development. (p. 98)

If all this agreement exists, why does teacher evaluation remain an extraordinarily controversial and disruptive influence within local school settings? In most instances the difficulties arise not with the concept or the general purposes, but from the way evaluation is carried out. Actual evaluation is most often directed by the requirements of the evaluation system. And herein lies trouble, because in most cases the system is the problem (McGreal, 1983).

The major difficulties associated with developing effective teacher evaluation systems are well-documented. They include such problems as poor teacher-administrator attitudes toward evaluation (Wagoner & O'Hanlon, 1968), the difficulties in separating formative and summative evaluation (Raths, 1982), inadequate measurement devices (Popham, 1981), lack of reliable and consistent teaching criteria (Travers, 1981), the lack of reliable data collection techniques (Scriven, 1981), the fallibility of standard feedback mechanisms (McKeachie, 1976), and the general lack of training for teachers and supervisors in the evaluation process (McGreal, 1983). The number and complexity of these problems would make it seem an impossible task to develop an effective and useable evaluation system.

But regardless of these difficulties, school systems must have a functioning teacher evaluation system. Within newly developed career ladder programs the major focus on evaluation of teacher performance will shift from evaluation for improvement or termination to evaluation to reward performance or for career advancement. Consequently, additional pressure is placed on the existence of an acceptable plan. The question for local school districts and state educational organizations is: "Given the fact that it is unlikely that there exists now or in the near future any totally reliable teacher evaluation system, what can be done to develop the most realistic, practical, and effective system possible?"

Fortunately, our knowledge about the supervision/evaluation of teaching has grown dramatically in recent years (McGreal, 1983; Medley, Coker, & Soar, 1984; Millman, 1981). While the definitive system seems beyond our reach, a series of events over the last 15 years has provided us the opportunity to become more confident in our ability to reliably assess levels of competence in teaching. These events include the growing picture of effective teaching being generated by the research on teaching (Wittrock, 1986), increased accuracy in recording both student and teacher classroom behaviors (Acheson & Gall, 1980), and a renewed interest in the critical analysis of various evaluation practices and overall systems (McGreal, 1983; Wise & Darling-Hammond, 1984).

By combining information gained from careful reviews of the growing body of literature in teacher evaluation with what has been learned through various analyses of functioning teacher compensation programs (Cornett, 1985), there appears to be a set of six commonalities that are emerging as fundamental to the successful development of appropriate and effective evaluation procedures for use within career ladder programs. The six commonalities will each be discussed separately in the next section of this chapter. It should be noted that the length of discussion following each commonality will vary. Neither the length of the discussion nor the ordering of the commonalities should be construed as indicating increased importance. Each of the six could stand independently, and all have important implications for local school districts and state departments whether taken alone or as a group. The length of discussion is related only to the amount of information needed to explain the meaning and the use of the commonality. It is not necessary that all six be present before a system can be judged effective or potentially effective. Indeed, only a handful of programs would have evaluation systems that reflect all six. These commonalities can be best used to provide a perspective, an awareness of alternatives, and if need be, a set of directions to follow.

BASIC COMMONALITIES OF EFFECTIVE EVALUATION PLANS FOR USE IN CAREER LADDER PROGRAMS

Career ladder plans need effective teacher evaluation systems and thus should reflect the best in evaluation practice. Six commonalities of effective evaluation plans will be discussed in this section: (a) density of leadership, (b) clear criteria, (c) the use of alternative data sources, (d) the use of multiple evaluators, (e) concern for both formative and summative evaluation, and (f) evaluations systems linked to the staff development program.

Density of Leadership

The role strong leadership plays in the development of effective evaluation systems is well-documented (Iwanicki, 1981; McGreal, 1983; Wise & Darling-Hammond, 1984; Zimmerer & Stroh, 1974). There would appear to be several ways that this necessary leadership manifests itself. The most obvious need for leadership appears to be that which emanates from the top. Much of the effective schools literature points to the importance of the principal in providing instructional leadership at the school level. The same concept can be extrapolated to suggest the importance of top-level leadership when dealing with district-wide or state-wide improvement initiatives.

At the local level there is increasing evidence that the role of the superintendent is every bit as crucial to school effectiveness as is the building principal (Murphy & Hallinger, in press). It has long been held by those who serve as outside consultants to school districts that the likelihood of the successful implementation of a school improvement effort is in direct proportion to the amount of involvement and commitment shown by the superintendent. Successful leadership from the top must be active leadership. Superintendents and central office staff must be physically and emotionally involved in the school-wide process of planning, developing, and implementing a local evaluation plan.

At the state level, it seems especially important that leadership from the top be focused and obvious. The nature of most state-mandated career ladder or merit pay programs makes it very difficult for top-level leadership to be visible. Too often leadership in state-level programs becomes diffused because of the perceived need everyone has to want to claim credit or responsibility for the program. This spreading of responsibility has a tendency to make it difficult for one person or a small group of persons to emerge as the major spokesperson for the proposed programs. As more individuals or groups feel the need or desire to assume a leadership role, the more difficult it is to develop the understanding and commitment within workers in state-level educational organizations and local schools that is necessary to foster an environment conducive to change. It is likely that the most effective statewide career ladder programs will be those where leadership has emerged through educational channels rather than through legislative mandates that grew out of a political process. Since this is not the case in most states, it becomes particularly important for state officials to identify and encourage influential educational leaders to serve as the major spokespersons for the movement.

Additionally, the history of successful implementations suggests that while it is necessary to have strong leadership from the top, it is not sufficient. Leadership must be dispersed throughout the organization. This depth of leadership generally needs to be developed, for it does not appear to be a natural phenomenon. At the local level, this is one of the main purposes served by having strong involvement on the part of the staff. One of the reasons that staff involvement through the committee or advisory group process is so important and useful is that the process helps develop leadership in the members of these groups. They display this leadership by influencing the rest of the staff. This depth becomes increasingly important the more dramatic or threatening the proposed program may be.

In those states that have chosen to develop statewide evaluation programs, this leadership density must be purposefully sought and nurtured. The size and nature of most state educational organizations precludes serious commitment to any one program. State workers who have many responsibilities and divided loyalties, and who have grown accustomed to the vagaries of the political process, are not inclined to enter into the development of new programs with the enthusiasm and energy necessary to influence others. Special attention must be given to identifying those individuals within state departments who can be pulled together into a small working group who will assume the major share of responsibility for dissemination and training in the evaluation phase of a career ladder program. They should be chosen on the basis of their interest, commitment, and influence rather than on their location within the organization. In this way you can begin to develop a cadre of state-level workers who have the knowledge and the willingness to generate enthusiasm and involvement in others.

It seems clear that the density of leadership that appears so important to the success of developing an effective evaluation plan can occur most readily in local school settings. If the option is still available, most states should allow local schools to develop their own evaluation procedures. Evaluation plans that are required by the state with mandated procedures and training programs are far less likely to be successful. This would appear to be the case if for no other reason than the difficulty of generating the depth of leadership necessary to encourage acceptance of new programs.

Clear Criteria

An essential element of any effective evaluation system is the existence of a clear, visible, and appropriate set of evaluation criteria. There are two clear reasons for the existence of these criteria. First, as Strike and Bull (1981) indicated, it is the responsibility of an employing school district and the right of an employed teacher to have a fully developed and explicit set of criteria or expectations that define the role of teacher. Secondly, the criteria provide a standard against which actual performance can be measured.

Most often, local negotiated contractual arrangements require the existence of a set of evaluation criteria. In addition, many states have mandated a set of criteria that must be present before local teacher evaluation systems can receive state approval. An example of a state-required set of criteria listed in the form of a set of essential teaching competencies is displayed in Table 1.

Since many school districts have a tendency to submit local plans for state approval that contain the basic minimums required, these and similar criteria developed in other states are serving as the models for districts to use. While the criteria as represented in Table 1 are appropriate expectations for a generic description of a part of a teacher's job (correctly as, these competencies are drawn from the research on teaching—see McGreal, 1983, for a fuller rationale for using the teaching research as criteria for assessing and describing teacher classroom performance), they are really not full enough descriptions to serve the purpose of a comprehensive teacher evaluation system. The criteria in Table 1 focus

Table 1
Essential Teaching Competencies With Sample Descriptors and Indicators

1. The Teacher Communicates Accurately and Effectively in the Content Area and Maintains a Professional Rapport With Students By:
   A. Communicating accurate and up-to-date knowledge of subject
   B. Providing accurate oral and written communications compatible with and acceptable in the classroom setting
   C. Communicating to students the instructional intent or plan at the beginning of a learning experience
   D. Communicating involvement and interest in the lesson
   E. Giving clear directions and explanations relating to lesson content and procedures
   F. Communicating clearly, concisely, and in a manner appropriate to the level of the students
   G. Demonstrating confidence in his/her abilities by knowing what to do and how to do it
   H. Modeling and encouraging constructive behavior patterns
2. The Teacher Obtains Feedback From and Communicates With Students in a Manner Which Enhances Student Learning and Understanding By:
   A. Assuring that learners recognize the purpose and importance of topics and activities
   B. Clarifying directions and explanations when students do not understand
   C. Giving reasonable explanations for actions, directions, and decisions when appropriate
   D. Encouraging appropriate student-to-student, as well as student-to-teacher interactions
   E. Reinforcing and encouraging students' own efforts to maintain involvement
   F. Communicating regularly with students about their needs and progress
   G. Providing constructive feedback to students about their behavior
3. The Teacher Appropriately Utilizes a Variety of Teaching Methods and Resources for Each Area Taught By:
   A. Selecting content and a variety of materials and media for lessons which are appropriate to the lessons and the learners
   B. Using teaching methods, materials, and media which address student learning levels, rates, and styles
   C. Providing opportunities and materials for students to apply or practice the knowledge and skills learned
   D. Implementing learning activities in a logical sequence
   E. Working with individuals, small groups, and large groups as appropriate
   F. Providing opportunities for students to work independently
4. The Teacher Encourages the Development of Student Involvement, Responsibility, and Critical Thinking Skills By:
   A. Using techniques to arouse student interest
   B. Using appropriate questioning techniques
   C. Providing opportunities for the active involvement of students
   D. Allowing opportunities for student thought, speculation, and creativity
   E. Using student responses and questions in teaching
   F. Giving students opportunities to make appropriate choices and take responsibility for their own learning
   G. Providing reteaching, impromptu learning, or other adjustments when necessary
5. The Teacher Manages the Classroom to Ensure the Best Use of Instructional Time By:
   A. Handling routine tasks promptly and efficiently
   B. Minimizing distractions and interruptions
   C. Having materials or media ready for student use
   D. Handling behavior problems individually when possible
6. The Teacher Creates an Atmosphere Conducive to Learning, Self-Discipline, and Development of Realistic and Positive Self-Concepts By:

Table 1 Continued

A. Establishing and stating expectations for behavior utilizing input from students
B. Allowing opportunities for students to express personal ideas, needs, and interests
C. Being sensitive to the needs and feelings of students
D. Acknowledging student achievements
E. Assuring each student some success

attention on only the classroom instructional practices of teachers. While this may be the most important part of a teacher's job, it does not cover all of their responsibilities.

It is crucial that evaluation criteria, job descriptions, and minimum expectations be fully developed so that they cover all the elements upon which one can and will be evaluated. In the case of career ladders, there must exist a baseline set of criteria that presents a thick picture of all the elements which must be satisfied before advancement can occur. In effect, this is the criteria for a district's regular, ongoing teacher evaluation system. Advancement, especially on the first steps of a career ladder, cannot be made or maintained without continuous and consistent meeting of these fundamental minimum expectations.

A full presentation of evaluation criteria for use as a generic description should include personal, organizational, professional, and performance-directed criteria. All may not be equally important in determining the overall worth or value of a teacher, but they contribute to the overall view of what a teacher is minimally expected to do and to be. Examples of criteria generated by two local districts are presented in Tables 2 and 3. Both present a set of minimum expectations or standards selected by the districts that provide the basic guidelines for the evaluation of performance.

The evaluation criteria displayed in Table 2 represent minimum expectations in a series of relatively general statements. However, all four types of criteria (personal, professional, organizational, and performance-directed) are covered, and both the responsibilities of the district and the rights of the teacher are met by this presentation style.

The evaluation criteria displayed in Table 3 represent a more detailed, more explicit set of criteria. General qualities are listed and then are broken down through a series of more specific descriptors. The qualities and the accompanying competencies are directed primarily towards performance-oriented criteria, but eventually items that represent all four types are presented.

Table 2
Evaluation Criteria in District #1

An integral part of both tenured and nontenured staff's employment in the school district is an ongoing and continuous appraisal by their supervisor of the staff members' ability to meet minimum performance expectations. As appropriate to the various jobs performed by staff in the school district, the minimum performance expectations include, but are not necessarily limited to, the following:

1. Meets and instructs the student(s) in the locations and at the time designated.
2. Develops and maintains a classroom environment conducive to effective learning within the limits of the resources provided by the district.
3. Prepares for classes assigned, and shows written evidence of preparation upon request of the immediate supervisor.
4. Encourages students to set and maintain high standards of classroom behavior.
5. Provides an effective program in instruction in accordance with the adopted curriculum and consistent and with physical limitations of the location provided and the needs and capabilities of the individuals or student groups involved to include:
   A. Review of previously taught material
   B. Presentation of new material
   C. Evaluation of student progress on a regular basis
   D. Use of a variety of teaching materials and techniques
6. Strives to implement by instruction the district's philosophy of education and to meet instructional goals and objectives.
7. Takes all necessary and reasonable precautions to protect students, equipment, materials, and facilities.
8. Maintains records as required by law, district policy, and administrative regulations.
9. Assists in upholding and enforcing school rules, administrative regulations.
10. Makes provision for being available to students and parents for education related purposes outside the instructional day when necessary and under reasonable terms.
11. Attends and participates in faculty and department meetings.
12. Cooperates with other members of the staff in planning instructional goals, objectives, and methods.
13. Assists in the selection of books, equipment, and other instructional materials.
14. Works to establish and maintain open lines of communication with students, parents, and colleagues concerning both the academic and behavioral progress of all students.
15. Establishes and maintains cooperative professional relations with others.
16. Performs related duties as assigned by the administration in accordance with the district policies and practices.

Some steps on a career ladder include additional professional responsibilities beyond regular classroom instruction. Specific criteria for these additional duties are also required. Typically, the additional duties on functions assigned on higher career ladder levels tend to be less specific or definable than the basic teaching function. Such functions or responsibilities as facilitating, coordinating, or supervising are often very difficult to define in terms of specific job behaviors.

Consequently, the general job description presented for each level often will become the most definitive statement of evaluation criteria for

Table 3
Evaluation Criteria in District #2

I. Teaching Qualities
  A. Instructional Skills
    1. Demonstrates knowledge and skills of subject matter
       a. Presents material to students in an understandable, meaningful, and interesting manner
       b. Uses examples appropriately
       c. Accurately responds to student questions
    2. Implements district curriculum
       a. Follows course outlines
       b. Follows district curriculum guidelines
       c. Meets course objectives
    3. Organizes and plans instruction
       a. Establishes intermediate and long-range objectives
       b. Maintains organized lesson plans
       c. Provides for an orderly sequence of concepts and skills
       d. Implements planned activities effectively
       e. Uses class time effectively
       f. Provides for appropriate pacing of instruction
    4. Uses a variety of teaching methods
       a. Uses a variety of questioning techniques which require students to use varying levels of thinking skills
       b. Uses an effective variety of media materials and equipment
       c. Extends the learning environment beyond the classroom
       d. Utilizes a variety of supplemental materials and resources
       e. Uses a variety of presentational techniques such as discussion (small/large group), dramatization, lecture, simulation
       f. Uses supervised study constructively
       g. Understands and uses appropriate and effective balance of oral and written presentations
    5. Provides for individual differences and needs
       a. Adjusts learning activities appropriately to include remedial and enrichment instructions
       b. Utilizes appropriate support staff
       c. Provides and uses a wide range of appropriate materials
       d. Utilizes available data on students
    6. Evaluates and communicates student progress
       a. Establishes a consistent, accurate, timely and objective procedure in determining student grades
       b. Explains expectations and procedures to students and parents
       c. Follows established guidelines for evaluation and grade reporting
       d. Uses evaluation to improve student performance
       e. Constructs and uses tests which reflect course materials taught
  B. Classroom Management Skills
    1. Directs the student learning process
       a. Establishes realistic expectations for the individual and the group

Table 3 Continued

---

       b. Encourages students to pursue realistic goals

       c. Guides students toward the achievement of their personal goals

   2. Maintains student behavior conducive to student learning

       a. Establishes clear, understandable and reasonable rules and procedures

       b. Deals directly, fairly and effectively with student behavior problems

       c. Provides positive reinforcement for acceptable behavior and performance

       d. Responds constructively to student needs and concerns

   3. Maintains a pleasant, healthful, safe, and orderly environment conducive to learning

       a. Adjusts the physical environment to maximize learning (e.g. light, temperature, seating arrangements)

       b. Senses student needs for pleasant, healthful surrounding and adjusts the environment to meet those needs

       c. Takes necessary and reasonable precautions to protect students' equipment, materials and facilities

       d. Systematically structures classroom activities to best utilize facilities

 C. Communication Skills

   1. Deals constructively with parents

       a. Initiates contact with parents when necessary

       b. Responds promptly, constructively and professionally to parent-initiated concerns

       c. Demonstrates effective conferencing skills

       d. Involves parents in the learning process

   2. Establishes and promotes rapport with students

       a. Encourages students to share ideas and concerns

       b. Is open to reasonable student suggestions and opinions

       c. Shows respect for students

       d. Uses criticism constructively

   3. Demonstrates effective oral and listening skills

       a. Speaks clearly

       b. Speaks articulately

       c. Modulates voice appropriately

       d. Uses correct grammar and diction

       e. Balances listening techniques with oral presentations

       f. Listens attentively

       g. Responds tactfully and appropriately

   4. Demonstrates effective writing skills

       a. Prepares meaningful and effective written materials

       b. Writes in a clear, concise, neat and accurate form

       c. Uses correct grammar and spelling

       d. Structures communications tactfully, appropriately, and professionally

II. Professional Qualities

 A. Responsibilities

Table 3 Continued

---

   1. Performs duties in accordance with Board of Education, administrative, school, and department policies and contractual agreement
     a. Knows policies, procedures and information governing teacher duties, responsibilities, rights and privileges
     b. Demonstrates punctuality, accuracy, and responsibility in fulfilling professional obligations
   2. Contributes productively in professional activities and organizations
     a. Supports, attends and participates in a variety of school functions
     b. Participates in professional organizations
B. Behavior
   1. Exhibits a professional attitude and behavior in interpersonal relationships
     a. Deals professionally with supervisors and administrators
     b. Deals professionally with colleagues
     c. Deals professionally with support personnel
     d. Maintains professional conduct and decorum
     e. Makes suggestions for changes or improvements through appropriate channels
   2. Shows responsibility for self-improvement and professional growth
     a. Recognizes areas for self-improvement
     b. Initiates, constructs and completes meaningful professional growth activities
     c. Attends and participates in professional conferences and workshops
     d. Applies knowledge gained from self-improvement activities
     e. Shares professional expertise
   3. Shows willingness to accept responsibility
     a. Accepts and fulfills department, building, district and professional obligations
     b. Assumes responsibility for supervising student behavior throughout the school

---

performance at that level. While not particularly desirable, this condition will continue to exist until such time as more explicit behaviors can be identified that accurately reflect such "soft" functions as facilitating and coordinating.

For the purpose of illustration, a sample career ladder plan is displayed in Table 4. While the descriptors for eligibility and requirements relate to evaluation, additional descriptors for titles, compensation, and rewards are included.

Regardless of the way the roles and responsibilities of each step on a career ladder are designed, it must be remembered that the baseline set of expectations is always functioning. Teachers at every level should be expected to satisfy the criteria of the basic minimum expectations for a teacher. This is especially true of the personal, organizational, and professional expectations. These criteria will remain appropriate no matter what level a teacher occupies. Job performance criteria may change as the teacher assumes responsibilities outside the classroom but

Table 4
Sample Career Ladder Plan

RUNG 1: PROVISIONAL

A. Eligibility
1. Hold a valid South Carolina professional or temporary certificate
2. One year or less teaching experience in South Carolina or any other state
B. Requirements
1. Teach
C. Compensation
1. Base salary

RUNG 2: ANNUAL

A. Eligibility
1. Successfully completed requirements of the Provisional rung
2. One–two years teaching experience
B. Requirements
1. Teach
C. Compensation
1. Base salary
2. Plus appropriate step

RUNG 3: CONTINUING

A. Eligibility
1. Hold a valid South Carolina certificate
2. If employed by CCSD after 1983–84, must have met all requirements of Provisional and Annual Contract Teachers
B. Requirements
1. Teach
C. Compensation
1. Base salary
2. Plus appropriate step

RUNG 4: CAREER STEP I

A. Eligibility
1. Four years of teaching experience
2. Valid certificate
3. Continuing contract status
4. Advanced training of at least three graduate hours or the equivalent, beyond recertification requirement within five years of application to participate at this rung
5. Superior score on the Teacher Performance Assessment Program Instrument
6. Outstanding participation in extracurricular activities
7. Low absentee rate average over the three years preceding application to the rung
8. Satisfactory performance on site visits/interviews
9. Completion of the Application Packet

Table 4 Continued

B. Requirements
   1. Teach
   2. May be assigned as a Cooperating Teacher
   3. May be a "Buddy-Teacher" to a Provisional or Annual Teacher at the home school
   4. Prepare materials to be used by other teachers and staff
C. Compensation
   1. Base salary
   2. Plus appropriate step
   3. Plus $1,000
D. Rewards
   1. Recognition
   2. Certificate
   3. Pin

RUNG 5: CAREER STEP II

A. Eligibility
   1. At least three years at Career Step I (But with a fast track, teachers with 25 or more years experience may qualify with one year at Career Step I.)
   2. Earn at least nine graduate credit hours or the equivalent, beyond the recertification requirement, within five years of application to this rung
   3. Maintain superior score on most recent evaluation
   4. Maintain low absentee rate within three years preceding application
   5. Perform satisfactorily any duties assigned during the period at Career Step I
   6. Willing to accept an extended day/week not to exceed three additional hours per week on the average
   7. Current membership in state and/or national curricular organizations, e.g., ASCD, NCTM, NCTE, IRA
   8. Complete Application Packet
B. Requirements
   1. Teach
   2. Become involved in leadership positions in the school/district to include but not limited to:
      a. Chair of study or program committees
      b. Department or grade level chair
      c. Faculty chairperson to organize inservices or other faculty identified programs
      d. School representatives for principal or district
      e. Coordinator of special school/district projects
      f. Approved tutorial programs
C. Compensation
   1. Base salary
   2. Plus appropriate step
   3. Plus $3,000
   4. Plus additional compensation capped at $2,000 for extended day/week service

Table 4 Continued

D. Rewards
1. Course tuition reimbursement for "A" grades in courses taken beyond state-required certification courses
2. Publicity
3. Certificate
4. Pin

RUNG 6: CAREER STEP III

A. Eligibility
1. At least three years at Career Step II (But with a fast track, teachers with 25 or more years may qualify with two years at Career Step II.)
2. Earn at least nine graduate credits or the equivalent, beyond the recertification requirements, within the five years preceding the application to this rung
3. Maintain superior performance rate on the Teacher Performance Assessment Program Instrument
4. Maintain low absentee rate
5. Perform satisfactorily duties assigned at Career Step II
6. Actively participate in national and/or state curricular organizations, e.g., ASCD, NCTE, NCTM, IRA by doing at least one of the following:
   a. Attend conferences
   b. Publish journal articles
   c. Hold office
   d. Make presentation at a conference
   e. Serve on a committee
B. Requirements
1. Teach
2. Perform additional duties of leadership to include but not limited to:
   a. Summer school principal
   b. Visiting professorship at local colleges as instructor of teachers and administrators
   c. Curriculum planning and development
   d. Internship with central staff administrator (summer only)
   e. Direct a learning lab and/or teacher center
   f. Conduct workshops for provisional and annual contract teachers for summer remediation clinic
3. Plan programs with the approval of committees in one's area of expertise or experience(s)
C. Compensation
1. Base salary
2. Plus appropriate step
3. Plus $8,000
4. Plus additional compensation capped at $3,000
D. Rewards
1. Eligible for awards to defray expenses at conferences, professional meetings, travel grants, exchange programs, etc.

these performance criteria would continue in effect for that portion of the time upper-level teachers continued to be involved in classroom instruction.

The Use of Alternative Data Sources

At this early stage in the development of career ladder plans it would appear that there is a growing consensus that the use of a variety of sources of data will become common practice within the evaluation component of these plans.

In order to make the best possible judgments regarding the quality of job performance, the fullest possible picture of that performance must be developed. While observation has been the dominant method of collecting formal data about teaching, there are other data gathering methods that can be helpful if not essential to the establishment of an effective evaluation effort. Teaching and learning are complex acts that occur in many forms and contexts. To be studied in as full a manner as possible, teaching needs to be looked at in a variety of ways.

There are eight broad techniques for collecting data for teacher evaluation. These eight techniques are (a) paper and pencil test, (b) self-evaluation, (c) parent evaluation, (d) peer evaluation, (e) student performance, (f) student evaluation, (g) artifact collection, and (h) observation. None of the eight have been proven in and of themselves to be reliable for making summative judgments. However, it is felt that judgments based on data collected from multiple sources provide increased reliability (Epstein, 1985). Each of the eight have a certain degree of logic and value, but not all are as practical, especially from a logistical or resource utilization perspective. **In an increasing order of value,** the eight techniques are discussed in the sections that follow.

Paper and Pencil Tests

A number of states have begun to mandate some type of teacher competency test as a basis for teacher certification. The basic concern here has been with what is labeled teacher illiteracy and ignorance of the content of the school curriculum. As a result, most of these tests are tests of subject-matter knowledge rather than of professional knowledge. Although it is possible to suggest that these tests do provide information that can be used as a basic screening device for entry into teaching, it must be noted that all efforts to show that scores on such tests are related to effective teaching have failed (Medley, Coker, & Soar, 1984). In addition, the validity of paper and pencil tests for measuring other kinds of knowledge, such as knowledge of how pupils learn and how they may be taught most effectively, has also not been established (Quirk, Witten, & Weinberg, 1973). There is also no evidence that any written test can measure or predict the ability to apply either subject matter or professional knowledge in the classroom (Medley, Coker, & Soar, 1984).

The conclusion to be drawn is that while there may be some value in using tests as some form of certification screening, their contribution is more political than substantive. As indicated, there is no evidence to suggest that they have a place in either formative or summative teacher evaluation.

Self-Evaluation

Brighton (1965) summarized the major reasons for using self-evaluation:

1. When self-evaluation is utilized, the teacher shares with his professional colleagues the responsibility for improving his performance.
2. Teachers, particularly those aspiring to enhance professional status, regard self-evaluation as the most acceptable type of evaluation.
3. Self-evaluation is the ultimate goal of any teacher evaluation program that seeks to promote better performance and enhance professional status. Teachers are like other professional people. The best and only effective motive for change comes from within. (p. 67)

Brighton (1965) also listed the major problems of self-evaluation:

1. Many teachers, particularly those who are marginal or insecure, tend to overrate themselves.
2. Emotionally secure teachers tend to underrate themselves.
3. Few are able to be objective in assessing their own performance, with the result that self-evaluation is both inaccurate and unreliable. (p. 68)

It is difficult to ascertain the success of systematic attempts to foster self-evaluation, primarily because so few effective examples exist. (See Bodine, 1973, or Carroll, 1981, for discussions of systematic self-assessment models.) Unfortunately, in looking at most self-evaluation efforts in schools, more problems and cautions emerge than promise.

Increasing the teacher's ability to be self-reflective should be a desired outcome of any effective evaluation system. It appears to be most useful when it happens naturally rather than being required. When a focused staff development effort is provided with a formative-oriented evaluation system, self-evaluation is likely to happen spontaneously (McGreal, 1983).

Parent Evaluation

Recent research has pointed out the usefulness and desirability of collecting parents' evaluations of their children's teachers (Epstein, 1985). However, the number of studies in this area are few and the evidence does not point to input that is significantly different from that available from other, more easily obtained sources (Becker & Epstein, 1982). It would also appear that the most useful data from parents involves their description of those activities which relate to their relationship with the teacher (ease of contact, level of communications, etc.) rather than their evaluation of the teacher's performance in the classroom (McGreal, 1983).

Peer Evaluation

There is a paucity of information on the state of peer evaluation. The information that does exist is confusing because of the interchangeable use of the terms "peer evaluation" and "peer supervision." By definition, these terms represent different activities, although they occur basically in the same form. A number of successful peer supervision programs can be identified (Alfonso, 1977; Goldsberry, 1980). However, there is an almost unanimous objection to the concept of observation and evaluation of a teacher's classroom performance by peers (McGreal, 1983). Cohen and McKeachie (1980) indicated that "any type of peer evaluation can provide only a partially valid assessment of teaching effectiveness since faculty are not in a position to evaluate all the aspects of the colleague's teaching." Bergman (1980) similarly questioned the reliability of peer evaluation by stating that "there is obviously considerable opposition to peer review, primarily because judgments all too often are based on personal, irrelevant factors." In addition, if a school district or a state implements some form of peer evaluation, the cost of training and released time to conference, observe, analyze, and report must be considered. "Peer evaluators must be properly trained in methods of observing, recording, and analyzing teacher behaviors" (McGee & Eaker, 1977).

It cannot be denied that there is a surface logic and an obvious value in having peers evaluate each other's work. In many respects peer evaluation is one of the major parts of any definition of what should characterize a profession. Nevertheless, local districts and state departments should weigh heavily the fiscal and political costs of requiring peer evaluation against the questionable reliability of the data.

Student Performance

The use of student performance data as a means of summatively evaluating teacher performance is a classic illustration of what H. L. Mencken meant when he said that every complex problem has a simple, obvious answer which is wrong.

Medley, Coker, and Soar (1984) reject the notion of the **summative** use of student performance in evaluating teachers because of problems associated with pupil variability, the regression effect, and the limitations of achievement tests presently available. Their excellent review of these problems would indicate that there is not sufficient support to justify the use of student performance as a form of summative evaluation. While there are available suggestions as to how to reduce the dangers (Millman, 1981), the recommended procedures seem beyond the training levels and time constraints of local administrators.

There is, however, support for the value of including student performance data for use as input in the **formative** evaluation of teaching. Millman (1981) offered an excellent description of how student data can be used formatively.

There is logic to the value of using student achievement as a summative measure of teacher competence. But prevailing opinion seems to be that the inherent problems in the process (inadequate tests, confounding influences on student growth, lack of reliable statistical measures) prevent product models from being appropriate. Used properly, student scores can be a valuable source of input (but the key words are used properly).

Student Evaluation

In the judgment of many, collecting information from students is a powerful source of data about classrooms (Farley, 1981; McNeil & Popham, 1973; Walberg, 1969). However, the average school teacher is uncomfortable with the concept (McGreal, 1983). Teachers generally lack faith in the student's ability to accurately rate their performance. In many respects their fears are justified. There is not a great deal of support, especially at the elementary and secondary level, for the accuracy of student ratings. The support that does exist is not strong enough to justify using student ratings in any summative sense.

The kind of data collected and how they are used are the key elements in the acceptability and usefulness of student input. The major ingredient for the successful use of student evaluations is the acceptance of the idea that students are much more reliable in describing life in the classroom than they are in making evaluative judgments of the teacher. Walberg (1974) reinforced that view when he indicated that a series of studies has demonstrated that student perceptions of the classroom learning environment can be measured reliably. The key phrase is "student perceptions of the learning environment," not student perceptions or judgments of the teacher's performance.

A number of established instruments for measuring student perceptions of the learning environment are available. The Learning Environment Inventory (Anderson, 1973; Maguire, Goetz, & Manos, 1972) and the Class Activities Questionnaire (Walberg, House, & Steele, 1973) are perhaps the best and most useful. School districts and state departments would do well to make these instruments available to their teachers and supervisors or to train them in the construction of such instruments for their individual use.

Artifact Collection

As time as a variable of learning has become a more visible concept, the way teachers and students spend their instructional time in classrooms has been studied in a more systematic and accurate fashion (Rosenshine, 1980). Current data suggest that K–12 students spend as much time interacting with teachers' materials as they do being directly taught by the teacher (McGreal & Collins, 1985). These realities of classroom life make it imperative that teacher evaluation procedures include the systematic analysis and discussion of classroom materials (McGreal, 1983).

Teaching artifacts include all instructional materials teachers use to facilitate learning. This includes everything from textbooks, workbooks, and supplementary texts to learning kits, maps, audiovisual aids, films, dittoed material, study guides, question sheets, worksheets, problem sets, quizzes, and tests. Typically, teachers assume the responsibility for collecting the artifacts for an entire teaching unit, or for a two- to three-week period from a single class. Following the collection, the teacher and supervisor meet to review, analyze, and discuss the materials.

Much research is needed to learn more about the effect of teachers' artifacts on teaching and learning. At this point, the most positive benefit seems to be the high level of technical-professional talk it generates between teachers and supervisors. While frameworks for use in adding the analysis of artifacts are available (McGreal, Broderick, & Jones, 1984), it should be assumed that the major impact of artifact collection and analysis is in formative evaluation.

Observation

Classroom observation is the most practical procedure for collecting formal data about teacher performance. The quality of observations and the ways supervisors collect and share data with teachers are major factors in the success and effectiveness of teacher evaluation systems.

Much of the usefulness of observation can be attributed to the fact that it is a learned skill. In reviewing many of the excellent sources available regarding classroom observation (for example, Acheson & Gall, 1980; Borich, 1977; Rosenshine & Furst, 1973; Stallings, 1977), there appear to be four practical ways for supervisors to improve their observational skills and to use the data once they are collected.

1. The reliability and usefulness of classroom observation is directly related to the amount and type of information supervisors have prior to the observation. (This suggests training in the techniques that are imbedded in clinical supervision.)
2. The narrower the focus supervisors use in observing classrooms, the more likely they will be able to accurately describe the events relating to that focus. (This is an encouragement for goal-setting

models and the use of the research on teaching to help focus attention on effective teaching behaviors.)

3. The impact of observational data on supervisor-teacher relationships is directly related to the way data are recorded during observation. (Observers must learn to record descriptively rather than judgmentally and should be introduced to the different types of observation instruments available.)

4. The impact of observational data on supervisor-teacher relationships is directly related to the way feedback is presented to the teacher. (This suggests the need for training in conferencing skills and the ability to write summative evaluations that contain supporting facts for all value terms used.)

Traditionally, observation has been the dominant method for collecting data about teaching. The general acceptance of observation by teachers and the fact that, under certain conditions, it is reasonably reliable, should make it remain the dominant source of formal data. However, local schools and state departments must be prepared to provide the necessary training to make it as effective as it can and should be.

Encouragement and training in the use of alternative sources of data is clearly a commonality of any effective evaluation system. The increased pressure for discriminatory judgments that is encountered within career ladder or merit pay plans only serves to increase the importance of looking totally at job performance. Common sense dictates that the most reliable and valid judgments are going to be made in direct relation to the amount and quality of data available. All of the possible sources of data discussed are most appropriate within the context of formative evaluation. Taken together, they can provide the fuller, richer picture of performance that is necessary for making summative decisions.

It must be noted that the alternative sources of data discussed in this section are directed primarily at the collection of data for use in evaluating **teaching** performance. At upper levels in career ladder plans teachers often assume additional responsibilities that do not involve direct teaching. Consequently, many of the data sources presented here are less appropriate.

In most cases, teachers placed in the upper career levels perform many different functions. This fact tends to complicate the use of typical evaluation procedures that rely on similar and consistent sources of data. It becomes almost necessary to develop evaluation procedures that are individualized to meet the unique roles of each teacher at the upper career levels. Certainly, those teachers performing the same basic duties could be evaluated similarly. But when roles and responsibilities differ, it is suggested that procedures combining the alternative sources of data discussed in this section with the use of multiple judges and teacher developed portfolios as discussed in the next section be the form that upper-level teacher evaluation takes. This issue is discussed in more detail in the next section.

The Use of Multiple Evaluators

Instead of judgments by one individual on few occasions, it is frequently suggested that multiple judges could rate teachers more reliably (Darling-Hammond, Wise, & Pease, 1985; Educational Research Service, 1983). While there appears to be a general consensus that multiple evaluators would add to more accurate judgments about performance, few have actually attempted to determine empirically what multiple judges could contribute to the evaluation of teachers (Epstein, 1985). In the absence of empirical support and with the practicalities in mind of the logistic and resource problems inherent in using multiple evaluators, it seems reasonable to find some middle ground in deciding on one or multiple judges.

Successful practice would suggest that the use of multiple evaluators might follow the form of a U-shaped curve. That is, multiple judgments are most useful at the entry or probationary levels and at the upper career levels.

At the entry level and during the first years of teaching it is important that schools be concerned about collecting reliable summative data since decisions about retention are more easily made before teachers enter into the various forms of continuing contractual service (tenure). Collecting data of this nature can be aided by different perspectives on the skills that these beginning teachers have and, perhaps more importantly, their potential for growth. Additionally, teachers in these early stages would undoubtedly profit from the more intensive, directed relationship that is possible when some form of team approach is used. Two possible models are available: (a) an adaptation of the Manatt marginal teacher assistance team (Manatt, 1984) or (b) a program similar to the California Mentor Teacher program (Wagner, 1985).

Once teachers enter into a continuing contractual situation (a tenure-track position) their personal and professional lives change along with their status in the career ladder program. During this stage they begin to accumulate additional formal training, actual years of experience, and hopefully, more advanced teaching skills. This accumulating set of skills and experiences begins to prepare them to meet the minimum expectations and requirements for advancement into the upper levels of the career ladder.

In this earlier career stage, the most productive supervision/evaluation relationship is generally achieved through a one-to-one involvement with a supervisor. The evaluation process should have a heavy orientation towards formative evaluation with the teacher playing a significant part in the process. Because of the tenure situation, summative evaluation becomes far less of an issue. This type of formative, mutually involved process is best encouraged through individual goal-setting models that put a supervisor and a teacher into a closer, more collegial environment. These types of evaluation procedures are almost always most productive when the teacher is responsible to only one supervisor rather than several. (See McGreal, 1983, for a more detailed discussion of goal-setting models involving single evaluators.)

In making evaluative judgments regarding entry and retention at the highest career levels, the nature of the criteria would suggest the usefulness of multiple sources of data (see preceding section) as well as multiple judges. There are two issues involved in developing evaluation procedures for the upper career levels. These issues involve (a) the way and the type of data that are collected and (b) who takes responsibility for collecting and presenting the data. Typically data collection is the responsibility of the administration, carried out by administrators, or by officially designated "others" such as peers or parents. This is most easily done when the teacher is performing a single function such as regular classroom instruction. In this instance all the data collected can be focused on an act that is familiar and repetitive. However, at upper levels within career ladders, the selected staff assume functions and responsibilities outside of regular instruction. Many standard data collection techniques become less appropriate and useable. For example, observation becomes far less valuable when career level teachers are involved in tasks that are not related to direct classroom teaching. Additionally, teachers qualified for or already holding upper-level positions tend to be more mature, more experienced, and more competent than others. It would seem that the typical models for evaluation that rely on administrative overseeing and monitoring would be less necessary and less appropriate.

The group of people who are qualified to assume advanced career level positions should be allowed and encouraged to take the responsibility of selecting and, in some cases, collecting the data from which judgments of their performance can be made. This process, often labeled the portfolio approach, is clearly a significant and emerging trend.

In this process the teachers take the responsibility for collecting the data that they feel provide an accurate picture of their performance. This may include such alternative sources of data as administrator write-ups of teaching performance as determined through observation, student test scores, student evaluations, parent letters, recommendations and comments from peers, etc. This collection of data is collected and placed in a "portfolio" which is then reviewed by a jury of evaluators. This procedure encourages the treatment of upper career level applicants or job holders as professionals by allowing them the option of collecting and selecting the sources of data about their performance.

This section clearly is suggesting a form of differentiated evaluation that matches procedures to the maturity, competence, and location within the career ladder of the teachers. This recommended way of addressing the issues of alternative data sources and multiple judges seems to be emerging as a viable and effective means for improving evaluation procedures.

Concern for Both Formative and Summative Evaluation

The making of evaluative judgments about advancement and retention within career ladders is a necessary activity. But this need for summative judgments should not be allowed to completely shape the form and substance of the evaluation system. The most effective evaluation systems within career ladder and merit pay plans have consciously built their systems with an emphasis on formative evaluation techniques while still allowing for the needed summative judgments.

As decisions become increasingly important for job differentiation and as money and responsibility become rewards, there is a tendency for the summative aspect of evaluation to become increasingly emphasized. However, experience in building regular teacher evaluation suggests that maintaining an emphasis on instructional improvement promotes greater teacher involvement, a higher likelihood of changes in teacher classroom behavior, and better teacher-supervisor attitudes toward evaluation (Harris, 1986; McGreal, 1983; Medley, Coker, & Soar, 1984; Redfern, 1980). For purposes of building new evaluation systems within career ladder plans, these characteristics of formatively oriented systems seem to be able to exist without interfering with the ability to make summative judgments. On the other hand, systems that are built with procedures and processes that focus predominately on summative outcomes seem to seldom be accompanied by these characteristics (McGreal, 1983).

The practicality of formative procedures is in many ways a reflection of the realities of our ability to reliably evaluate teacher performance. Evidence still suggests that our ability to collect data about teaching to improve performance is far more reliable than our ability to summatively rate teaching performance (Medley, Coker, & Soar, 1984). Almost all of the training available to supervisors to enhance their supervision and evaluation skills is drawn from formative techniques (clinical supervision; classroom observation skills such as scripting and category system; artifact collection; conferencing skills). This does not mean that valuing cannot or should not occur, but it does mean that the attitudes which determine the way evaluation systems take shape and the training that accompanies new systems must take into account the importance of allowing and encouraging formative and summative evaluation to be complementary activities, not competing (see McGreal, 1983, and Medley, Coker, & Soar, 1984, for suggestions as to the use of formatively collected data in making summative judgments).

Evaluation Systems Linked to the Staff Development Program

This commonality is present in discussions of both evaluation systems and effective staff development programs. It seems obvious that you cannot put the same supervisors (same in the sense that no specific training has been provided to them) in a new evaluation system and expect changes, let alone improvement, to occur. It is equally inappropriate to think that additional supervisory training will promote significant improvement if supervisors come back to an evaluation system whose procedures and required processes do not encourage or allow good practice to happen.

Ideally, the necessary relationship between evaluation and staff development is fostered by a vision that sees career ladder plans as a subset of a bigger movement within a local district or throughout a state. This bigger movement involves the development of a three- to seven-year plan that has as its major focus the enhancement of classroom instructional practices within the schools. The first stage in the plan is the identification and implementation of training programs that would provide a series of interventions and experiences that by intent and design provide research-based information on effective teaching and supervisory practices. Examples would include such programs as those based on the work of Madeline Hunter (Hunter, 1985), the training programs that have emerged from the teacher effects research (Evertson & Emmer, 1984; Kerman & Martin, 1980; Mohlman, Kierstead, & Gundlach, 1982; Rosenshine, 1983), and training in clinical supervision and its various derivatives (Acheson & Gall, 1980; Glatthorn, 1984; Glickman, 1980). As the training in one or more of these programs is implemented, then the introduction of new regular evaluation systems and career ladder plans can be seen as being complementary to and a reflection of the bigger movement towards enhanced teaching and learning.

Staff development provides the consistency of common definition of terms and language, and a focus on instruction and the supervision of instruction that is necessary for the development of successful supervisor-teacher interaction. The evaluation system provides for the continuous and ongoing focus on the skills and practices developed during the staff development experiences. In many respects the evaluation system within the career ladder program becomes the maintenance vehicle for staff development after the trainers have all left.

This symbiotic relationship must be recognized and allowed to happen. Early attempts at building career ladder programs, especially those at the state level, failed to develop this bigger plan whereby career ladders could be seen as a natural part of a more positive and educationally sound movement. Instead career ladders were developed as another of a series of relatively independent acts designed to "reform" educational practice. The programs by their hasty implementation separated professional development from evaluation. Training that was provided or required was generally given only to the evaluators and not to the teachers. This practice virtually assures that communication and understanding between supervisor and teachers will be difficult to obtain.

This symbiotic relationship is absolutely essential to the successful development of career ladder programs. Local districts and state agencies would do well to be sure that the larger vision of improved practice drives a coordinated effort in meshing career ladder programs and staff development.

RECOMMENDATIONS

Career ladder programs have the potential to address a number of teacher and teaching issues. Central to the success of career ladder programs are the type and quality of evaluation procedures that exist within those programs. Despite their checkered past, evaluation systems still offer the best opportunity for improving the quality of teaching and learning. Research in this area is growing and effective practices already exist. Knowledge of the research when combined with the best information about successful practice can greatly enhance the likelihood that newly developed career ladder programs can be effectively implemented. This chapter and this book have been developed to aid in the dissemination of this knowledge and information. Recommendations are listed below to guide the planning and developing of evaluation practices for use in career ladder plans.

1. Density of Leadership
    A. Successful leadership must be active leadership.
    B. Superintendents and central office staff must be physically and emotionally involved in the school-wide process of planning, developing, and implementing a local evaluation plan.
    C. At the state level, leadership from the top must be focused and obvious.
    D. It is important for state officials to identify and encourage influential educational leaders to serve as the major spokespersons for the evaluation.
    E. Leadership must also be dispersed throughout the organization.
    F. Special attention must be given to identifying those individuals within state education departments who can be pulled together into a small working group who will assume the major share of responsibility for dissemination and training in the evaluation phase of a career ladder program.
    G. If the option is still available, most states should allow schools to develop their own evaluation procedures.
2. Clear Criteria
    A. Clear, visible, and appropriate criteria must be identified.

B. It is crucial that evaluation criteria, job descriptions, and minimum expectations be fully developed so that they cover all the elements upon which teachers can be evaluated.

C. Criteria for advancement in a career ladder plan should be detailed and descriptive.

D. A full presentation of evaluation criteria for use as a generic description should include personal, organizational, professional, and performance-directed criteria.

E. The job description presented at each level of the career ladder actually will become the most definitive statement of evaluation criteria for performance at that level.

F. Teachers at every level should be expected to satisfy the criteria of the basic minimum expectations for a teacher.

3. The Use of Alternative Data Sources

   A. For the evaluation of teaching, several alternative sources of data should be used including:
      (1) Paper and pencil tests
      (2) Self-evaluation
      (3) Parent evaluation
      (4) Peer evaluation
      (5) Student performance
      (6) Student evaluation
      (7) Artifact collection
      (8) Observation

   B. For the evaluation of additional professional duties that are typically performed by teachers at upper levels in career ladders, individualized procedures combining alternative data sources with multiple judges and teacher collected portfolios provide the most reliable form of evaluation.

4. The Use of Multiple Evaluators

   A. Multiple evaluators are most useful at the entry or probationary levels and at the upper career levels.

   B. Collecting summative data for teachers in their early years can be aided by different perspectives (different evaluators) on the skills that the beginning teachers have and on their potential for growth.

   C. In the early years of a teacher's career, the most productive supervision/evaluation relationship is generally achieved through a one-to-one involvement with a supervisor with a heavy focus on formative evaluation.

D. In making evaluation judgments regarding entry and retention at the highest career levels, the nature of the criteria would suggest the usefulness of multiple sources of data as well as multiple judges. Thus it would seem that the typical models of evaluation that rely on administrative overseeing and monitoring would be less necessary and less appropriate.

E. The group of people who are qualified to assume advanced career level positions should be allowed and encouraged to take the responsibility of selecting and, in some cases, collecting the data from which judgments of their performance can be made. This process is often labeled the portfolio approach. This procedure encourages the treatment of upper career level applicants or job holders as professionals by allowing them the option of collecting and selecting the sources of data about their performance.

5. Concern for Both Formative and Summative Evaluation
   A. It is necessary to make evaluative judgments about advancement and retention within a career ladder plan.
   B. There should be an emphasis on formative evaluation while still allowing for the needed summative judgments.
   C. Formative and summative evaluation should be complementary activities, not competing activities.

6. Evaluation Systems Linked to the Staff Development Program
   A. Staff development programs should be designed to address research-based information on effective teaching and supervisory practices.
   B. The introduction of new, regular evaluation systems within a career ladder plan can then be seen as complementary to and a reflection of the bigger movement towards enhanced teaching and learning.
   C. The evaluation system should provide for continuous and ongoing focus on the skills and practices developed during the staff development experiences.
   D. This symbiotic relationship between staff development and evaluation must be recognized and allowed to happen.
   E. Local school districts and state agencies should have a larger

vision of improved practice that drives a coordinated effort in meshing career ladder programs and staff development.

REFERENCES

Acheson, K., & Gall, M. (1980). *Techniques in the clinical supervision of teachers.* New York: Longman.

Alfonso, R. (1977). Will peer supervision work? *Educational Leadership, 33,* 593–595.

Anderson, G. (1973). *The assessment of learning inventory.* Halifax, Nova Scotia, Canada: Atlantic Institute for Education.

Becker, H., & Epstein, J. (1982). Parent involvement: A study of teacher practices. *The Elementary School Journal, 83,* 85–102.

Bergman, J. (1980). Peer evaluation of university faculty. *College Student Journal, 14,* 57–61.

Bodine, R. (1973). Teacher's self-assessment. In E. House (Ed.), *School evaluation: The politics and process.* Berkeley, CA: McCutcheon.

Bolton, D. (1973). *Selection and evaluation of teachers.* Berkeley, CA: McCutcheon.

Borich, G. (1977). *The appraisal of teaching.* Reading, PA: Addison-Wesley.

Brighton, S. (1965). *Increasing your accuracy in teacher evaluation.* Englewood Cliffs, NJ: Prentice-Hall.

Carroll, J. G. (1981). Faculty self-evaluation. In J. Millman (Ed.), *Handbook of teacher evaluation.* Beverly Hills, CA: Sage.

Changing course: A 50-state survey of reform measures. (1985, February). *Education Week, 4*(2), 11–30.

Cohen, P., & McKeachie, W. (1980). The role of colleagues in the evaluation of college teaching. *Improving College and University Teaching, 28,* 147–150.

Cohn, M., & Natriello, G. (1984). *Critical issues in the development of a merit pay system.* Paper presented at the annual meeting of the American Educational Research Association, New Orleans, LA.

Cornett, L. (1985). Trends and emerging issues in career ladder plans. *Educational Leadership, 43,* 6–10.

Darling-Hammond, L., Wise, A., & Pease, S. (1985). Teacher evaluation in the organizational context: A review of the literature. *Review of Educational Research, 53,* 283–328.

Educational Research Service. (1983). *Merit pay plans for teachers: Status and descriptions.* Arlington, VA: Author.

Epstein, J. (1985). A question of merit: Principals' and parents' evaluations of teaching. *Educational Researcher, 14,* 3–10.

Evertson, C., & Emmer, E. (1984). *Organization and management for elementary teachers.* New York: Holt, Rinehart & Winston.

Farley, J. (1981). Student interviews as an evaluation tool. *Educational Leadership, 39,* 185–187.

Glatthorn, A. (1984). *Differentiated supervision.* Alexandria, VA: Association for Supervision and Curriculum Development.

Glickman, C. (1980). *Developmental supervision.* Alexandria, VA: Association for Supervision and Curriculum Development.

Goldsberry, L. (1980). *Colleague consultation.* Unpublished doctoral dissertation, University of Illinois, Champaign-Urbana, IL.

Harris, B. (1986). *Developmental teacher evaluation.* Newton, MA: Allyn & Bacon.

Hunter, M. (1985). Knowing, teaching, and supervising. In P. Hosford (Ed.), *Using what we know about teaching*. Alexandria, VA: Association for Supervision and Curriculum Development.

Iwanicki, E. (1981). Contract plans. In J. Millman (Ed.), *Handbook of teacher evaluation*. Beverly Hills, CA: Sage.

Johnson, S. M. (1984). Merit pay plans for teachers: A poor prescription for reform. *Harvard Educational Review, 54,* 175–185.

Jordon, K., & Barkow, N. (1983). *Merit pay for elementary and secondary teachers: Background discussion and analysis of issues*. Washington, DC: Congressional Research Service, Library of Congress.

Kerman, S., & Martin, M. (1980). *Teacher expectation and student achievement — TESA*. Bloomington, IN: Phi Delta Kappa.

Maguire, T., Goetz, E., & Manos, J. (1972). *The evaluation of two instruments for assessing classroom climate for primary grades*. Alberta, Canada: Alberta Human Resources Council.

Manatt, R. (1984). *Supervising the marginal teacher* (Video Cassette Recording). Alexandria, VA: Association for Supervision and Curriculum Development.

McGee, J., & Eaker, R. (1977). Clinical supervision and teacher anxiety. *Contemporary Education, 49,* 24–30.

McGreal, T. (1983). *Successful teacher evaluation*. Alexandria, VA: Association for Supervision and Curriculum Development.

McGreal, T., Broderick, E., & Jones, J. (1984). Teacher artifacts. *Educational Leadership, 42,* 30–33.

McGreal, T., & Collins, C. (1985). *Seatwork: A perspective for teacher trainers and supervisors*. Unpublished manuscript.

McKeachie, W. J. (1976). Psychology in America's bicentennial year. *American Psychologist, 31,* 819–833.

McNeil, J., & Popham, W. J. (1973). The assessment of teacher competence. In R. Travers (Ed.), *Second handbook of research on teaching*. Chicago, IL: Rand-McNally.

Medley, D., Coker, H., & Soar, R. (1984). *Measurement-based evaluation of teacher performance*. New York: Longman.

Millman, J. (Ed.). (1981). *Handbook of teacher evaluation*. Beverly Hills, CA: Sage.

Mohlman, G., Kierstead, J., & Gundlach, M. (1982). A research-based model for secondary teachers. *Educational Leadership, 40,* 16–19.

Murphy, J., & Hallinger, P. (in press). The superintendent as instructional leader: Findings from effective school districts. *The Journal of Educational Administration*.

Popham, W. J. (1981). *Teacher evaluation: The wrong tests for the right job*. Paper presented at the annual meeting of the American Educational Research Association, Los Angeles, CA.

Quirk, T., Witten, B., & Weinberg. (1973). Review of studies of the concurrent and predictive validity of the National Teachers Examinations. *Review of Educational Research, 43,* 89–113.

Raths, J. (1982). Research synthesis on summative evaluation of teaching. *Educational Leadership, 39,* 310–313.

Redfern, G. (1980). *Evaluating teachers and administrators: A performance objectives approach*. Boulder, CO: Westview Press.

Rosenshine, B. (1980). How time is spent in elementary classrooms. In C. Denham & A. Lieberman (Eds.), *Time to learn*. Washington, DC: U.S. Government Printing Office.

Rosenshine, B. (1983). Teaching functions in instructional programs. *The Elementary School Journal, 83,* 335–351.

Rosenshine, B., & Furst, N. (1973). The use of direct observation to study teaching. In R. Travers (Ed.), *Second handbook of research on teaching*. Skokie, IL: Rand-McNally.

Scriven, M. (1981). Summative teacher evaluation. In J. Millman (Ed.), *Handbook of teacher evaluation.* Beverly Hills, CA: Sage.

Stallings, J. (1977). *Learning to look.* Belmont, CA: Wadsworth.

Strike, K., & Bull, B. (1981). Fairness and the legal context of teacher evaluation. In J. Millman (Ed.), *Handbook of teacher evaluation.* Beverly Hills, CA: Sage.

Travers, R. M. W. (1981). Criteria of good teaching. In J. Millman (Ed.), *Handbook of teacher evaluation.* Beverly Hills, CA: Sage.

Wagner, L. A. (1985). Ambiguities and possibilities in California's mentor teacher program. *Educational Leadership, 43*(3), 23–29.

Wagoner, R., & O'Hanlon, J. (1968). Teacher attitudes towards evaluation. *Journal of Teacher Education, 19,* 471–475.

Walberg, H. (1969). Predicting class learning: A multivariate approach to the class as a social system. *American Educational Research Journal, 4,* 529–540.

Walberg, H. (Ed.). (1974). *Evaluating educational performance.* Berkeley, CA: McCutcheon.

Walberg, H., House, E., & Steele, J. (1973). Grade level, cognition, and affect: A cross section of classroom perceptions. *Journal of Educational Psychology, 74,* 250–260.

Wittrock, M. (Ed.). (1986). *The handbook of research on teaching* (3rd ed.). New York: Macmillan.

Wise, A., & Darling-Hammond, L. (1984). *Evaluation: A study of effective practices.* Santa Monica, CA: Rand.

Zimmerer, T., & Stroh, T. (1974). Preparing managers for performance appraisal. *Advanced Management Journal, 39,* 36–42.

Chapter 8

PROMOTING THE PROFESSIONAL DEVELOPMENT OF TEACHERS

GEORGEA MOHLMAN SPARKS

Why consider the issue of professional development in a book on career ladders? What should be the goals and content of a professional development program that supports career ladder plans? What do we need to know about teachers as adult learners? How should the professional development activities be conducted to ensure that teachers grow and improve? Recent research, experience, and common sense will be combined to answer these questions in the following sections. The chapter will conclude with recommendations for how professional development programs can support career ladder systems.

WHY INCLUDE PROFESSIONAL DEVELOPMENT IN CAREER LADDER SYSTEMS?

Career ladders as described in this book clearly require teachers to (a) improve teaching skills and to (b) learn new skills required by their new position on the ladder. When teachers are approaching eligibility for promotion to a higher level on a career ladder, they should have the opportunity to attend sessions where the critical skills they will be evaluated on are reviewed and practiced. These workshops or study groups also provide a source of moral support (Little, 1982) as teachers help each other prepare for the impending evaluation.

Once a teacher has reached a new level in the career ladder, new skills may be needed. Among these may be skills in supervision, mentoring for new or struggling teachers, evaluating eligible teachers, staff development, curriculum development, collaborative planning, research, and managing the change process. Most teachers who have been doing little else than teaching will not have the expertise to accomplish the tasks

163

required of them in their new positions. If a career ladder system is to succeed, extensive staff development support must be provided so teachers can both move up the ladder and successfully fulfill their new roles as they move up.

WHAT ARE THE GOALS OF
PROFESSIONAL DEVELOPMENT?

Before asking how we should conduct professional development activities, a more important question needs to be asked. That is, what are the goals or outcomes of professional development programs? We've said that there are two purposes for career-ladder-related staff development programs—improving teaching and developing leadership skills in curriculum and training. Let us first deal with the improvement of teaching.

If the goal for teacher improvement is to create a cadre of teachers who all teach according to a predetermined set of "effective" practices, the delivery system will look one way. If the goal is to create thoughtful, reflective professionals capable of making decisions based on a large bank of research and practical knowledge, then the staff development processes will look quite different. If we are serious about developing truly professional teachers then the latter goal will guide our design of staff development activities. Classrooms are too complex and students vary too widely for any one set of content or prescriptions to be very helpful. Teachers can, however, be given opportunities to develop a framework for interpreting what happens in their classrooms so they can make the most productive decisions possible.

The outcomes of the second aspect of career-ladder-related staff development programs also need to be examined. Training for leadership roles in staff or curriculum development can also be accomplished in a more or less prescriptive way. For example, when training teachers to become trainers in effective teaching workshops, two approaches can be taken. In the first, the teacher watches another person deliver the workshops, participates in the workshops, teams with a more experienced presenter, and eventually takes on full training responsibilities. Such training-of-trainers models often lack a critical ingredient—a deep understanding of the research and theory that underlie the recommended teaching strategies. Ideally, professional development for such school leaders would include in-depth study of research methods, findings, and contexts so that the workshop leader can handle questions from a deep store of knowledge of effective teaching.

When thinking of the goals of professional development it is important to keep in mind that teachers are much less receptive to learning anything new when they are fearful or defensive. They may become fearful because they (a) think they will lose their job or earn less money unless they teach or perform in a rigid, predetermined way; (b) think that the professional development activities are not really for their growth, but, rather for their evaluation; or (c) believe that the career ladder system is unfair or biased. Many teachers in career ladder programs may react this way to any attempt to provide professional development opportunities. A major challenge for career ladder developers and implementers is to create an environment where teachers feel professionally esteemed rather than demeaned. One way to create such a nonthreatening environment is to allow flexibility for teachers' individual differences and to clearly respect their competence when establishing program goals.

WHAT SHOULD BE THE CONTENT OF PROFESSIONAL DEVELOPMENT PROGRAMS THAT SUPPORT CAREER LADDERS?

Of course, the answer to this question will rely heavily on (a) the locally developed evaluation instruments which reflect the school or district's definition of effective teaching and (b) the skills required in teachers' new roles at the higher levels of the career ladder.

Professional Development Programs in Effective Teaching

Each area of teaching that is evaluated in a career ladder plan will typically have various levels of competency, from minimal performance to exceptional performance. Professional development programs naturally will want to gear their content to the areas of teaching assessed and to the operational definitions of acceptable performance in those areas.

There is a caution needed, however, regarding using only minimum performance levels to guide the design of staff development programs. The minimum criteria—the "bare bones" indicators of proficiency—should not limit what is offered in staff development programs nor should it limit definitions of effective teaching at the higher levels of the career ladder. It is impossible for any evaluation system to reflect all aspects of the artistry of teaching (see Gage, 1985). Just because an element of teaching is not included in an evaluation instrument used at the lower levels of the career ladder does not mean that this strategy should not be included at higher levels or that it should be excluded as a training topic.

For example, while the use of cooperative learning strategies (Johnson & Johnson, 1984; Slavin, 1980) may not be required for promotion to a lower level, the research indicates that these techniques are especially helpful in multicultural and heterogeneous classrooms. Teachers should have the opportunity to add cooperative learning to their repertoire of teaching strategies as they approach the middle of the career ladder. Other promising teaching approaches (e.g., content-area reading strategies) should also be included in the professional development programs regardless of whether they are included in the evaluation criteria.

Many states are drawing in part on the research on teacher effectiveness to guide their development of standards for classroom teaching performance. The research has highlighted several topics for staff development programs including proactive classroom management (Emmer & Evertson, 1981), discipline (Kounin, 1970), teacher expectations (Good, 1981), student learning styles (Dunn & Dunn, 1978), questioning strategies (Hunter, 1976), cooperative learning (Johnson & Johnson, 1984; Slavin, 1980), motivation and reinforcement, and designing lessons to ensure mastery of objectives (Hunter, 1976). The list could go on and on.

Teachers may find they need to polish their instructional and classroom management skills for at least three reasons: (a) to improve or acquire skills that will be assessed for promotion, (b) to perform a supervisory role at their new career level, and (c) to design and deliver workshops on effective teaching. A thorough knowledge of the instructional process is clearly needed to perform these tasks.

An understanding of how the effective teaching research was done can lead to the thoughtful use of this content in staff development programs. The research on teaching has not highlighted every effective practice imaginable nor has it yielded statements about effective teaching that apply in all teaching situations (Gage, 1985). For these reasons, it is best to use the research as a springboard for encouraging teacher reflection rather than as a source of prescriptions for practice.

There are many teaching practices that have been shown to relate to and/or cause improved student achievement test scores in basic skills.

These include strategies for organizing the classroom (Evertson, Emmer, Sanford, & Clements, 1984); the concept of Academic Learning Time (Denham & Lieberman, 1980); the use of praise (Brophy, 1983); the influence of teacher expectations on students' opportunity to learn (Good & Brophy, 1984); learning styles (McCarthy, 1981); cooperative group learning strategies (Johnson, Johnson, & Maruyama, 1983); and the teaching functions of reviewing, presenting content, guided practice, feedback and correctives, and independent practice (Rosenshine & Stevens, 1986). For an in-depth review of the research on teaching, see the **Handbook of Research on Teaching** (Wittrock, 1986).

It is important to recognize that the methods used in the effective teaching research required that teaching behavior be measured using reliable and valid observation instruments. Thus, any behavior that could not be consistently seen or assessed was not included as a research variable. Clearly, there are many important aspects of teaching (e.g., communication styles) that are difficult to measure reliably and objectively. The fact that certain subtle teaching practices do not appear in the research findings does not mean they are not important to consider in career ladder or in staff development programs.

It is also important to recognize that the outcomes studied have almost always been standardized achievement test scores. Again, the fact that other important educational outcomes (e.g., critical thinking) have not appeared in the research does not mean that such outcomes should not be considered in the professional development of teachers or in career ladder plans.

The upshot of this discussion is that effective teaching research provides some valuable insights into the teaching behaviors that are likely to work when the goal is improved test scores. It provides a common language and a set of concepts that can be helpful in analyzing the teaching act. For these reasons, it provides excellent content for staff development programs. When effective teaching research is used as the only way of looking at teaching or as a source of prescriptions, however, it does a disservice to the professional competence of teachers.

Content for Professional Development Programs in Subject Areas

Content mastery is another of the many areas assessed by career ladder systems. With so many teachers teaching subjects for which they have little or no preparation, assessing competence in this area takes on added importance. Workshops on teaching critical concepts and skills in math, science, writing, reading, or social studies may be needed by teachers who see themselves as weak in subject matter expertise. With the current emphasis on the teaching of higher level thinking, new understandings and skills may be needed by teachers who, heretofore, were not asked to teach such content. The resurgence of interest in the arts also indicates a need for programs in this area. Again, I would refer the reader to the **Handbook of Research on Teaching** (Wittrock, 1986) for a summary of recent research on the teaching of subject matter.

Content for Professional Development Programs in Knowledge and Skills Needed to Perform New Tasks

The skills needed by teachers as they move up to new levels on the career ladder will be dictated by the unique characteristics of the particular career ladder system. Among the new roles taken on by teachers might be: assisting with teacher preparation in cooperation with a local university or college (e.g., pre-student teaching or student teaching supervision), serving as a mentor for other teachers, assisting in the continuing professional development of other inservice teachers, providing inservice training, developing inservice training materials and programs, developing curriculum programs and materials, and conducting research and program evaluation tasks. The roles of teachers and administrators are discussed at length in Chapter 5.

The training content for teachers taking on the role of staff developer might include skills and knowledge listed in Table 1.

TABLE 1
Skills Needed at Higher Levels of Career Ladders

Supervisory Skills

   a. Clinical supervision (Cogan, 1973)
   b. Developmental supervision (Glickman, 1985)
   c. Differentiated supervision (Glatthorn, 1984)
   d. Peer coaching processes (Showers, 1985; Wolfe, 1985)

Staff Development and Training Delivery

   a. Research on effective staff development (Sparks, 1983a; Joyce & Showers, 1983)

b. Adult learning theory (Burden, 1985; Knowles, 1978; McCarthy, 1985)

Aspects of Change

a. Stages of concern related to change (Hall & Loucks, 1978)
b. Collaborative planning (Peters & Waterman, 1982)
c. Consensus building (Lindaman & Lippett, 1979)

Effective Teaching

a. Effective teaching research (Wittrock, 1986)
b. Instructional design (Gagne, 1977)

The research related to many of these topics is summarized in this book.

Teachers taking on the role of curriculum developer will need training in instructional design (Gagne, 1977), content-specific effective practices (see Wittrock, 1986), and program evaluation procedures (Cook & Campbell, 1979). As teachers near the top of the career ladder and begin to share administrative responsibilities, they will need training in leadership skills (Shulman & Sykes, 1983), e.g., planning, preparing budgets, and conducting meetings.

WHAT DOES ONE NEED TO KNOW ABOUT ADULT LEARNING WHEN PROMOTING THE PROFESSIONAL DEVELOPMENT OF TEACHERS?

Before considering the organizational climate and the delivery systems of career-ladder-related professional development programs it is important to pause and consider the learner—the professional adult. Four topics related to adult learning are discussed here: teacher concerns, adult learners' development and preferences, teachers' conceptual levels, and teachers' attitudes toward change.

Teacher Concerns

Being sensitive to the needs and concerns of the participants in a professional development program is a major key to success. Planners and trainers will want to use the Concerns-Based Adoption Model (CBAM) (Hall & Loucks, 1978) to continuously monitor participants' concerns and adapt the planned activities to those needs. When teachers have personal or informational concerns (e.g., "How long do I have between the training and the time I'll be evaluated on my classroom use of the new techniques?"), they will make little progress until these needs are addressed through clear communication of expectations and policies related to career ladders.

When teachers are concerned with management of newly learned strategies (e.g., "It's taking me forever to plan my lessons using the required format!"), they need concrete demonstrations, and guided practice with feedback. When teachers are finally at the impact stages (e.g., "It's making a difference with my kids!") or higher (e.g., "I think I've found a better way to do this"), they are ready to begin to help others and to take a stronger leadership role (Glickman, 1985; Hall & Loucks, 1978). Thus, being in touch with the predominant concerns of participants in career ladder staff development programs allows maximum growth with the least discomfort on the part of the learner. Monitoring concerns can also aid in identification of those teachers ready to become staff developers.

Adult Learning

It is important to consider the principles of adult learning when promoting the professional development of teachers. One assumption arising from research in this area is that adults naturally strive toward greater competence and feelings of self worth (Levine, 1985). Two strands of adult learning research relate to staff development: developmental stages and needs experienced by adults of all ages.

Teacher Development

As adults progress through various age-related stages, they experience different interests and needs which impact their perceptions of work (Levinson, Darrow, Klein, Levinson, & McKee, 1978; Sheehy, 1976). In the mid-twenties, first commitments are made to work and family. In the late twenties and early thirties, long-range commitments are carefully examined. After a period of settling down in the thirties, the forties usher in a period of uncertainty regarding values and priorities. Stabilization with family, friends and personal interests characterize the late forties and fifties. Later, adults mellow and increase their commitment to relationships (Burden, 1986).

Teachers progress through developmental stages in their careers. Based on Burden's (1986) summary of the research on teacher development, three stages seem apparent. In the beginning stage, the new teacher is struggling for survival; in the middle stage, the teacher is adjusting, growing, and exploring; in the final stage, the teacher is a mature professional.

These age and career stages can be related to teachers' professional development needs (Levine, 1985). For example, a beginning teacher will typically exhibit a high degree of energy and a desire to learn. Professional development activities will capitalize on this youthful exhuberance through providing mentors and opportunities to experiment with a variety of roles. Teachers in the middle stages tend to be concerned with the development of competence and career advancement. These teachers will need opportunities to take on new responsibilities, for example through mentoring or providing inservice training. Teachers nearing the end of their careers will express interest in health and retirement issues (Krupp, 1981). Opportunities for nurturing younger colleagues and students will be especially valuable for late-career teachers.

Professional development can work hand in hand with career ladders to meet the needs of teachers at different developmental stages. Teachers at similar stages can be brought together to share their experiences and to determine their goals regarding career stages. Teachers moving from one stage to the next can share their experience and wisdom with teachers just entering that stage (Levine, 1985).

Preferences of Adult Learners

Adult learners share many preferences when it comes to professional development programs. Among these are a desire for job-relevance, active involvement with concrete practices, control over their own learning, small-group informal sharing, and a safe nonthreatening environment (Levine, 1985; Wood & Thompson, 1980). Adults will feel committed to learning new concepts and practices when they find that the new learnings are job-related and help make their classroom more successful. Thus, providing specific ideas or techniques that are successful with students is critical to maintaining the motivation of teachers (Knowles, 1978).

But, learning a new strategy in a workshop does not guarantee that it will be used with success in the classroom; and if the latter never happens, motivation to continue learning is lost. Thus, active involvement with the new practices in simulated situations (e.g., role-playing) and on-site assistance with classroom implementation are important elements of staff development (Joyce & Showers, 1981). This need for concrete practice becomes even more apparent when one realizes that many adults may be operating at Piaget's concrete operational stage rather than the formal operational stage of intellectual development (McKinnan, 1976).

Teachers also prefer to exercise control over their own learning. Because most teachers have been performing their teaching tasks with little or no on-the-job training, they see themselves as competent professionals and resist any intimation or action that indicates otherwise. Thus, mandated programs and prescribed sets of teaching practices are likely to be rejected. If we wish to develop professionals, we need to give teachers an active role in decision making and a choice of goals and activities. Teachers need to be involved in goal setting and planning related to professional development programs and career ladders. A useful model for collaborative staff development planning is provided by Wood, Thompson, and Russell (1981; also see Sparks, 1985).

Many adults seem to prefer small-group informal learning situations where there is intimacy and an opportunity to share their experiences with others (Sparks, 1983a; Wood & Thompson, 1980). In such situations, teachers find they have something (an experience or an effective technique) to offer other teachers; this, in turn, is a great self-esteem booster. Just as important, they often pick up something new to try from their colleagues. Such support groups also provide a safe, nonthreatening environment where risk taking and experimentation are encouraged (Sparks, 1984; Stallings, 1982). To meet the professional needs of teachers, small-group sharing, peer visitations, and mentoring systems will be extremely effective.

Teachers' learning styles (McCarthy, 1985) will also influence the selection of activities and learning situations. Some teachers learn best by pondering, others learn by watching, and others acquire new skills only by doing. Such preferences in learning styles should also be explored and considered when designing career-ladder-related professional development programs.

Teachers' Conceptual Levels

Knowing teachers' level of intellectual functioning (Hunt, 1975) can help determine what kind of professional development experiences are best for them. Teachers who typically think at lower levels of abstraction may need concrete demonstrations and carefully guided practice and feedback to learn new practices or ways of thinking. Teachers at higher levels of abstraction will need less direct assistance and an environment that encourages innovation and adaptation with new practices or ideas (Glickman, 1985).

Of course, the goal is to create professional development programs that move teachers to higher levels of conceptual functioning where they become more reflective, analytical decision makers. In fact, research indicates that teachers at higher conceptual levels were more adaptive in their teaching style, used a wider variety of teaching approaches, and were more sensitive to their students' emotions (Hunt, 1971).

Such higher levels of functioning can be developed through encouraging experimentation, reflection, and action research. Sprinthall and Thies-Sprinthall (1980) have identified training activities that develop greater cognitive complexity in teachers: experiences in a variety of roles, guided reflection on one's experience, and assessment of cognitive complexity. They also suggested that programs continue for at least one year and that personal support and challenge be provided. Teachers need opportunities to develop and test new techniques, ideas, and programs (Glickman, 1985). Career ladder plans offer a structure in which such growth producing activities can be provided for all teachers.

Teachers' Attitudes Toward Change

Teachers make a conscious decision whether they will or will not try out or adopt a new practice. What influences this decision? Doyle and Ponder (1977) suggested that three criteria influence teachers' decisions regarding implementation. The first, instrumentality, refers to the extent to which the teaching practice or idea is stated clearly and specifically. Previous comments regarding the need for concrete, practical suggestions support this factor.

The other two criteria refer to the philosophical acceptance a teacher feels toward the recommended practices and the perceived effort required to make the change. Recent research (Mohlman, Coladarci, & Gage,

1982) has indicated that when teachers object to innovations either on the grounds that (a) they are inconsistent with their philosophy of teaching (e.g., "Having classroom rules is too authoritarian") or (b) they require too much work (e.g., "If I try Mastery Learning, I'll be planning for three hours every night"), they are unlikely to implement new practices.

Structured professional development activities can, however, dissolve much of this resistance. In small supportive groups, teachers typically feel comfortable enough to challenge the philosophical basis of a new technique or to express their concern about the work required to make a change. As a result of sincere thoughtful discussions with their peers, the strength of the objection will often diminish and teachers will decide to try the new idea. The leader also can provide articles and videotapes that support the effectiveness of a particular strategy. Finally, giving teachers time to plan how they will use new ideas during the workshop or during release time may allay the concerns about the time required to try something new.

There is some provocative research (Crandall & Associates, 1982; Guskey, 1985) to indicate that attitudes may not need to be changed before a teacher will try something new. Rather, it appears that if we can just get the teacher to try the new technique, a change of attitude will follow. The acceptance of the new practice, however, will occur only if it is fairly easy to use in the classroom and if it is immediately clear that it has the desired effect (i.e., improved student learning or behavior).

This change in attitude relates to another aspect of teachers' professional growth—self efficacy, or the feeling that one is able to control what happens in one's classroom. When staff development experiences help teachers develop confidence and a belief in their ability to deal effectively with classroom events, dramatic improvements are often seen (Sparks, 1983b). Teachers showing the greatest growth in Stallings' Effective Use of Time Workshops (Stallings, 1980) said, "I now realize I have control over many things I thought I had no control over" and "I no longer feel powerless" (Sparks, 1984). Because these teachers had learned one or two simple techniques that improved their students' behavior, they began to feel "in charge" and went on to make other changes and improvements.

Summary of Adult Learning Theory and Research

Five topics related to adult learning have been examined. The first topic was teacher concerns—how teachers react to trying something new. Teachers at the early stages of change will typically have personal or informational needs and will require informational sessions and clear policies. Teachers with management concerns will benefit from clear demonstrations and direct assistance with classroom implementation. Teachers at the final impact stages will reflect on the effectiveness of the techniques and adapt them or share them with others.

Adult developmental stages related to ages and careers are also important considerations when designing professional development programs. Younger beginning teachers will have high energy and a thirst for learning. Middle-career teachers will want to develop new skills and advance their careers, while late-career teachers will focus on retirement and nurturing other teachers.

Adults also share several preferences for their own professional development. They want the new skills or information to be relevant to their everyday classroom problems. They prefer active involvement with concrete ready-to-use practices and having control over decisions regarding their own learning. They also want to share ideas and experiences with other teachers in a nonthreatening learning environment.

Teachers' levels of cognitive complexity will also affect the impact and design of professional development activities. Teachers at lower conceptual levels will need concrete demonstrations and structured guided practice with new techniques. Those at higher conceptual levels will need less structure and will benefit from opportunities to innovate and adapt new strategies. Teachers will grow in cognitive complexity through developmental assessment, role-taking experiences, reflection, continuous programs, and support for risk taking.

Teachers' attitudes toward a new practice will play a strong part in whether they adopt that practice. For a new skill or idea to be implemented, it should be concrete, philosophically acceptable, and relatively uncomplicated to use. Sharing of ideas and problems in a small support group can often help dissolve some teachers' resistance to change. When teachers take the risk of trying something new and find that they are successful, attitudes often change and a greater sense of control and assertiveness develops.

HOW DOES THE ORGANIZATIONAL CLIMATE RELATE TO THE SUCCES OF PROFESSIONAL DEVELOPMENT PROGRAMS?

Studies of teacher change have found unanimously that organizational climate is critical to the success of change efforts. Little (1982) highlighted school norms of experimentation and collegiality as important for positive staff development. Stallings and Mohlman (1981) found that teachers improved most in schools where the principal was supportive of teachers and was clear and consistent in communicating school policies. The Rand researchers (Berman & McLaughlin, 1978) concluded that the major factor affecting success of innovations was administrative support from both principals and superintendents.

These findings point clearly to the necessity of adequate organizational support for professional development when career ladder plans are established. Loucks-Horsley and Hergert (1985) identified several support functions provided by principals and district administrators in successful improvement efforts. These support functions include: (a) clarifying the goals of the school and the change program, (b) protecting teachers from competing demands on their time ("running interference"), (c) providing easy-to-locate materials and advisors, (d) making the changes a high priority by publicly emphasizing their importance, and (e) having a person in a leadership position "manage by walking around" (Peters & Waterman, 1982) to get feedback and input.

While it is widely accepted that principals and administrators should attend training programs with their teachers, it is less commonly acknowledged that these same leaders may need special training in skills required to support the change process. Administrators who understand the Concerns-Based Adoption Model (CBAM) (Hall & Loucks, 1978) will be more likely to accept the slow pace of change and to be responsive to the concerns of teachers. Training in consensus- and team-building strategies, conducting effective meetings, group processing and communication skills, and other organizational development concepts will help school and district administrators provide more effective leadership for teachers' professional development.

For any professional development program, a major initial activity is to develop a sense of trust and ownership among teachers. Gathering staff input regarding professional development needs and concerns will help meet this goal. Several studies of organizational factors and change have concluded that the levels of trust and commitment, and the rates of implementation of new practices were higher in programs where participants were involved in project decisions (Berman & McLaughlin, 1978; Lawrence, 1974; Stallings & Mohlman, 1981).

Several models exist for including teachers in decisions regarding school improvement and staff development (e.g., Hough & Urick, 1981; Loucks-Horsley & Hergert, 1985; Wood, Thompson, & Russell, 1981). The models share two elements: extensive teacher input and a systematic set of steps for accomplishing the changes. The steps typically include (a) an initiation phase where data are collected to help identify a goal and a plan is subsequently written, (b) an implementation phase where the plan is implemented and follow-up support is provided, and (c) an institutionalization phase where the changes become a regular part of the school program.

Evaluations of such school-based change efforts (e.g., Sparks, Hough, & Urick, 1984) are encouraging. Teachers typically report making substantial progress toward their goals and dramatic improvements in school climate and communication. Collaboratively planned systematic professional development programs appear to be highly promising for districts with career ladders. Groups of teachers who decide to work together toward a career-ladder-related goal are likely to reap great benefits in skills, collegiality, and morale.

HOW SHOULD THE PROFESSIONAL DEVELOPMENT ACTIVITIES BE CONDUCTED?

The design of activities for the professional growth of teachers will clearly reflect the district's or state's philosophy regarding the goals of staff development programs. If the goal is to create thoughtful, reflective professionals who are capable of making decisions after consideration of a large bank of research and practical knowledge, then the staff development processes will support growth in that direction. Glickman (1985) outlined several avenues by which a teacher can grow professionally: clinical supervision, curriculum development, inservice education, and action research (cooperative study groups).

Professional Development Through Supervision

Supervision is defined as one-to-one assistance provided by an expert for the purpose of improving teaching. While there are many ways to view supervision (see Sergiovanni, 1982), the most commonly used is clinical supervision. Cogan (1973) and Goldhammer (1969) described the steps of clinical supervision as: (a) establishing a relationship, (b) planning with the teacher, (c) planning for observation, (d) observing instruction, (e) analyzing the data, (f) planning the conference, (g) conducting the conference, and (i) renewed planning for the next cycle (Garman, 1982). Madeline Hunter (1983) has advocated clinical supervision as a vehicle for assisting teachers with the implementation of her instructional skills program.

Glatthorn (1984) and Glickman (1985) have extended the early work on supervision by introducing the ideas of "differentiated" supervision and "developmental" supervision. Glatthorn (1984) believed that not all teachers need clinical supervision and that they should have opportunities for cooperative professional development, self-directed development, and administrative monitoring. The needs of the teacher and the available resources of the organization determine which approach is taken. Glickman (1985) described different styles of supervision, from more directive to less directive, depending on the developmental level of the teacher.

This brief overview of supervision indicates that in career ladders a variety of approaches to supervision ought to be considered, with a matching of the appropriate strategy to the needs and developmental level of the teacher.

Professional Development Through Curriculum Development

Curriculum development should not be ignored as a vehicle for professional growth. As teachers collaborate to design, pilot test, and disseminate subject-matter-related materials and programs, they develop a greater understanding of the complexity of teaching and learning. Teachers can also profit from examining curriculum alignment, the match between what is actually taught in the classroom, what is intended to be taught, and what is tested. Through this process, they discover gaps and inconsistencies and band together to develop a more systematic educational program (see Robbins, 1985). Career ladder plans that give teachers the opportunity to examine and develop curriculum offer a valuable learning experience.

Professional Development Through Inservice Education

Inservice education has the unfortunate fate of being seen as useless, one-shot dog-and-pony shows that have little real influence on the competence of teachers. Nevertheless, numerous studies (see Gage, 1985) indicate that significant teacher growth in effectiveness can result from well conceived inservice training programs. The more recent term, "staff development," is often used to refer to long-term training efforts, although many define this term more broadly.

Structured experiences for teachers' professional growth may take the form of workshops or they may be more individualized. Many teachers will become quite resistant when required to attend workshops on topics in which they have no interest. Their level of cognitive complexity or development (see Burden, 1986) makes their interests and needs quite different from those of other teachers. Fortunately, these teachers are often quite enthusiastic about pursuing their own professional goals, either individually or in small study groups. This section and the next will address both types of professional development programs—workshops and cooperative study groups.

One of the most common means of promoting the professional development of teachers is through workshops. What is known about providing workshop-based training that results in greater professional competence?

Planning Inservice Workshops

As workshops are planned, several issues need to be considered. These include decisions about who should provide the training, how the workshops are scheduled, and how large the group should be when conducting the workshops.

Who should provide the training? There is no firm agreement on this issue. Some researchers have found that the most effective trainers tend to be those who have developed and used the new strategies extensively (Loucks-Horsley & Hergert, 1985). Such trainers have high credibility with teachers, either because they have only recently left the classroom or because they have not left it at all. Researchers who make it clear that they have spent many hours in classrooms and understand the everyday realities of teaching are also well received. Teachers seem to be least trusting of consultants or others who "breeze in and breeze out" of the school or district and seem to know little about the local situation.

Trainers who have recently learned to provide workshops and lack a deep understanding of the rationale and research behind the techniques often lose teachers' respect when they are unable to answer questions that require such a fund of knowledge. Thus, when career-ladder teachers are asked to provide inservice workshops, they will need extensive training not only in the new program, but also in the theory and research underlying it.

How should the workshops be scheduled? Note that we are assuming that there will be more than one workshop in a well designed program. The research is quite clear that little growth occurs as a result of a single workshop on a given topic (Berman & McLaughlin, 1978; Lawrence, 1974). Providing a one-event workshop that lasts three or four days with no follow-up sessions is hardly better. The best schedule seems to be to offer several two- to six-hour workshops separated by two or three weeks (Sparks, 1983a; Stallings, 1982).

When workshops are spread out over time several desirable things happen. First, a sense of teamwork and collegiality is bound to develop when the same people join together for a common purpose over an extended period of time. Sharing of concerns, group-generated solutions to instructional problems, and professional friendships result. A second reason for spreading the content of workshops over several sessions is to avoid the sense of information overload that so often accompanies workshops. If teachers are capable of digesting and trying out only a few new things at a time, then it is more appropriate to have several short workshops rather than one or two long ones.

A third reason for planning several workshops relates to the concept of "mutual adaptation" (Berman & McLaughlin, 1978). As teachers try out new techniques they adapt them to fit their unique teaching situations. In turn, as teachers experiment with a new way of teaching, their way of thinking about teaching and learning may change. Let's assume that teachers are taught about cooperative learning strategies at a workshop. During the next two weeks each teacher tries one or two versions of cooperative learning and makes note of student responses. At the next workshop the participants discuss what they tried and how it worked. As a result of this cycle of learn, experiment, modify, share, and try again, teachers develop a more proactive and reflective approach to teaching (Simmons & Sparks, 1985).

How large should the group be when conducting workshops? Almost every study of what teachers like best about inservice workshops has identified "sharing ideas with other teachers" as a favorite aspect (Holly, 1982). Yet, too often, workshops are planned for large groups of 40 or 50 who spend most of the time passively listening or doing very structured group tasks. If we truly believe that teachers can learn from other teachers, then group sizes should be kept small enough to encourage sharing and thoughtful discussion.

Groups of eight or fewer are ideal for encouraging trust and sharing. Research on small-group interaction (Menlo & Gill, 1982) has indicated that more personal sharing and risk taking occurs in groups of eight or fewer as compared to groups larger than eight. When workshops are planned for large groups, teachers can be divided periodically into groups of eight or fewer. It is helpful to have a skilled facilitator for each group to keep the participants solution-oriented (rather than gripe-oriented) and to make sure each person has a chance to talk.

While some people advocate keeping secondary and elementary teachers in separate groups, experience has shown that joining them results in a greater understanding and acceptance of the differences between the levels. And, often, the two groups are amazed at how much they can learn from each other. Of course, when working on curriculum or lesson design, it may be more productive to group teachers according to the grade or subject taught.

Workshop Activities

What types of training activities should be included in workshops? An extensive body of research by Joyce and Showers (1981, 1982, 1983) indicates that providing theory, demonstrations, practice, feedback, and coaching will ensure that the majority of teachers transfer the newly learned skills into their classrooms. Others (Sparks, 1983a; Stallings, 1982) suggest adding one other activity—small-group sharing of (a) how the theories and practices relate to teachers' everyday teaching, and (b) "nuts and bolts" descriptions of how teachers use the new ideas and practices in their classrooms.

Provide theory and research. Most teachers are quite curious about where the recommended practices come from. They have been through enough educational about-faces and abandoned programs to be rather skeptical about anything hailed as new and effective. When teachers are given the details about how the research was conducted, some of this natural skepticism dissipates. Teachers also will be more receptive when the research is presented not as a basis for a prescription, but rather as an idea to be thought about and used when needed.

For example, the concepts and research behind academic learning time (Denham & Lieberman, 1980) help teachers think about their own use of time. Understanding that the research was correlational and conducted in elementary-level basic skills subjects helps teachers realize that no hard-and-fast rule regarding engaged rate or success rate can be made. The finding that these variables relate strongly to student achievement does, however, prompt teachers to analyze their own use of class time.

When participants are given no opportunity to examine the theory or research underlying the recommended practices, many teachers feel talked down to, devalued, and insulted. They also wonder how much the trainer actually understands about the strengths and weaknesses of the workshop's theory or research base. Experience (Gage, 1985; Stallings, 1980) has shown that teachers enjoy and benefit from reading summaries of research and hearing researchers present the results of their studies. Such presentations are especially well received when they are followed by immediate discussions of the practical applications of the findings.

Modeling/Demonstrations. One of the most powerful workshop experiences occurs when the participants actually experience the techniques or ideas being recommended. For example, a workshop leader may teach a session on mastery learning using the same mastery learning techniques that are being recommended. Unfortunately, this kind of modeling is not always possible, for example in workshops on classroom management and discipline. The leaders can model efficient use of time allocated for learning, but actual use of discipline strategies must be demonstrated in simulated situations or on videotape. Another argument for providing modeling and simulations is that the various learning styles of participants are more likely to be met.

Discussing Implications and Applications. When hearing a presentation about any teaching strategy, participants are almost always saying to themselves, "That strategy relates to what I typically do in (this) way." The tendency to relate any new idea to our existing framework of teaching experiences is irresistable. Teachers need opportunities to express their reactions, concerns, and questions regarding newly presented techniques. They also will want to share how the new idea relates to what they are already doing in their classrooms.

For example, when teachers learn about the potential negative effects of teacher expectations and differential treatment of students, they begin to question whether they act in a biased manner toward their students. At the same time, teachers realize that it is necessary to adapt their teaching to the students' strengths and weaknesses. Then teachers are faced with a conflict. When is it alright to have differing expectations for students?

Small-group guided discussions provide an opportunity for teachers to pursue this provocative question. During these discussions they will also begin to share techniques for making sure they do not unintentionally provide unequal learning opportunities to their students. For instance, one teacher might explain how he or she uses a seating chart to keep track of who is called on. Another teacher might describe a way of rotating the seating arrangement so that no student spends the entire year sitting in the rear of the room. In groups of 10 or more, such candid sharing of concerns and techniques is unlikely to occur. Again, small groups are preferable.

Such small-group discussions are most productive when guided by a facilitator or leader who keeps the group focused on finding solutions and sharing ideas rather than allowing the group to get sidetracked into talk about school policies or individual students. Other responsibilities of the leader are to make sure one or two people do not dominate the discussion, to clarify important points, and to contribute ideas for problem solutions.

Practice and Feedback. When the strategies presented in the workshop require a significant departure from how teachers typically teach, then it is important to provide in-workshop practice of the new strategies with feedback (Joyce & Showers, 1980). For example, when teachers are learning the skills of mentoring as part of their new career-ladder status, they will need much guided practice on supervisory techniques. After giving the rationale and research behind a supervisory model and demonstrating its use, teachers would pair up to analyze a videotaped lesson and design and role-play a post-conference. Peers and/or the workshop leader provide both reinforcement of correct procedures and suggestions for improvements.

Another way of providing in-workshop practice is through microteaching. If teachers were learning questioning strategies to get every student involved in the learning, they would practice whole-group response techniques (e.g., signaling answers) by trying them out with a small group of workshop participants. Such practice would be especially necessary to overcome the common habit of asking the question and calling on a volunteer.

In-classroom Support for Implementation. Even when participants demonstrate the ability to use a new technique in a workshop, this does not guarantee that it will be used appropriately in the classroom. Joyce and Showers (1983) refer to the importance of developing "executive control" over new practices. In short, teaching strategies are only effective when they are used thoughtfully and at the right time—what some (e.g., Gage, 1985) would acknowledge as the essential "artistry" of teaching. How is such artistry developed?

Peer coaching and clinical supervision by a trainer have been two of the most commonly suggested means for providing follow-up to workshops. Later, it will be argued that small cooperative study groups (who may or may not engage in peer coaching) are also beneficial for developing "executive control" over new practices.

Joyce and Showers (1982) have described the process of coaching as providing companionship, giving of technical feedback, analyzing when to apply a model, examining the effects of its application, adapting of the model to the needs of students, and giving interpersonal support during the practice period. Such coaching could be provided by administrators, curriculum supervisors, college professors, or teachers (Showers, 1985).

Recent evidence (Sparks, in press) indicates that teachers may benefit more from a peer's coaching than from a workshop leader's coaching. Surprisingly, teachers who engaged in peer observations showed more improvement in their teaching than did another group who received coaching by the trainer. These results can be explained in several ways. First, the collegiality that existed among the peer coaching group (presumably because they had taken the risk to allow a peer in their class) was much greater than in the other group. Second, the experience of coding and analyzing a peer's teaching behavior may have caused the observers to be more analytical about their own teaching. Teachers who have recently learned classroom systems often report a heightened awareness of their own teaching behavior and its effects on students (Stallings, 1985).

Typical peer observation activities might include the coding of teacher-student interactions to study the distribution of questions among students, analyzing the behavior of one or two problem children, watching a peer try out a new technique and coding the responses of students, or seeing a new strategy demonstrated by a peer. One way to make sure teachers are comfortable with the process is to begin with observation forms that focus on student activities rather than on teacher activities. For example, teachers might code student time-on-task during different kinds of activities (Stallings, 1985). When the teacher knows the observer is watching the students the entire process is less threatening.

Several conditions need to be met before the success of peer coaching can be ensured. Confidentiality and trust must be established prior to the observations. This can be done by having teachers select the person who will observe them and by having peer observers sign pledges of confidentiality. The administrator in charge of teacher evaluation must also make it clear that all completed observation forms are the property of the teacher observed and that no information resulting from peer observations will be used for evaluation. Peer coaching must be seen as a staff development activity focused on improving professional skills, not as an evaluation activity (Showers, 1985; Sparks, 1983a; Stallings, 1985).

Peer coaching can be made most comfortable for teachers when a substitute teacher covers the observer's class while he or she is observing another teacher. During the next instructional period, the substitute moves to the room of the teacher just observed while that teacher observes his or her colleague. Rotating the substitute in this manner can help make peer observations more convenient for teachers. It is also important to schedule a short post-observation meeting where the two teachers examine and interpret the data collected.

The Match Between the Design and Goals of Inservice Programs

There is no magic formula that tells us how many sessions need to be planned for a particular topic or how many of the above activities are necessary to achieve a particular inservice goal. There is, however, some research (e.g., Joyce & Showers, 1980; Mohlman, Coladarci, & Gage, 1982) that can help guide such decisions. A good rule of thumb is this: When the skills and ideas to be learned are quite different from what teachers are already doing, more workshops and more in-depth follow-up assistance will be needed. When the inservice content is familiar to teachers and the aim is "fine-tuning" of already established teaching practices, fewer workshops and less follow-up is needed.

Evertson, Emmer, Sanford, and Clements (1983) found that teachers made dramatic improvements in their classroom management after only one workshop held before the start of the school year and one follow-up session three weeks after school began. In contrast, Joyce and Showers (1983) have found it necessary to provide several workshops and extensive follow-up coaching before teachers transfer the "models of teaching" strategies to the classroom. Successful inservice programs focusing on effective teaching, teacher expectations, or cooperative learning typically spread four or five workshops over several weeks and offer opportunities for in-classroom coaching.

Professional Development Through Cooperative Study Groups

There are several alternatives to traditional workshop-based inservice programs; these will be referred to here as "cooperative professional development" activities. Such cooperative staff development is characterized by the joining together of two or more teachers or administrators to solve a perceived problem. Such activities capitalize on and facilitate the creative problem-solving capacity of teachers. Unfortunately, traditional workshops often fail to take advantage of the collective expertise of the participants. Cooperative professional development may occur through action research groups, teachers centers, or mini-grants.

Action Research

Action research groups (e.g., Watts, 1985; Westbrook, Loomis, Coffina, Adelberg, Brooks, & Ellis, 1985) provide one of the best illustrations of the concept of cooperative professional development. The group focuses on defining the problem, identifying conditions related to the problem, generating potential solutions, and systematically testing the effects of one or more solutions. Individually or in pairs, teachers design and implement such action research projects (see also Simmons & Sparks, 1985).

A person experienced in research methods and knowledgeable about classrooms facilitates the action research group. This person typically has expertise in a specific area, for example, in the teaching of reading.

In one action research model (Smith, 1985) teachers generate a list of topics they would like to learn more about. Each teacher then identifies one problem in their classroom that they would like to solve. The facilitator and teachers then find and share resources (videotapes, speakers, articles, books, etc.) that bear on the identified problems and topics.

As the group works through the information, each teacher begins to clarify and refine his or her problem statement. Then an action research plan is written which includes the proposed strategies and a method of evaluating their effects. After the group has reviewed each person's plan and made suggestions for improvement, the teachers implement their plans. Other teachers in the group may be asked to collect data in a peer's classroom to evaluate the effects of the changes. In the remainder of the sessions, teachers report progress made on the action research projects and share effective strategies.

Teachers Centers

Teachers Centers (Devaney, 1977) provide a stimulating environment for teachers to join together to learn about a particular area. Small study groups often arise spontaneously as teachers begin to share their classroom problems and their desire for solutions. Soon, resources are found and teachers are taking specific actions to solve their problems. Such open, stimulating environments where teachers can informally share and learn together are a powerful vehicle for staff development.

Mini-Grants

A slightly different form of cooperative professional development is the professional conference or individually chosen workshop. The needs and interests of many teachers are often quite different from what is offered by the local professional development programs. Thus, teachers should be encouraged to apply for mini-grants to attend outside conferences and workshops. Teachers may submit a proposal that includes a description of the activity, a statement of the anticipated benefits, and a description of how the new skills or ideas will be shared with colleagues afterwards. One highly successful school improvement plan (Sparks, Nowakowski, Hall, Alec, & Imrick, 1985) included the provision that teachers who attended staff workshops on effective teaching would be eligible for a mini-grant to pursue a topic of their own choosing. In this way, teachers were provided a means of pursuing their own individual interests.

RECOMMENDATIONS FOR THE PROFESSIONAL DEVELOPMENT OF THE CAREER LADDER TEACHER

There is definitely a critical role for professional development in career ladders. Any system that (a) assesses and rewards educators' on-the-job performance or (b) promotes teachers into new roles and responsibilities will require an extensive staff development component. Without such a support structure, few would rise to higher levels of the career ladder. The following list of recommendations will be helpful in building professional development opportunities into career ladder plans.

1. **Goals of Career Ladder Professional Development**
   A. The goal of professional development programs in career ladder systems is growth in teachers' ability to use knowledge, research, and experience to make enlightened decisions regarding teaching and learning. Rigid prescriptions for the practice of teaching should be avoided in favor of broad principles and concepts that guide decisions during teaching.
2. **Content of Professional Development Programs that that Support Career Ladders**
   A. Provide professional development opportunities in (a) improving teaching for those who want to move up one level on the career ladder (teaching skills would relate to the criteria specified for promotion) and (b) knowledge and skills necessary to perform new duties as part of a new level on the career ladder (skills such as mentoring or curriculum design).
   B. Do not limit the topics, skills, and principles included in the professional development program to only those required as minimum to move up on the career ladder. Offer opportunities for teachers to develop a wide repertoire of teaching strategies and to develop high levels of artistry in their teaching, even when these skills are not necessarily part of the career ladder criteria.
   C. If the research on effective teaching is used as a basis for professional development programs, caution is required. These findings relate mostly to skills required to raise test scores and not

every effective practice has been specified. Effective teaching research is best used as a set of concepts to help teachers analyze their own teaching and student learning.

D. Subject-matter mastery is a viable goal for professional development programs in a career ladder, especially in the light of existing and anticipated shortages in many areas.

3. **Adult Learning**

A. At the beginning of any change effort (and throughout), assess teachers' concerns about the new program through interviews and questionnaires. Tailor the career ladder and professional development activities to the expressed concerns. For example, information and personal concerns may be expressed about evaluation procedures, salaries, and other issues that affect teachers directly. Little growth in skills is likely to occur until these concerns are addressed through clear information about policies and procedures. Management concerns will require in-classroom assistance, whereas impact concerns signal that the teacher is ready to begin helping others.

B. Adult learners respond best to professional development programs that are directly related to their jobs, that get teachers actively involved with concrete practices, that give teachers a choice among goals and activities, that include small-group informal sharing in a safe, nonthreatening environment, and that develop confidence in teachers' ability to make a difference in their classrooms.

C. Tailor activities to match teachers' levels of concrete or abstract thinking. Design professional development opportunities that move teachers toward more abstract, reflective thinking about instructional decisions.

D. Allow teachers to identify and critique their objections to trying a new idea through small-group discussions of the philosophical or practical implications of using a given practice. Such discussions are appropriate for teachers considering a new classroom management/instructional technique or a supervisory strategy.

4. **Organizational Support and Professional Development**

A. Professional development programs within career ladders must be seen not as an evaluative but rather as a growth-producing activity. Because of the strong evaluation component inherent in career ladders, many teachers will be distrustful of the professional development activities that support the career ladder program. Program developers and administrators will need to make the purposes of the evaluation and professional development components of career ladder programs clear.

B. Provide monetary, logistical, and psychological support to teachers and administrators in career-ladder-related professional development programs. Protect teachers from other demands on their time during staff development activities, publicly emphasize the importance of professional development, and give formal recognition to participants. Hire an advisor to assist teachers with concerns and skills related to the career ladder and professional development programs.

C. Appoint a well respected administrator to be in charge of the professional development program. This person should be a strong advocate of the program and should contact participants frequently to monitor progress.

D. Train principals and other administrators in the skills and principles necessary to support change (e.g., knowledge and skills about team-building, conducting meetings, organizational development, supervision, research on teaching, evaluation, and leadership styles). These skills will be especially useful when developing and implementing career ladders.

E. Consistently solicit participant input to help guide professional development and career ladder decisions. Collaborative strategies for goal setting, planning, and implementation can be valuable tools for developing ownership and commitment to career-ladder-related professional development activities.

5. **How to Conduct Professional Development Activities**
   A. Use curriculum development as a vehicle for professional development, especially on the higher rungs of the career ladder.
   B. Provide inservice education to assist with (a) improving teaching to reach a new level on the career ladder and (b) developing skills needed to succeed on a new rung of the ladder. Inservice workshops should be (a) spread over time, (b) provided by a credible competent leader, and (c) focused on small-group sharing of reactions and experiences.
   C. For each technique recommended in inservice workshops, (a) provide the underlying theory and research, (b) model and demonstrate its use, (c) have participants discuss application of the new

idea, (d) provide opportunities to practice the skill and get feedback, and (e) provide in-classroom support for implementation.

D. Encourage peer coaching, which produces collegiality and a thoughtful, analytical approach to the improvement of teaching. This process works best when it is voluntary, confidential, unrelated to evaluation, student-centered, and made convenient through the use of release time.

E. Consider less extensive training schedules, activities, and follow-up when the purpose is to fine-tune already existing skills (e.g., questioning skills). More elaborate training is needed when unfamiliar skills are being learned or when an entirely new role is taken on (e.g., the role of staff developer).

F. Include alternatives to traditional workshop-based professional development. Cooperative or individual staff development activities could include small study groups, action research, or mini-grants to attend conferences.

G. Teachers Centers provide a gathering place that is free from evaluation where teachers can support one another and learn from one another. Such centers may be even more important to career-ladder teachers who find the pressure of evaluation and promotions somewhat stressful.

When well conceived professional development programs are included in career ladder plans, teachers and administrators will have both the motivation and support for their continuing professional growth.

REFERENCES

Berman, P., & McLaughlin, M. (1978). *Implementing and sustaining innovations: Federal programs supporting educational change* (Vol. 8) (Prepared for the U.S. Office of Education, DHEW). Santa Monica, CA: Rand Corporation.

Brophy, J. (1983). Classroom organization and management. *Elementary School Journal, 83,* 265–286.

Burden, P. (1986). Teacher development: Implications for teacher education. In L. Katz (Ed.), *Advances in teacher education* (Vol. II). Norwood, NJ: Ablex Publishing Co.

Cogan, M. (1973). *Clinical supervision.* Boston: Houghton-Mifflin.

Cook, T., & Campbell, D. (1979). *Quasi-experimentation: Design and analysis issues for field settings.* Chicago: Rand McNally.

Crandall, D., & Associates. (1982). *People, policies, and practices: Examining the chain of school improvement.* Andover, MA: The NETWORK.

Denham, C., & Lieberman, A. (Eds.). (1980). *Time to learn.* Washington, DC: National Institute of Education.

Devaney, K. (1977). Warmth, concreteness, time, and thought in teachers' learning. In K. Devaney (Ed.), *Essays on teachers centers.* San Francisco, CA: Teachers' Center Exchange, Far West Laboratory for Educational Research and Development.

Doyle, W., & Ponder, G. (1977). The practicality ethic and teacher decision making. *Interchange, 8,* 1–12.

Dunn, R., & Dunn, K. (1978). *Teaching students through their individual learning styles: A practical approach.* Reston, VA: Reston.

Emmer, E., & Evertson, C. (1981, January). Synthesis of research on classroom management. *Educational Leadership.*

Evertson, C., Emmer, E., Sanford, J., & Clements, B. (1983). Improving classroom management: An experiment in elementary classrooms. *Elementary School Journal, 84,* 173–188.

Evertson, C., Emmer, E., Sanford, J., & Clements, B. (1984). *Classroom management for elementary teachers.* Englewood Cliffs, NJ: Prentice Hall.

Gage, N. L. (1985). *Hard gains in the soft sciences.* Bloomington, IN: Phi Delta Kappa.

Gagne, R. (1977). *The conditions of learning.* Chicago: Holt, Rinehart, & Winston.

Garmon, N. (1982). The clinical approach to supervision. In T. Sergiovanni (Ed.), *Supervision of teaching.* Alexandria, VA: Association for Supervision and Curriculum Development.

Glatthorn, A. (1984). *Differentiated supervision.* Alexandria, VA: Association for Supervision and Curriculum Development.

Glickman, D. (1985). *Supervision of instruction: A developmental approach.* Newton, MA: Allyn & Bacon.

Goldhammer, R. (1969). *Clinical supervision.* New York: Holt, Rinehart & Winston.

Good, T. (1981). Teacher expectations and student perceptions: A decade of research. *Educational Leadership, 38,* 415–422.

Good, T., & Brophy, J. (1984). *Looking in classrooms* (3rd ed.). New York: Harper & Row.

Guskey, T. (1985). Staff development and teacher change. *Educational Leadership, 42*(7), 57–60.

Hall, G., & Loucks, S. (1978). Teacher concerns as a basis for facilitating and personalizing staff development. *Teachers College Record, 80,* 36–53.

Holly, F. (1982, February). Teachers' views on inservice training. *Phi Delta Kappan,* pp. 417–418.

Hough, W., & Urick, R. (1981). Leadership, educational change, and the politicalization of American education. In P. Houts & D. Meyer (Eds.), *Education in the eighties: Curriculum changes.* Washington, DC: National Institute of Education.

Hunt, D. (1971). *Matching models in education.* Toronto: Ontario Institute for Studies in Education.

Hunt, D. (1975). Person-environment interaction: A challenge found wanting before it was tried. *Review of Educational Research, 45,* 209–230.

Hunter, M. (1976). *Rx improved instruction.* El Segundo, CA: T.I.P. Publications.

Hunter, M. (1983). Script-taping, an essential supervisory tool. *Educational Leadership, 41*(3), 43.

Johnson, D., & Johnson, R. (Eds.). (1984). *Structuring cooperative learning: Lesson plans for teachers.* New Brighton, MN: Interaction.

Johnson, D., Johnson, R., & Maruyama, G. (1983). Interdependence and interpersonal attraction among heterogeneous and homogeneous individuals: A theoretical formulation and a meta-analysis of the research. *Review of Educational Research, 52,* 5–54.

Joyce, B., & Showers, B. (1980). Improving inservice training: The messages of research. *Educational Leadership, 37,* 379–385.

Joyce, B., & Showers, B. (1981). *Teacher training research: Working hypotheses for program design and directions for further study.* Paper presented at the annual meeting of the American Educational Research Association, Los Angeles, CA.

Joyce, B., & Showers, B. (1982). The coaching of teaching. *Educational Leadership, 40,* 4–10.

Joyce, B., & Showers, B. (1983). *Power in staff development through research on training.* Alexandria, VA: Association for Supervision and Curriculum Development.

Knowles, M. (1978). *The adult learner: A neglected species.* Houston, TX: Gulf.

Kounin, J. (1970). *Discipline and group management in classrooms.* New York: Holt, Rinehart & Winston.

Krupp, J. A. (1981). *Adult development: Implications for staff development.* Manchester, CT: Author, 40 McDivett Drive.

Lawrence, G. (1974). *Patterns of effective inservice education: A state of the art summary of research on materials and procedures for changing teacher behaviors in inservice education.* Tallahassee: Florida State Department of Education. (ERIC Document Reproduction Service No. ED 176 424)

Levine, S. (1985). Translating adult development research into staff development practices. *The Journal of Staff Development, 6*(1), 6–17.

Levinson, D., Darrow, C., Klein, E., Levinson, M., & McKee, B. (1978). *The seasons of a man's life.* New York: Alfred A. Knopf.

Lindaman, E., & Lippett, R. (1979). *Choosing the future you prefer.* Washington, DC: Development Publications.

Little, J. (1982). Norms of collegiality and experimentation: Workplace conditions of school success. *American Educational Research Journal, 19,* 325–340.

Loucks-Horsley, S., & Hergert, L. (1985). *An action guide to school improvement.* Alexandria, VA: Association for Supervision and Curriculum Development.

McCarthy, B. (1981). *The 4Mat system: Teaching to learning styles with right/left mode techniques.* Barrington, IL: Excel.

McCarthy, B. (1985, April). What 4Mat training teaches us about staff development. *Educational Leadership,* pp. 61–68.

McKinnan, J. (1976). The college student and formal operations. In C. Rinner (Ed.), *Research, teaching, and learning with the Piaget model.* Norman, OK: University of Oklahoma Press.

Menlo, A., & Gill, S. (1982). *Antecedents to member participation within small groups: A review of theory and research.* Paper presented at the Finley Carpenter Research Conference, The University of Michigan School of Education, Ann Arbor, MI.

Mohlman, G., Coladarci, T., & Gage, N. L. (1982). Comprehension and attitude as predictors of implementation of teacher training. *Journal of Teacher Education, 33,* 31–36.

Peters, T., & Waterman, R. (1982). *In search of excellence.* New York: Harper & Row.

Robbins, P. (1985). Improving instruction: The Napa County Follow-Through Project. *The Journal of Staff Development, 6*(2), 6–17.

Rosenshine, B., & Stevens, R. (1986). Teaching functions. In M. Wittrock (Ed.), *Handbook of research on teaching* (3rd ed.). New York: Macmillan.

Sergiovanni, G. (Ed.). (1982). *Supervision of teaching.* Alexandria, VA: Association for Supervision and Curriculum Development.

Sheehy, G. (1976). *Passages: Predictable crises of adult life.* New York: Dutton.

Showers, B. (1985). Teachers coaching teachers. *Educational Leadership, 42*(7), 43–48.

Shulman, L., & Sykes, G. (Eds.). (1983). *Handbook of teaching and policy.* New York: Longman.

Simmons, J., & Sparks, G. (1985). Using research to develop professional thinking about teaching. *The Journal of Staff Development, 6*(1), 106–116.

Slavin, R. (1980). Cooperative learning. *Review of Educational Research, 50,* 315–342.

Smith, R. (1985, November). Improving reading instruction through action research. *The Developer,* p. 3–4.

Sparks, G. (1983a). Synthesis of research on staff development for effective teaching. *Educational Leadership, 41*(3), 65–72.

Sparks, G. (1983b). Inservice education: Training activities, teacher attitude, and behavior change (Doctoral dissertation, Stanford University, 1983). *Dissertation Abstracts International.* (DEP83-20778)

Sparks, G. (1984). *Inservice education: The process of teacher change.* Paper presented at the annual meeting of the American Educational Research Association, New Orleans, LA. (ERIC Document Reproduction Service No. ED 244 930)

Sparks, G. (in press). The effectiveness of alternative training activities in changing teaching practice. *American Educational Research Journal.*

Sparks, G., Hough, W., & Urick, R. (1984). *Evaluation of a six-step staff development model for school improvement.* Paper presented at the annual meeting of the American Educational Research Association, New Orleans, LA. (ERIC Document Reproduction Service No. ED 254 954)

Sparks, G., Nowakowski, M., Hall, B., Alec, R., & Imrick, J. (1985). School improvement through staff development. *Educational Leadership, 42*(6), 59–62.

Sparks, D., & Sparks, G. (1985). *School improvement through staff development* [Videocassette]. Alexandria, VA: Association for Supervision and Curriculum Development.

Sprinthall, N., & Thies-Sprinthall, L. (1980). Educating for teacher growth: A cognitive developmental perspective. *Theory into Practice, 19*(4), 278–286.

Stallings, J. (1980). Allocated academic learning time revisited, or beyond time on task. *Educational Researcher, 8*(11), 11–16.

Stallings, J. (1982). Effective strategies for teaching basic skills. In D. Wallace (Ed.), *Developing basic skills programs in secondary schools.* Alexandria, VA: Association for Supervision and Curriculum Development.

Stallings, J. (1985). Effective elementary classroom practices. In M. J. Kyle (Ed.), *Reaching for excellence: An effective schools sourcebook.* Washington, DC: U.S. Government Printing Office.

Stallings, J., & Mohlman, G. (1981). *School policy, leadership style, teacher change, and student behavior in eight schools, final report.* Washington, DC: National Institute of Education.

Watts, H. (1985). When teachers are researchers, teaching improves. *The Journal of Staff Development, 6*(2), 118–127.

Westbrook, C., Loomis, A., Coffina, J., Adelberg, J., Brooks, S., & Ellis, S. (1985). Classroom research: A promising model for staff development. *The Journal of Staff Development, 6*(2), 128–132.

Wittrock, M. (Ed.). (1986). *Handbook of research on teaching* (3rd ed.). New York: Macmillan.

Wolfe, P. (1985, April). Colleague coaching. *The Developer,* p. 4.

Wood, F., & Thompson, S. (1980). Guidelines for better staff development. *Educational Leadership, 37*(5), 374–386.

Wood, F., Thompson, S., & Russell, F. (1981). Designing effective staff development programs. In B. Dillon-Peterson (Ed.), *Staff development/organization development.* Alexandria, VA: Association for Supervision and Curriculum Development.

Chapter 9

CHANGING THE WORK ENVIRONMENT OF TEACHERS

Jean L. Easterly

Improving working conditions for teachers is a critical component in attracting and retaining the best and the brightest. One way to enhance the professional work environment for teachers is through career ladders. This approach suggests that outstanding teachers are identified, given additional responsibilities, and provided rewards commensurate with their new responsibilities.

Career ladders cannot effect a total change in the work environment of teachers. Therefore, the implementation of career ladders must be supported by a series of profound educational changes. These changes need to address: (a) shortages or inadequacies of books, supplies, equipment, and buildings; (b) too many classroom interruptions; (c) insufficient preparation time; (d) heavy teaching loads; (e) lack of parental interest; (f) overcrowded classrooms; (g) too many non-teaching duties; (h) inadequate salaries; (i) lack of job mobility; (j) lack of offices or work areas for planning periods; (k) lack of qualified personnel to provide special services and counseling for students; (l) lack of well qualified substitute teachers; and (m) misassignments (assignments of positions to teachers who lack the appropriate subject area preparation).

While career ladders cannot do the job alone, there are a variety of working conditions which they can address. These include: (a) a front-loaded career, (b) an unstaged career, (c) loneliness in the workplace, (d) powerlessness, (e) evaluation by inspection, and (f) role stress. Each will be described at some length. The ability of career ladders to change these working conditions will be discussed and specified recommendations for implementation will be made.

A FRONT-LOADED CAREER

Dan Lortie (1975) suggested that financial rewards in teaching are quickly received and subsequent rewards are less impressive. As a result there is "a sense of relative deprivation among those who persist in teaching and work at above-average levels of work" (Lortie, 1975, p. 86).

While there are differences in salary structure, new teachers begin at a relatively high level compared to their highest earning potential. As Schlechty and Vance (1983) noted, teachers who attain the top of the salary schedule, after about 15 years of service, are only slightly older than doctors completing their residencies.

This aspect of "topping-out" is particularly troublesome for teachers who face increasing financial needs as they age and move through their careers. Many of these teachers have growing children. As a result, they experience sharply rising costs, especially as their children enter college. Since most salary increases come early in their careers (if they seek the master's degree), many experienced teachers do not find salary increases adequate to meet escalating financial needs. Many leave teaching and seek higher paying jobs.

While salaries may be the most obvious aspect of frontloading, the issue of working conditions cannot be ignored. Many districts provide identical incentives for first-year teachers and 20-year teachers alike. As a result, mature teachers who seek to gain expertise and improve professional practice are severely limited. Often, they must do so on their own time and with their own money, while paying for their own substitutes. It is not uncommon to hear of a teacher taking a sick day to attend a professional conference. Worse yet are teachers who have been elected to serve on state and national boards and committees because of their recognized leadership abilities. Some of these outstanding educators have been prevented from attending meetings because they have exceeded the number of personal and professional days given to all teachers in equal number.

In addition to being front-loaded in terms of rewards, teaching often socializes newcomers by asking them to assume the most difficult jobs. Over and over again, new teachers are given the least motivated students while more experienced hands work with more motivated students. This is due to the fact that teachers already employed by the district are given opportunities to transfer to other schools or classrooms when openings exist. As a result, many experienced teachers transfer to classrooms they perceive to be less difficult or challenging. Thus, it is quite possible that new teachers may begin at less desirable schools with the most difficult students. The reality of inverse beginner responsibilities and relatively early reward systems conspire to make teaching a front-loaded profession.

AN UNSTAGED CAREER

Structures for supporting teachers, as they mature professionally, are not generally found in most school districts. The celebration of individual teacher excellence is almost nonexistent. From the one-dimensional salary scale to identical duties and responsibilities, the conglomerate, with individuals in that conglomerate, is perceived as equal. Here, equality is carried out to its most ugly extreme, **a cookie cutter profession** where all who profess are amazingly equal. "For the teacher, no feature of the teaching occupation is more destructive of the long-term prospects for improvement than the current reality that to move up, you must move out" (California Commission on the Teaching Profession, 1985, p. 13).

When teachers do assume new responsibilities, they are apt to experience disdain from their colleagues. As one teacher (Easterly, 1984b, p. 71) explained: "Many [the staff] are resentful of the special program [I'm directing]."

Changes in existing structures must be supported by a fundamental and wide-sweeping change of heart. Teachers who assume new duties must be rewarded, not hurt.

Career Stages in Teaching

Assisting teachers is an emerging knowledge base which describes career stages in teaching (Burden, 1986; Burke, Christensen, & Fessler, 1984; Fuller & Brown, 1975; Veenman, 1984; Watts, 1980). Research indicates that teachers do have different skills, knowledge, attitudes, and concerns at different points during their careers. Despite this evidence, teaching remains essentially unstaged in its administrative design and teachers are perceived to be equal. If teaching is to change in the near future, educators must possess an awareness, understanding, and acceptance of the stages of teacher development.

The first stage in the life history of a teacher is often called the survival stage (Burden, 1986; Watts, 1982). This stage begins during student teaching and usually continues well into the first year of teaching.

Some teachers never get beyond this stage while others return to it as a result of such events as reassignment to different grade levels or subject areas. During this stage teachers are struggling with problems of their own competence. Often these problems include classroom management, being liked, and being evaluated. Burden (1986) reported that first-stage teachers perceived themselves to be subject-centered. Teachers believed they had little professional insight and lacked confidence. They were unwilling to try new methods and found themselves conforming to a preconceived image of "teacher."

The second career stage may be described as an adjustment stage (Burden, 1986). During this period, teachers started to see children's complexities and sought new teaching techniques. They became more genuine with children and gradually gained confidence in themselves. Watts (1980) described the stage as characterized by an increasing sense of comfort and more attention to child-centered rather than teacher-centered activity.

In many ways the mastery stage is more difficult and elusive to define than the others. Watts (1982, p. 7) described the master teacher as one who "is working smoothly within the context of the school and of his/her own personality. . . . Probably one of the distinguishing marks of a master teacher is an unwillingness to stop growing, examining, and messing around with the job at hand." Burden (1986) reported that mature teachers believed they had a good command of teaching activities. They were willing to try new teaching methods and thought they could handle most new situations that might arise. Gradually they had relinquished their former image of "teacher."

Adult Development

The emerging literature on adult development offers a useful framework for understanding the life history of teachers (Hunt, 1971; Levinson, 1978; Loevinger, 1966; Sheehy, 1974). The socialization and cognitive development of adults offer perspectives which can inform the profession of teaching.

Loevinger (1966) examined ego development and described its impact on adults as they pass through stages and try to understand themselves. He reported that adults moved from conformity to emotional independence. When these findings are cast in a teacher socialization framework, it may be assumed that beginning teachers are at the conformist stage of ego development. As teachers grow in experience, they move to a more autonomous stage. Veenman (1984, p. 165) believes that "needs such as security, affiliation, and self-esteem must be satisfied first before beginning teachers can behave as autonomous or self-actualized persons. . . . " The evidence indicates that beginning teachers are different from experienced teachers. First-year teachers need time to adjust to the conditions of teaching and become socialized into appropriate professional behavior. Vehicles for accomplishing this are not generally available for beginning teachers.

Cognitive stages of development offer another framework for examining adult development. Hunt (1971) reported that adults at higher stages of development exhibited creativity, a wider range of coping behaviors, and a greater tolerance for stress. Teachers functioning at higher stages of cognitive development are able to perceive problems more broadly and can respond more accurately and empathetically to the needs of students, parents, and peers. When reviewing research on effective teachers, Veenman (1984, p. 162) reported that teachers at higher stages "may be more flexible, stress tolerant, adaptive, better able to assume multiple perspectives and to apply a greater variety of teaching strategies and coping behaviors than teachers at lower cognitive developmental levels. . . . " While teachers at advanced levels of cognitive development are more effective teachers, structures do not generally exist which utilize their expertise.

Conclusion

The life history of teachers can be understood from a number of different perspectives. Career stages in teaching are supported by research on adult development. Theories on adult stages include the socialization and cognitive frameworks. Both frameworks can provide guidance in designing opportunities and challenges which enhance the professional growth of teachers. If the profession is to prosper, it must find ways to match varying maturational levels of teachers with varying levels of responsibility. Career ladders may provide that match between levels of maturity and responsibility.

LONELINESS IN THE WORKPLACE

Teachers typically teach in rooms physically separated from each other. When they do emerge for planned breaks or lunch, their dialogue is frequently of a social rather than professional nature (Glickman, 1984–1985). Qualities that are seen as hallmarks of productivity in business— mutual help, exchange of ideas, cooperative work to develop better practices—are rare in schools. For this and other reasons, over half of entering teachers leave within five to seven years, with attrition particularly heavy after the first year or two (California Commission on the Teaching Profession, 1985, p. 13).

In many schools, teachers work together in the same building for years with virtually no knowledge of what their colleagues are doing. They do not share with each other nor take the opportunity to observe one another teach. As a result, there is no way of complementing each other's teaching or learning from each other. In his comprehensive study on schooling, Goodlad (1984, p. 187) found little "data to suggest active, ongoing exchanges of ideas and practices across schools, between groups of teachers, or between individuals even in the same schools."

Other factors contribute to the sense of isolation which many teachers feel. In a study of outstanding elementary teachers (Easterly, 1983), one teacher described how a parent had gone to the principal instead of going to her. Another teacher noted the lack of support from parents when their children were misbehaving. Many teachers encounter a lack of support on the part of principals or school specialists, as expressed in these ways by teachers in the Easterly (1983) study:

> I put an F on a child's . . . report card. Parents came in and said, . . . "Well, that woman can't give my child an F." . . . In front of the parents, without even having a conference with me, the principal said, "I agree with the parents." [He] handed me the report card and said, "Change it to a D." I changed it to a D. I wasn't going to fight the principal and the parents.
>
> . . . Another teacher was physically attacked during parent-teacher conferences with a knife by a parent. . . . Nobody contacted him even to see if he was all right. . . . That could happen to any one of us at any time.
>
> . . . I can think of one instance where I had a child who was very, very emotionally impaired. He was literally choking other children when he would get angry. . . . This went on and on and I could just feel the

frustration growing and the feeling of helplessness and not getting the help as soon as I thought I should get it is very stressful to me. (p. 10)

Given the preceding examples, it is not surprising that many teachers find their jobs to be lonely vigils rather than concerted team efforts to work effectively with students.

While isolation is common among all teachers, it is probably more acute for new teachers. Loneliness and even alienation are often the fate of beginning teachers. Afraid to expose their inadequacies, they often fail to reach out to senior teachers for assistance. Meanwhile, the culture of the school may mediate against experienced teachers offering to help, especially when the neophyte appears not to need assistance. Some experienced teachers believe that an offer to help insults the intelligence and skills of newcomers. As a result, they do not offer assistance unless asked.

Compounding this is the possibility that some beginning teachers have little respect for their older colleagues. Indeed, some may believe that older teachers are outdated whereas they, as beginners, are in touch with the truth. All of this conspires to keep people professionally separated from each other. As a result, many beginning teachers learn mostly by trial and error.

Much can be learned by examining the existing research on effective schools. These schools promote collegial relationships and sharing among all teachers. Rosenholtz and Smylie (1984) pointed out that teachers in collegial settings interact to a greater extent about professional rather than social concerns and do so more often and with a greater number of colleagues. Rosenholtz and Smylie (1984) reported that "the product of exchange in traditional settings is sympathy, [whereas] the product of exchange in collegial settings is ideas" (p. 157).

POWERLESSNESS

Teachers experience a sense of powerlessness because they have (a) little influence in setting directions for school districts or schools, (b) they are constrained in a number of ways even in their own classrooms, (c) they are limited in decisions they can make due to outside school influences, and (d) they rarely initiate their own research. Teachers need opportunities to participate in these important arenas of influence.

One important arena of influence for teachers is at the school and district levels. Goodlad (1984) reported that teachers in his study perceive themselves to be quite autonomous in their own classrooms while having less control in areas beyond their classrooms. One important area of influence is the selection of future colleagues. Typically, teachers are not asked to help in the interviewing process even though they may work side by side with colleagues for years. Teachers are not involved in the evaluation of colleagues yet are expected to work with some thought to be incompetent. Lack of influence over fiscal management is yet another area where teachers feel little influence.

A second area of influence is found in the classroom. Watts (1984) suggested that in the classroom teachers give orders while outside the classroom teachers take orders. While this statement seems generally true, it may be too simplistic a division. Even though teachers perceive themselves to be much more powerful in their own classrooms, it seems likely that teachers are limited in many subtle ways. Most teachers are not involved in decisions such as textbook selection and the formulation of policies concerning curriculum, staff development, discipline, homework, scheduling, and grouping. Bells, schedules, and school policies tend to routinize a teacher's day, causing an intellectually deadening effect on even the most dedicated teachers. Creativity is snuffed out when the main focus of teaching is covering textbooks and supervising workbook activities.

Outside influences also limit opportunities to participate in decision making. For example, achievement tests are especially troublesome when they are not aligned with the curriculum which teachers want to teach. As a result of misalignment, many teachers spend hours helping students prepare for tests when they could be using their instructional time in other ways.

Another arena of influence is educational research. While teachers occasionally contribute to the work of others, they rarely initiate their own research. Bird and Little (1985, p. 4) noted that teachers "accumulate such skills and wisdom as they can by themselves and then take their inventions with them when they leave. Superb teachers leave their marks on all of us, but they leave no mark on teaching."

Structures are needed which enable teachers to become full participants in the decision-making process. Their arenas of influence must expand. Goodlad (1984) concluded that a profession by its very nature involves autonomy in decision making.

EVALUATION BY INSPECTION

According to a Preliminary Report from the ASCD Task Force on Merit Pay and Career Ladders, most approaches to teacher evaluation "are oriented toward inspection rather than growth" (English, 1984–1985, p. 34). Schools are presently organized in such a way that only negative evaluations count since positive evaluations are not linked to any rewards that count. Teachers rated as outstanding are not paid any more than teachers rated as average or even below average (Lieberman, 1985). Schlechty (1984) noted that

> if positive evaluations are not used to enhance one's reputation or status, if positive evaluations are not used to make one eligible to accept new responsibilities and gain enriched job assignments, and if positive evaluations are not used to determine expanding career options, then the only evaluations that count are those that are negative. (p. 106)

Evaluation presently conducted in schools is primarily of a summative nature performed by a principal with an inspection focus. Typically, the intention of the evaluation is for retention rather than the determination of excellence or performance improvement. Goodlad (1984) found that principals, especially high school principals, are not in the best position to evaluate teachers. According to Goodlad (1984, p. 303), "the only models for evaluating teachers that have proven to be reasonably effective to date are those of peer review, as used by major universities."

For many years, the concept of the principal as an instructional leader has been held as an ideal. In addition to summative evaluation, principals are expected to conduct formative evaluations as well. This type of evaluation is done primarily to help teachers improve their professional skills and can be facilitated through the use of clinical supervision and coaching techniques. Formative evaluation must be based upon a trusting, supportive relationship between the evaluator and teacher. It is, therefore, essential that formative evaluation be separated from summative evaluation. Separation is accomplished by assigning the roles to different people.

Given the separation of formative evaluation from summative evaluation, it appears unlikely that one principal could or should be involved with both types of evaluation. In addition it probably is unrealistic to expect a principal to develop and maintain a first-rate school while serving as the role model for and the monitor of all teaching in that school (Goodlad, 1984). Ways must be found so that teachers, especially beginning teachers, are helped to grow professionally through both formative and summative evaluation. (The issue of evaluation is discussed more fully in another chapter in this book.)

ROLE STRESS

Gupta and Jenkins (1981) suggested that role stress can be present in many forms. These include unclear role expectations, incompatible role expectations, lack of time or ability to meet role expectations, the inability to use one's own skills, and inadequate resources to meet role expectations.

The findings of Gupta and Jenkins are illuminated by the following statements made by teachers who have identified areas in their professional lives that are in conflict (Easterly, 1983, pp. 4–5). One teacher, for example, pointed out a conflict between being organized and being flexible: "When I've spent all my time getting organized, ... I don't adjust well to someone saying, 'We're not going to have reading today, we've got something in the gym.'" Conflicts were identified by another teacher who felt torn between the need to listen to the concerns of the children and the need to attend to other classroom matters: "[There are] papers over here that need to be checked and I should get over and get this set up and I should get this group going and somebody is sitting here talking." A conflict between having compassion and being objective was described as one of the problem areas: "I am a caring person but at the same time I ... know the difference. I know when not to get too involved with it." The preceding examples document the ever-present pressure of making choices among conflicting values in the teaching profession. As one teacher noted: "It's really tough. It's like you have a lot of different roles to play. . . . I feel just like a juggler . . . waiting for all these balls to hit the ground."

Though role definitions are constantly changing, some teachers are able to reach out to their colleagues for support. However, many teachers experience stress because they lack adequate peer support in difficult social situations (Gupta & Jenkins, 1981). Presently, teachers have little support from overworked administrators. A vehicle is needed to enable teachers to provide maximum support for other teachers.

Another source of role stress is the conflict which exists between ideals of the teaching profession and realities of the workplace (Lanier, in press). Teachers struggle as they try to perform at high levels with little or no clerical help and limited professional development opportunities. Many become disillusioned and leave the profession.

IMPACT OF CAREER LADDERS ON WORKING CONDITIONS

The teaching profession has been described as a front-loaded and unstaged career where teachers encounter loneliness, powerlessness, role stress, and evaluation by inspection. Ways must be found to move from a front-loaded career to one that nurtures newcomers while providing rewards appropriate for the most senior teacher. Teaching must change from an unstaged career to one that is staged. Collegial interaction must replace loneliness, autonomy must replace powerlessness, and role congruence must replace role stress. Evaluation by inspection must be de-emphasized while increasing professional growth opportunities for teachers.

A Front-Loaded to a Future-Oriented Career

Relatively early reward systems and inverse beginner responsibilities make teaching a front-loaded career. Career ladders can provide rewards which are available later and are a result of individual commitment and expertise. Through career ladders, beginning teachers can be inducted slowly into the full ranks and responsibilities of teachers. These changes in orientation toward the future give teachers something to which they can aspire.

Career ladders provide different rewards for different levels of teaching responsibility, experience, and expertise. A recent monograph by the Association of Teacher Educators (1985), entitled **Developing Career Ladders in Teaching,** suggests that master teachers can earn salaries equal to and sometimes more than school administrators. These top salaries are reserved for teachers who have demonstrated their abilities to be outstanding classroom teachers and excellent instructional leaders. These positions are based on 12-month contracts and are supported by ever-increasing improvements in working conditions. For example, as teachers assume increased responsibilities, they will need additional secretarial support, time and travel funds to attend professional conferences, tuition assistance, and released time to carry out responsibilities related to their new roles.

Inverse beginner responsibilities cannot coexist with the concept of a career ladder. A career ladder, by its very nature, gives the least responsibility and maximum assistance to its newest teachers. In order to accomplish this, first-year teachers should be given reduced teaching loads. This reduction will provide beginning teachers time to observe more experienced teachers and receive individual help from senior teachers assigned as mentors.

Career ladders need to be supported by a commitment from local school districts and superintendents to intervene when schools are at risk. In a recent report, the California Commission on the Teaching Profession (1985, p. 30) recommends that "failure to make improvements within a reasonable time should constitute grounds for dismissal of the school principal or, when the problem is determined to be at the district level, the superintendent."

Unstaged Career to Staged Career

Teachers have different skills, knowledge, attitudes, and concerns at different points during their careers. An expanding knowledge base documents changes which follow regular developmental patterns. Career ladders can provide challenge, variety, and support for teachers at each stage of their careers. A description of one career ladder model is presented here. (A fuller description of career ladder features and teachers' roles can be found in Chapters 4 and 5.)

Career ladders offer a wealth of career options which correspond to regularly occurring stages of teacher development. The first-year teacher or intern will have a reduced teaching load more consistent with the apprenticeship or intern model. Teachers at the second rung of the career ladder, associate teachers, are responsible for instructing students. They may supervise student teachers and serve as mentors for interns. Senior teachers, those at the third rung of the career ladder, may teach in staff development programs and help reassigned teachers (those recently assigned to a different school or grade level).

Teachers at the last step of the career ladder, master teachers, are essentially instructional leaders. Their new roles will shape the direction of the school program and teaching as a profession (Association of Teacher Educators, 1985). Their responsibilities may include coordinating summer school programs for teachers and conducting demonstration lessons for others while working in their own classrooms with their own students.

In order to provide time to work with other teachers, master teachers may spend up to half of their time out of the classroom. At the elementary level, two master teachers might share the same classroom, and at the secondary level, the master teacher might teach half the normal load of classes. In that way, the delivery of instruction will be provided in a consistent manner rather than by substitute teachers.

From Loneliness to Collegiality

Loneliness in the workplace is common for the beginning teacher and the experienced teacher as well. Contributing to the isolation of teachers is the physical separation from each other and lack of support from school specialists, principals, and colleagues. While career ladders cannot change the physically cellular nature of schools, they can provide new opportunities for collegial relationships and a network of solid support.

Career ladders offer systematic ways to provide practitioner help for teachers who are experiencing problems in their classrooms. Teachers at varying levels of the career ladder will work directly with other teachers who need assistance. Senior, associate, and master teachers will act as mentors who support and guide.

A clear separation will be made between the roles of mentoring and evaluating. Teachers receiving assistance from a mentor should not be evaluated by that mentor. With this separation of mentoring and evaluating, a trust relationship and bond can form between the giver and the receiver of help. This kind of assistance will be especially helpful to the beginning teacher who is caught needing help but often is afraid of being evaluated.

As a result of this special bond between mentor and mentee, a true collegial relationship can emerge. When two teachers are drawn together to consider a problem situation, both can identify needed changes and then work to make them happen. When both teachers feel free to reflect upon the usefulness of the assistance given, ways can be identified to strengthen their professional partnership.

Special approaches can be utilized which encourage long-term collegial relationships. One involves the use of clinical supervision. Throughout its cycle of pre-observation conference, observation, and post-observation conference, mentors can provide opportunities for teachers to define their own goals and to reflect on their own practices. When two teachers can crawl through observational data together, both can interpret what was happening and then make plans for the next time. When mentors can provide teachers with tools to change practice, the partnership can become a relationship between peers.

Given the importance of these special partnerships, it is imperative to select career ladder teachers who are willing to share their expertise with other teachers. This willingness to share breaks down the competitive aspect of career ladders while fostering and encouraging collegial relationships.

From Powerlessness to Autonomy

Career ladders offer many new and unique roles which will enable teachers to have a more direct influence on the direction of their schools and their profession. These roles include opportunities for (a) evaluating their own colleagues, (b) designing selection criteria for those who want to serve at various levels on the career ladder, (c) developing new ways of documenting selection criteria, and (d) taking leadership roles in designing career ladders.

Through career ladders teachers will be involved in the shared responsibility of evaluating their own colleagues. To accomplish this, senior, associate, and master teachers will be given the opportunity to participate in the evaluation of teachers in other school buildings. In addition, teachers must be involved in designing objective evaluation tools for a number of different roles. New approaches in evaluation will be needed as teachers assess both classroom teaching and instructional leadership skills.

Evaluation processes can be facilitated in a number of different ways. In each instance, every assurance of objectivity and maximum teacher input must be made. This will be essential since a positive evaluation in a career ladder will result in a sizable pay raise. While the primary rating that matters is presently retention, ratings of the future will have significant economic consequences.

One way to provide an objective evaluation system for classroom teaching is by selecting a team of educators including (a) one teacher with subject matter or grade level expertise which matches the background of the teacher to be evaluated, (b) an administrator who is presently serving at an appropriate level, and (c) a college faculty member with the appropriate background. All team members would have undergone extensive training themselves and have demonstrated their abilities to perform at high rates of inter-rater reliability using low-inference observational tools.

A single observation should not be used as the only means of evaluation. A minimum number of three observations appears to offer a fair method of assessment when supported by multiple sources of evaluation such as a structured interviewing process.

Teachers being evaluated must have ways of preserving their own dignity with some degree of control over their situation. For example, teachers being evaluated on teaching effectiveness should be able to choose the kind of lesson they wish to teach. In addition, teachers should participate in setting times for the observations and in approving the selection of observers. Educators assigned to an evaluation team should be randomly drawn from the existing pool of trained observers.

In addition to evaluating peers, teachers must be involved in designing selection criteria for those who wish to serve at various levels on the career ladder. (For more details, see Chapter Seven which discusses the identification and evaluation of teachers in a career ladder plan.) Given the challenging array of career options for teachers, these criteria must go far beyond a superior knowledge of subject matter, an above average knowledge of a general nature, and superior skills in teaching. Master teachers should (a) be willing to share their expertise with other teachers; (b) be able to work well with colleagues, administrators, and parents; (c) possess the ability to cause learning to occur; (d) be continual learners; and (e) possess certain clusters of personality characteristics. These clusters may include those personality characteristics identified by Sheehy (1981) as pathfinder characteristics and cited by Easterly (1984a) as applicable to identifying outstanding teachers. These include a willingness to risk change, a sense of right timing, an ability to be both responsive and nurturing as well as independent and assertive, a sense of purpose, and a perception of being happier now than when they were younger. Other factors include feeling appreciated by significant others (Easterly, 1984a) and having a support network (Easterly, 1984b).

Teachers need to take the initiative in developing ways to document selection criteria. It seems likely that some criteria may be verified by paper and pencil tests while others could be verified through observations, rating scales, questionnaires, letters from colleagues, structured interviews, and pre- and post-test instruments designed by teachers for specific classrooms. Careful attention must be given to the design of a multiperspective evaluation package which clearly identifies those individuals who will be prepared to assume new responsibilities on the career ladder. Documentation of evaluation procedures must be simplified "to reduce confusion and anxiety and to lessen the burden of paperwork preparation" (Handler & Carlson, 1985, p. 137).

In addition to evaluating and selecting peers, teachers need to take leadership roles in designing career ladders which offer many challenging options. The options include an opportunity to coordinate staff development programs and faculty involvement in curriculum development. Vehicles are needed which encourage teachers to become curriculum designers rather than persons who primarily implement curriculum. Teachers should participate in the selection of new faculty, staff, and administrators. Career ladders need to be designed so that teachers are given the time, support, and encouragement to conduct action research which improves practices. University researchers and teacher researchers may wish to form teams which will expand the knowledge base of the teaching profession. A new vocabulary may be needed to describe emerging roles such as peer facilitator, group facilitator, action researcher, peer evaluator, mentor, teacher trainer, and teacher educator.

As career ladders are considered by school districts, teachers need to initiate and monitor the design process. When teachers do this, they assume responsibility for the redesign of existing organizational structures. Through their efforts, career ladders can empower teachers to guide their own profession.

Professional Growth Instead of Inspection

Career ladders offer many new opportunities for professional growth. They provide specified preparation for teachers as they assume new roles and responsibilities and they separate professional growth from summative evaluation (inspection). In addition, career ladders provide staff development which meets needs of teachers at different stages of their professional careers.

Developing Career Ladders in Teaching (Association of Teacher Educators, 1985) recommends a year of transition which prepares teachers to assume new roles and responsibilities. Rather than hoping that teachers will be able to perform new duties at the next level on the career ladder, teachers will be given assistance, knowledge, and the chance to practice new roles before being evaluated for advancement to a new step on the career ladder. While they are learning, teachers will be supported and nurtured by other teachers as they improve specific observation, planning, communication, and leadership skills. This year of transition is a fundamental component of an effective career ladder plan.

In addition to assisting teachers during this important year, career ladders will provide a sharp contrast to the present situation. In most schools today, principals are caught in the middle between the roles of formal evaluator and professional developer (Parker, 1985). Career ladders will emphasize the separation of professional growth from inspection or summative evaluation. While principals will still be involved in formal evaluation, they will share that responsibility with teachers. Professional development will become more and more the domain of teachers as they assume mentorship roles. These long-term helping relationships will enhance the professional growth of the teacher seeking help and of the mentor who is there to provide the needed support and assistance.

A third avenue of professional growth is provided through staff development for specific target groups. (See Chapter 8.) Beginning teachers, new teachers to the school district, reassigned teachers, interns, and student teachers all have special needs. They may include such survival skills as classroom management and motivating students. Master teachers can provide the leadership in designing specific workshops for these and other target groups. As master teachers plan workshops together, they will have an opportunity to learn from each other and thus grow professionally as well as the clientele whom they serve.

Role Congruence vs. Role Stress

At first, career ladders may create additional role stress as new responsibilities are delineated and implemented. One of the stress points will certainly occur as the role of instructional leader begins to shift from the principal to teachers on the career ladder. As teachers join in shared decision making, initial conflicts may occur. Principals and teachers will need to work through common concerns so that new and more effective roles can emerge for both. (See the chapter on roles of teachers and administrators.)

As soon as potential conflicts are identified and resolved, career ladders can serve to reduce role stress for teachers. Structures will be provided for the support of teachers on an individual basis. When teachers can ask for assistance and get it quickly, stress is reduced.

Through the help of a caring mentor, many problems which cause role stress can be resolved.

When teachers have a solid support network, role conflicts and ambiguities can be explored and resolved. Career ladders provide released time for teachers to coordinate informal sharing times among colleagues. This precious time can be set aside to help teachers reflect on their own teaching, share these reflections with colleagues, and engage in "a collective struggle to learn more . . . " (Lieberman & Miller, 1984, p. 13). The environment provided will be a safe place to engage in dialogue, promote inquiry, and share dreams. This reshaping of the work environment is essential if role congruence is to occur.

In addition to individual and group support, career ladders create a bridge which spans the gulf between present working conditions and the highest ideals of the profession. Teachers will be recognized as professionals and supported with the necessary clerical and technical assistance. Teachers will become decision makers and leaders. Teachers will have the challenge and variety of many career options.

At this moment in history, teaching stands on the brink of becoming a true profession. When its members can participate fully, the present conflict between real and ideal can be resolved.

RECOMMENDATIONS FOR THE WORK ENVIRONMENT

The following recommendations are based upon improved working conditions outlined in **Developing Career Ladders in Teaching** (Association of Teacher Educators, 1985) and recommendations gleaned from the preceding chapter. These recommendations should be carefully considered prior to any design or implementation process. Improvements in working conditions include the following:

1. Support for continued professional growth
   A. Sabbatical leaves
   H. Released time to attend professional conferences
   C. Released time for other professional activities
   D. Travel funds for attending conferences
   E. Tuition assistance for advanced study
   F. Specific preparation for teachers when they seek advancement to a new step on the career ladder

    G. Staff development which meets needs of teachers at different stages of their professional careers

    H. Reduced teaching loads for beginning teachers so that they can observe more experienced teachers and receive individual help from senior teachers assigned as mentors

    I. Help for teachers who are experiencing problems in their classrooms

    J. Released time for teachers to coordinate informal sharing times among other teachers

    K. Released time to conduct action research which improves practice

2. Recognition of teachers' contributions
   A. Feedback from administrators, colleagues, students, the community
   B. Awards or certificates (e.g., Teacher of the Year)
   C. Trophies or plaques displayed in schools for teaching honors
   D. Special facilities (e.g., special parking areas, private offices)
   E. Salaries commensurate with roles and responsibilities

3. Nature of job assignment
   A. Reduction in noninstructional tasks or duties (e.g., recess duty, lunchroom supervision, some types of paperwork)
   B. Reasonable class sizes
   C. A daily block of time away from students for planning and preparation
   D. Released time to carry out responsibilities related to leadership roles within the career ladder
   E. A reasonable schedule
   F. Reduction in classroom interruptions
   G. Increased job mobility
   H. Reduction in misassignments (assignments of positions to teachers who lack the appropriate subject area preparation)
   I. Safe and orderly school environments

4. Work environment
   A. Adequate classroom space
   B. Offices or work areas for planning periods

5. Material resources
   A. Access to equipment (e.g., computers, typewriters, telephones, copy machines, audiovisual equipment)
   B. Adequate books, supplies, and buildings

6. Adequate assistance from personnel who support teachers

    A. Secretaries
    B. Teacher aides
    C. Administrators
    D. Other teachers
    E. Qualified personnel to provide special services and counseling for students
    F. Qualified substitute teachers
    G. Strong parental support and interest

7. Participation in school management (work control and shared decision making)

    A. Shared planning and decision making by administrators and teachers
    B. Opportunities to participate in selecting new faculty, staff, and administrators for the school
    C. Opportunities to participate in planning and conducting curriculum development, staff development, and other functions that determine the direction of the school and the school district
    D. Shared responsibility for evaluating their own colleagues
    E. Opportunities to participate in the summative evaluation of teachers seeking advancement to a new step of the career ladder
    F. Opportunities to participate in designing objective evaluation tools which assess both classroom teaching and instructional leadership skills
    G. Opportunities to participate in designing selection criteria for those who wish to serve at various levels on the career ladder
    H. Opportunities to assume leadership roles in designing career ladders

REFERENCES

Association of Teacher Educators. (1985). *Developing career ladders in teaching.* Reston, VA.

Bird, T., & Little, J. W. (1985). *School organization of the teaching occupation.* San Francisco: Far West Laboratory for Educational Research and Development.

Burden, P. R. (1986). Teacher development: Implications for teacher education. In L. Katz & J. Raths (Eds.), *Advances in teacher education: Vol. II.* Norwood, NJ: Ablex Publishing Co.

Burke, P. J., Christensen, J. C., & Fessler, R. (1984). *Teacher career stages: Implications for staff development.* Bloomington, IN: Phi Delta Kappa Educational Foundation.

California Commission on the Teaching Profession. (1985). *Who will teach our children? A strategy for improving California's schools.* Sacramento, CA.

Easterly, J. L. (1984a). Outstanding teachers: Pathfinders for the profession. *Action in Teacher Education, 6*(3), 1–5.

Easterly, J. L. (1984b). *Perceptions of outstanding elementary teachers about themselves and their profession* (Technical Report No. 1). Rochester, MI: Oakland University, The School of Human and Educational Services. (ERIC Document Reproduction Service No. SP 016 656)

Easterly, J. L. (1983). *Master teachers caught in conflict.* Paper presented at the Summer Workshop of the Association of Teacher Educators, LaCrosse, WI.

English, F. W. (1984-1985). Still searching for excellence. *Educational Leadership, 42*(4), 34-35.

Fuller, F. F., & Brown, O. H. (1975). Becoming a teacher. In K. Ryan (Ed.), *Teacher education: Seventy-fourth yearbook of the National Society for the Study of Education (Part 2)* (pp. 25-52). Chicago: University of Chicago Press.

Glickman, C. D. (1984-1985). The supervisor's challenge: Changing the teacher's work environment. *Educational Leadership, 42*(4), 38-40.

Goodlad, J. I. (1984). *A place called school.* New York: McGraw-Hill.

Gupta, N., & Jenkins, G. D. (1981). *Work role stress among female and male public school teachers.* Paper presented at the Annual Conference of the American Psychological Association, Los Angeles.

Handler, J. R., & Carlson, D. L. (1985). *Shaping Tennessee's career ladder program* (Part 2 Report, Improving Teacher Quality through Incentives Project). The University of Tennessee, Knoxville: U.S. Department of Education.

Hunt, D. E. (1971). *Matching models in education.* Toronto: Ontario Institute for Studies in Education.

Lanier, J. (in press). Research on teacher education. In M. C. Wittrock (Ed.), *Handbook of research on teaching* (3rd ed.). New York: Macmillan.

Levinson, D. J., Darrow, C. N., Klein, E. B., Levinson, M. H., & McKee, B. (1978). *The seasons of a man's life.* New York: Alfred A. Knopf.

Lieberman, A., & Miller, L. (1984). School improvement: Themes and variations. *Teachers College Record, 86*(1), 4-19.

Lieberman, M. (1985). Educational speciality boards: A way out of the merit pay morass? *Phi Delta Kappan, 67*(2), 103-107.

Loevinger, J. (1966). The meaning and measurement of ego development. *American Psychologist, 21,* 195-206.

Lortie, D. C. (1975). *School teacher.* Chicago: University of Chicago Press.

Parker, J. C. (1985). *Career ladder/master teacher programs: Implications for principals.* Reston, VA: National Association of Secondary School Principals.

Rosenholtz, S. J., & Smylie, M. A. (1984). Teacher compensation and career ladders. *The Elementary School Journal, 85*(2), 149-166.

Schlechty, P. C. (1984). Recommendations for improving the career opportunities of teachers in the Charlotte-Mecklenburg Schools: A constructive alternative to merit pay. *Journal of Children in Contemporary Society, 16*(3-4), 105-120.

Schlechty, P. C., & Vance, V. S. (1983). Recruitment, selection and retention: The shape of the teaching force. *Elementary School Journal, 83,* 469-487.

Sheehy, G. (1981). *Pathfinders.* New York: Bantam.

Sheehy, G. (1974). *Passages: Predictable crises of adult life.* New York: E. P. Dutton.

Veenman, S. (1984). Perceived problems of beginning teachers. *Review of Educational Research, 54*(2), 143-178.

Watts, H. (1980). *Starting out, moving on, running ahead, or how the teachers' center can attend to stages in teacher's development.* San Francisco: Far West Laboratory for Educational Research and Development. (ERIC Document Reproduction Service No. ED 200 604)

Watts, H. (1982). Observations on stages in teachers development. *MATE Viewpoints, 4*(1), 4-8.

Watts, H. (1984). The rewards of teaching. *Journal of Staff Development, 5*(2), 78-88.

Chapter 10

COSTS FOR A CAREER LADDER

GEORGE N. SMITH

Career ladder plans have swept across the United States in response to educational reform recommendations, accountability issues, efforts to establish more meaningful evaluations systems, and efforts to restructure the teaching career. One of the most important factors in establishing career ladder plans is the cost of such plans.

This chapter will include a discussion of (a) problems with teacher salaries now (without career ladders being established), (b) costs of career ladder plans, (c) models for career ladder salary systems, and (d) recommendations in relation to the costs of career ladder plans.

PROBLEMS WITH TEACHER SALARIES NOW

There are problems with the salaries that teachers are paid now, even without the establishment of career ladder plans. In fact, these problems are contributing factors why career ladders are being proposed at this time. This section will include a discussion of (a) problems with the salary structure for teachers and (b) problems with merit pay plans that have been proposed to address some of the salary problems.

Problems With the Salary Structure for Teachers

Beginning teacher salaries offered throughout the country are lower than beginning salaries offered in many other professions requiring comparable levels of training. For example, in Arizona the average beginning teacher salary in 1985–86 was $15,400. The starting salaries for other professions were higher, including: $19,960 for accountants; $23,280 for chemists; $26,556 for electrical engineers; $21,040 for financial analysts; and $23,280 for telecommunication analysts. It is difficult to compete for the best and the brightest people to go into the teaching career when the starting salaries of many other fields are so much higher than teaching.

The inequities remain throughout a teacher's career because the increase in the average starting teacher salary is exceeded by even larger increases in the average starting salary of other professions. For instance, beginning teacher salaries increased by 87.8% from 1973–74 to 1983–84. But in the same time frame, the beginning salaries for buyers increased by 120.8%, chemists by 132.4%, and engineers by 138.9%.

Furthermore, inequities between average salaries in teaching and average salaries in other occupations appear to increase over time. For example, average teacher salaries increased from $10,778 in 1973–74 to $21,935 in 1983–84. But the average salary of other professions increased at even a higher rate. For instance, from 1973–74 to 1983–84 the average salary for accountants went from $11,600 to $24,592; chemists went from $13,939 to $29,770; and engineers went from $15,252 to $32,223.

Again, the inequities remain through a teacher's career because the increase in the average salary of teachers is exceeded by even larger increases in the average salaries of other occupations. For example, the average salary for teachers increased by 103.5% from 1973–74 to 1983–84. But in the same time frame, the average salary for accountants increased by 112%, chemists by 113%, and engineers by 111.3%.

Problems With Merit Pay

Merit pay systems have been used in some school districts in an effort to pay talented teachers better salaries. But the results of merit pay plans have not been as successful as some people would prefer. The following is a brief list of reasons for the failure of merit pay as identified by school districts.

1. No measurable criteria or satisfactory instrument on which to base evaluations, making impartial ratings nearly impossible
2. Difficulty in determining who deserved a merit award
3. Insufficiently prepared evaluators
4. Inconsistency among evaluators and standards from school to school and from level to level within a school
5. Unilateral evaluations
6. Changes in the school system leadership and philosophy
7. Parents wanting their children to be taught by "superior" teachers

8. Quota systems provoking artificial cutoffs freezing out less experienced teachers
9. Negative publicity or confidentiality of merit recipients destroyed by publishing the recipients' names in local newspapers
10. Too many recipients, causing the "merit" concept to be lost
11. Too expensive to operate or maintain
12. Merit that became permanent, rather than requiring renewed recognition and awards
13. A difference in opinions between the board and administration regarding the reasons for implementing a merit pay program and its expected outcomes

COSTS OF CAREER LADDER PLANS

This section includes a discussion of (a) the types of costs that are involved when establishing career ladders, and (b) a review of actual experiences with costs in several states as career ladders have been implemented.

Types of Costs

Costs of a career ladder plan are an important consideration. They fall into three broad categories: (a) cost of developing the plan and the evaluation system, (b) the evaluation process, and (c) the incentives themselves (Weeks & Cornett, 1985). In addition, there are some non-salary costs that are involved when establishing career ladders. These four categories will be discussed in the sections that follow.

Costs for Development

Developmental costs are considerable, particularly if the evaluation system relies on multiple sources of data and if the state does not already have the evaluation instruments. For example, if the state decides to include classroom observation in the evaluation process, instruments must be designed. If the state wishes to test professional knowledge or knowledge of subject matter, tests must be developed or purchased.

Another aspect of developmental costs is the trial and error approach that is being used to establish career ladder plans in some districts and states. Trial and error techniques are often applied to move the various experiments from planning to implementation. The economics of these stages and the previously discussed costs cannot be ignored, though they would be difficult to define in terms of dollars and school district expense.

As decisions are made about the features of a career ladder plan during the initial planning, consideration must be given to the process and support of career ladders. A number of issues related to process and support were identified in **Developing Career Ladders in Teaching** (Association of Teacher Educators, 1985), and these are listed below. Most of the items have a cost inherent in the decision.

1. Who should be involved in planning and implementing the career ladder? Legislators? The state education agency? School board members? School administrators? Teachers? Teacher unions? Parents? Others?
2. How long will it take to develop and initiate a new system?
3. Will there be field tests? Pilot programs?
4. How much latitude and autonomy will each school district have? Each school-building unit?
5. Will the role of the personnel office need to be changed? How?
6. How will the selection and the assignment of teachers at various career steps be handled? By whom?
7. What will the role of the local and state teacher unions be?
8. Should other career ladder models be examined before developing a local plan?
9. Should representatives from a number of school districts considering a career ladder meet to deal with general concerns?
10. What policy and other mechanisms are needed to ensure due process for teachers?
11. What will be the role of various professional specialty groups?
12. How will the program be evaluated?
13. Should there be a research component at each step of the way?
14. What role will curriculum and supervision personnel have?
15. What budget will be required for new salary schedules?
16. What personnel will be required to manage the program? What competence will they need?
17. What budget will be required to train and maintain the personnel who will evaluate teachers?
18. Will monies for the program come from the local district? The state? Both? In what proportion?

Costs for the Evaluation Process

The evaluation process itself is an important consideration, and may vary widely depending upon how it is structured. Historically, local evaluations have been performed by principals, and often have consisted of completing a simple checklist. However, today's systems are more thorough and more complex. In some evaluation systems, a teacher must be observed by multiple observers, including peers, and sometimes the principal. Classroom observations must be accompanied by a conference with the teacher both before and after the observation. This requires a substantial commitment of personnel to the evaluation process itself. If a peer evaluation system is used, salaries must be paid to teacher-evaluators who would otherwise be in the classroom. Despite the costs, careful observation by trained evaluators is an essential component of performance-based plans.

Costs for the Incentives

Another cost consideration is that of the incentives themselves. The incentives must be large enough to be worth striving to achieve and, many would argue, they should be available to all who meet the standards. In addition, incentive supplements frequently are accompanied by across-the-board salary increases designed to make the package more attractive politically.

Non-Salary Costs

A number of non-salary costs have to be considered as career ladders are being implemented. These costs take the form of fears and concerns by teachers and administrators. Teachers may be (a) concerned that administrators will not be able to conduct an accurate evaluation of their performance, (b) fearful that the evaluators' professional objectivity will not be consistent, and (c) fearful that the collegiality of mutual support and sharing of ideas among teachers will be affected by paying teachers varying salaries based on performance evaluation. Administrators may be concerned that their district's evaluation process be adequately defined to substantiate and support proper implementation.

Experiences With Career Ladder Costs

Several states have moved from the developmental stages into implementation of performance-based incentive plans. The total costs of the programs vary from state to state depending on the size of the incentive increment and the proportion of teachers eligible. California has allocated $31 million for its Mentor Teacher Program, which provides $4,000 supplements to slightly less than 5% of the teachers in each participating district. It should be noted that, in each of the states, the pay plans were accompanied by large increases in overall school funding (Weeks & Cornett, 1985). The following is a review of the costs of career ladder plans being implemented in four states.

North Carolina

The 1985–86 pilot program for 16 North Carolina school districts was funded for $12 million. Teachers and administrators from the pilot districts participated in a 30-hour teaching training session. Each participant was paid a stipend of $500. Evaluation instruments were developed based on the effective teaching research. This instrument was field-tested in the pilot districts plus in 24 volunteer districts. Four teacher evaluations were conducted, two by the supervisor and two by the evaluator. Teachers assessed as being at Career Status I (the standard being determined at the state level) received one additional salary step over the salary schedule or the next year. Phasing in of Career Status II is in process.

Tennessee

Tennessee has funded its career ladder program at $50 million, $85 million, and $122 million for the first three years of the implementation in order to provide supplements of $1,000, $2,000, and $3,000 for Career Levels I, II, and III. The second full year of implementation (1985–86) was funded at $85 million without any changes in the program. However, the evaluation process is being revised. The state has hired additional evaluators to continue evaluation of teachers for the upper levels of the career ladder. Teachers who came close to qualifying are being reevaluated. Also, teachers who had applied but were not evaluated because the applicants exceeded capacity are being evaluated this year.

Texas

During the first year of implementation, about $90 million was paid in career ladder supplements for the approximately 45,000 teachers named in Career Level II. There are legislated increments of $2,000 at each level of the ladder. Plans are being developed to train appraisers for implementation of a statewide evaluation system.

Utah

During the first year, 48% of the career ladder funds went to extended contracts. Full implementation for 1985–86 was supported with a $36 million budget. Districts have elected to distribute 62% of their funds for performance bonus and career ladder placement, leaving 38% for extended year contracts.

MODELS FOR CAREER SALARY SYSTEMS

The Arizona Education Association (1986) developed five models for a career development compensation plan. In the career development models, the AEA used the terms establishment, adaptation, and extension to represent three steps in career development. In the summary of the five plans that follows, those terms will be replaced by the terms Career Step I, Career Step II, and Career Step III to indicate terms that might likely be used with a salary plan for career ladders.

Model I

This is a model which indexes the salaries for the three career steps. The salary schedule for Career Step I would be essentially the same as the single salary schedule now used in many districts and would have an index of 1.0. The salary chart would show different salaries based on the level of education (i.e., bachelors degree, BS plus 15 graduate credits, masters degree, MS plus credits) and on the number of years of teaching experience (shown in yearly steps). The salary schedule for Career Step II would take the same format, but would have salaries which are one and a half times those in the schedule for Career Step I. Therefore, the salary index would be 1.5 for Career Step II. The salary schedule for Career Step III would again take the same format, but would have a salary index of 2.0 (i.e., the salaries would be two times of those listed in Career Step I). For example, a teacher earning $20,000 at Career Step I would earn $30,000 at Career Step II (cost index of 1.5) and $40,000 at Career Step III (cost index of 2.0).

Model 2

This is a model that adds on certain dollar amounts as teachers move from Career Step I to II and to III. Once again, the salary schedule based on level of education and years of teaching experience that is now widely used would be the basis of this salary plan. Teachers at Career Step I would be placed on that salary schedule based on their level of education and years of teaching experience. When approved to move to Career Level II, teachers would remain at the same location on the salary schedule at the time of the move, but each figure on the Career Level II salary schedule would represent a $3,000 increase over the comparable position on the salary chart used for Career Step I. Similarly, each figure on the salary schedule chart for Career Level III would represent a $4,000 increase over the comparable position on the salary chart used for Career Step II (thus representing a total of $7,000 over Career Step I). For example, a teacher earning $20,000 at Career Step I would earn $23,000 at Career Step II and $27,000 at Career Step III.

Model 3

This is a model which represents a variation of the typical single salary schedule and would display a salary range for each position on the schedule. The range would represent salaries that would be provided at the three career steps. For example, a given point on the salary schedule might display $24,000–$26,000 as the salary. What that means is that those teachers at Career Step I would earn $24,000, those at Career Step II would earn $25,000, and those at Career Step III would earn $26,000.

Model 4

This model replaces the typical single salary schedule with a display of the total range of salary that a person could earn at a given career step. The salary a teacher would receive within a career step would be determined by years of experience at that level. For example, the range given for Career Step I might indicate $22,000–$32,000. That means that year one on Career Step I would be $22,000, year two would be $23,000, year three would be $24,000, and so on. The salary range for Career Step II might be $33,000–$43,900. Year one on Career Step II would be $33,000, year two would be $34,000, and so on. The salary range for Career Step III might be $44,000–$54,000. Year one on Career Step III would be $44,000, year two would be $45,000, and so on. Other factors besides experience could be used to determine the salary within the range for the career steps. These factors could include education or demonstration of skills.

Model 5

This model is similar to Model 4, except that it does not have the range at each of the three levels. Only the starting salary is listed for each of the career steps. Movement from one career step to the next would be based on skill development, and teachers would not receive annual increases except those negotiated.

RECOMMENDATIONS

As decisions are being made about implementing career ladders, careful consideration needs to be given to the area of costs. Problems that have been experienced with merit pay plans should be avoided as salary issues are decided with career ladders. One clear concern is to simply have enough money in the budget to pay for the extra costs that are part of a career ladder plan.

Along with the background information in this chapter, the following recommendations are provided to aid decision makers concerning the costs of career ladders.

1. Before implementation, identify all expected cost areas and carefully calculate estimates.
2. Before implementation, select a model that will be used for determining teacher salaries on all career ladder steps.
3. Arrange for sufficient funding.

REFERENCES

Arizona Education Association. (1986, February). *The career development system.* Tucson, AZ: AEA/NEA Research.

Association of Teacher Educators. (1985). *Developing career ladders in teaching.* Reston, VA: Author.

Weeks, K., & Cornett, L. (1985, March). Planning career ladders: Lessons from the states. In *Career Ladder Clearinghouse.* Atlanta, GA: Southern Regional Education Board.

ADDITIONAL READINGS

American Association of School Administrators. (1983). *Superintendents respond to merit pay.* Washington, DC: Author.

Association for Supervision and Curriculum Development. (1985). *Incentives for excellence in America's schools.* Alexandria, VA: Author.

Astuto, T. A., & Clark, D. L. (1985). *Merit pay for teachers: An analysis of state policy options* (Educational Policy Study Series). Bloomington, IN: Indiana University, School of Education.

Bacharach, S. B., Lipsky, D. B., & Shedd, J. B. (1984). *Paying for better teaching: Merit pay and its alternatives.* Ithaca, NY: Organizational Analysis and Practice.

Calhoun, F. S., & Protheroe, N. J. (1983). *Merit pay for teachers: Status and descriptions.* Arlington, VA: Educational Research Service.

Cresap, C., McCormick, M., & Paget, D. (1984). *Teacher incentives: A tool for effective management.* Reston, VA: National Association of Secondary School Principals.

Hatry, H. P., & Greiner, J. M. (1984). *Issues in teacher incentive plans.* Washington, DC: The Urban Institute Press.

Johnson, H. C., Jr. (Ed.). (1985). *Merit, money and teachers' careers: Studies on merit pay and career ladders for teachers.* Lanham, MD: University Press of America.

Johnson, S. M. (1984). Merit pay for teachers: A poor prescription for reform. *Harvard Educational Review, 54*(2), 175–185.

McGuire, K., & Thompson, J. A. (1984). *The costs of performance pay systems.* Denver, CO: Education Commission of the States.

Palaich, R., & Flannelly, E. (1984). *Improving teacher quality through incentives.* Denver, CO: Education Commission of the States.

Porwoll, P. J. (1979). *Merit pay for teachers.* Arlington, VA: Educational Research Service.

Robinson, G. E. (1983, May). Paying teachers for performance and productivity: Learning from experience. *ERS concerns in education.* Arlington, VA: Educational Research Service.

Robinson, G. E. (1984, March). Incentive pay for teachers: An analysis of approaches. *ERS concerns in education.* Arlington, VA: Educational Research Service.

Rosenholtz, S. J., & Smylie, M. A. (1984). Teacher compensation and career ladders: Policy implications from research. *Elementary School Journal, 85*(2), 149–167.

Vroom, V. (1964). *Motivation and work.* New York: Wiley.

Chapter 11

CAREER LADDERS: AN NEA PERSPECTIVE

MARY H. FUTRELL

To consider the issue of career ladders, this chapter will include a discussion of (a) problems with semantics, (b) attractiveness of the teaching career, (c) problems with job ladders, (d) features of career development plans, and (e) a summary.

PROBLEMS WITH SEMANTICS

The National Education Association (NEA) is very precise in the semantics it uses to characterize various compensation and development proposals, and with good reason. One of the more disappointing aspects of the reform movement is that many proposals that are labeled as "career ladders" have turned out to be, in practice, harmful to both teachers and the field of education.

The first problem is that few people are talking about the same thing when they use the term, a factor which makes endorsement of even the concept quite dangerous. The second problem is that career ladders—in terms of how they have developed in states through the mid-1980s—have had very little to do with education reform. In essence, they have been variations on old and failed merit pay themes. Attempts by the NEA to point out the inherent flaws of these plans have often been treated as opposition to reform, rather than as opposition to unsound practices.

One of our organization's primary goals is to find and promote reform ideas which establish teaching as a valued and attractive profession. But NEA cannot support hierarchical ladder plans that set quotas on development opportunities. Many of the proposals that people have promoted as "career ladders" can actually have a negative impact on the ability of schools to attract and retain competent teachers, and to provide quality instruction.

What Has Happened to Career Ladder Plans

There is a great paradox in any discussion of career ladders. Few reform ideas have as much positive potential as genuine career ladders— that is, systems which promote career development. Yet in practice these ideas have led to the waste of much public money and good will.

It is a useful first step to examine what has happened when the concept of career ladders has been translated into actual programs. As the reform movement has developed in the 1980s, there have been more career ladder failures than successes. In Florida, several former state teachers of the year failed to qualify as "master teachers" in the state's merit plan. One teacher, commenting on the evaluation process, told the **Fort Myers News-Express** that the program required someone to be "a super teacher for 110 minutes a year."

Tennessee's venture into the career ladder system also has had difficulty, according to several surveys taken a year after the program was introduced. In a survey by the **Chattanooga Times,** the program even received negative marks from a majority of teachers selected for the upper levels of the ladder.

Fortunately, the problems with career ladders have not totally discredited the idea that teaching must be considered and developed as a **career.** The failures also have helped clarify just what works and doesn't work, and why. Unfortunately, with each failure it becomes increasingly uncertain as to whether career ladders will become an integral part of a genuine movement of educational renewal, or just another gimmick paraded under the banner of reform.

ATTRACTIVENESS OF THE TEACHING CAREER

Problems with the teaching career will be discussed in this section and suggestions to respond to the problems will be provided.

Problems With The Teaching Career

The debate over career ladders is bringing to the forefront a number of issues that bear directly on the attractiveness of teaching as a career. Consider these figures:

1. In Florida, 80% of those who begin teaching don't stay in the profession long enough to qualify for retirement.

2. In 1981 and 1982, emergency certificates represented 20% of all certificates issued in Texas.
3. In 1982, 56% of all math and science teachers nationwide were not certified in their fields.
4. The nation's 16,000 school districts employ a total of 12,000 physics teachers—that's one teacher for every 3,600 students. The supply of physics teachers is projected to drop.
5. Over 200,000 teachers are now teaching outside their major field of preparation.

As alarming as those figures are, they do not reflect the full severity of the situation. In a 1983 nationwide teacher opinion poll, 43% of teachers said that if they were given the chance to start over again, they probably would not become teachers.

In short, all available evidence indicates that the nation is experiencing something far more critical than a teacher shortage. The truth is that the necessary infrastructure of the teaching profession—experienced, dedicated personnel—is in a period of serious decline. Something must be done to respond to this problem.

Possible Solutions

To deal with these problems, we must begin asking what can we do to attract and retain people in the teaching profession. I think the basic answer is rather straightforward: We must make teaching a more attractive and more satisfying career.

First, providing better salaries for teachers is, of course, a necessary step toward any effort to upgrade the teaching profession. Teaching is the lowest paid profession requiring a college education, and the longer one teaches, the greater the gap grows between teaching and other occupations that demand similar training, skills, and responsibilities. But money alone will not solve the nation's educational dilemma. The National Education Association believes that a more comprehensive solution is necessary.

Second, the NEA supports programs that have, as their centerpiece, a commitment to long-term, adequately funded career development for teachers. Without such a commitment to **career development**, you don't have a career ladder plan. Instead, you either have what amounts to a traditional merit pay plan, or you have what Cornell University professor Samuel Bacharach has appropriately labeled a "job ladder"—that is, a ladder that leads right out of the classroom, one rung at a time (Bacharach, Lipsky, & Shedd, 1984).

The following sections consider problems with job ladders and also provide recommended features of career development plans.

PROBLEMS WITH JOB LADDERS

It is important to understand the nature of job ladder plans, if only to identify the flaws that distinguish them from genuine career development programs.

First, a flaw with job ladders is that a quota is usually set on the number of teachers who can be singled out for reward and advancement. By setting this quota, the job ladder approach poisons the academic atmosphere by setting teacher against teacher. NEA cannot support hierarchical ladder plans that set quotas on development opportunities.

A second flaw with job ladders is that they "promote" quality teachers right out of the classroom. As teachers advance up the steps of a job ladder, they have the option of becoming involved in additional professional responsibilities. Some of these responsibilities may require the teacher to be out of the classroom for a period of time. This process sends a very subtle, yet very dangerous, message throughout a school system. Bacharach has noted that a job ladder says that the functions of classroom teaching "are less professional or less important than the duties that have been reserved for the next higher level (on the ladder)—duties that invariably involve work **outside** the classroom."

Those designated "master teachers"—or whatever the label given to the highest rung on a job ladder may be—might continue to do some teaching, Bacharach adds, "but it's their **other** duties that justify their higher status or pay." This, concludes Bacharach, "is a peculiar way of upgrading the status of the profession."

FEATURES OF CAREER DEVELOPMENT PLANS

Career development plans possess several features. The features are discussed in the sections that follow.

No Quotas for Advancement

In contrast with job ladders, a career development plan emphasizes achievement of individual excellence and therefore does not have quotas for the number of teachers who are approved to certain steps of a career ladder. Each teacher has the potential to advance regardless of the performance of other teachers. This eliminates any reason for one teacher to regard another as a rival or as an obstacle to advancement.

Do Not Promote Beyond Teaching

Under career development plans, quality teachers are promoted **within** the classroom. They advance in their careers by improving such skills as mastery of subject, ability to manage a classroom, and ability to contribute to their school district's overall education program. As they advance, their expertise is used not to compete with other teachers, but rather to help other teachers.

We must abandon the idea that if you're really good at teaching, then you should be promoted **beyond** teaching. Effective career development programs do not take this approach. A true career development plan promotes the continuous refining of **teaching** skills. Through that refinement process, pride is built in the teaching profession.

Focus on Assistance

In any well-designed career development plan, evaluations have a central role to play. While merit pay and job ladder plans issue summary judgments through summative evaluation, career development plans should focus on assistance to help identify teachers' strengths and weaknesses for purposes of future skill enhancement.

The career development approach to evaluation is one way we can finally rid our schools of the "sink-or-swim" treatment of beginning teachers. In a career development program, new teachers would be expected to make mistakes and they would receive crucial support and advice from experienced instructors. The ability of experienced teachers to provide this formative assistance, in turn, would be acknowledged as a skill in itself.

Promote a Congenial Atmosphere

Career development plans provide a strategy for achieving teaching excellence. They promote the type of congenial, professional atmosphere that makes for quality schools. Teachers become allies rather than rivals. Schools once again become storehouses of educational expertise.

Career development plans treat the individual teacher fairly and promote greater harmony in the school. Teachers who work in collaborative settings are more likely to find their careers rewarding, more likely to improve their skills, and more likely to stay in the profession.

Involve Teachers and Administrators in the Planning

While there is no role model for career development proponents to follow—and indeed, experimentation is necessary and desirable—one element must always be present for the success of any plan: meaningful teacher involvement.

The involvement of teachers must not be limited to the planning stages. The process must involve principals or other administrative personnel, but it also means that those who teach must play a primary role.

It is safe to say that the millions of dollars that have been wasted on merit pay and job ladder programs around the country could have been saved had teachers and their associations been consulted. Attempts by the NEA to point out the inherent flaws of these plans have often been treated as opposition to reform, rather than as opposition to unsound practices.

Involve Teachers in Determining Evaluation Guidelines

No career development plan—however labeled—can be successful if teachers are not actively involved in determining the purpose of the evaluative process, the elements of teaching that will be evaluated, and the people who will be conducting the evaluations.

SUMMARY

There is a long-range benefit from fully involving teachers in the creation and maintenance of career ladder or career development plans. Such involvement creates professional pride. No longer do teachers feel they are at the mercy of forces outside their profession. When teachers are given a sense of dignity and some measure of control over their field, they will be much more likely to stay in the profession. And that will be good for not only teachers, but America as well.

A summary of recommendations for features of a career development plan is outlined below.

1. Do not identify quotas for advancement.
2. Do not promote teachers beyond teaching.
3. Focus on formative evaluation.
4. Promote a congenial atmosphere.
5. Planning a career development plan must include teachers, principals, and other administrative personnel.
6. Involve teacher associations in planning career development plans.
7. Teachers need to be actively involved in determining aspects of the evaluation, including the following:
   A. The purposes of the evaluative process
   B. The elements of teaching that are to be evaluated
   C. The people who will be conducting the evaluations

REFERENCES

Bacharach, S. B., Lipsky, D. B., & Shedd, J. B. (1984). *Paying for better teaching: Merit pay and its alternatives.* Ithaca, NY: Organizational Analysis and Practice, Boardman House.

Chapter 12

SUPPORT FOR CAREER LADDERS FROM TEACHER ASSOCIATIONS: NEW SCHOOLS, NEW TEACHERS

Albert Shanker

S ince career ladder plans have been proposed in a number of states to address problems with the teaching profession, teacher associations can do much to promote and establish career ladder plans. This chapter will include discussions of (a) the condition of the teaching profession, (b) traditional solutions to the problems, (c) views for restructuring the school and the teaching profession, and (d) a set of recommendations for what teacher associations can do to help establish and maintain career ladders.

WHERE WE ARE NOW IN THE TEACHING PROFESSION

The prophets of education have given us ample warning. Editorials, news stories, and scholarly studies have all cried out about the impending crisis in the teaching profession because of (a) teacher shortages in critical subject areas, (b) difficulties of recruitment and retention, and (c) the declining quality of newcomers just out of college. This section will include discussions of initial responses to the problems, and prospects for the future.

Initial Responses to the Problems

All of the news reports, along with some now-famous reports on the general state of education, have helped inspire a wave of reform that has swept the country. One state after another has implemented packages of legislation to upgrade schools, with particular emphasis on faculty improvement through some sort of combination of tougher requirements, testing, salary increases, incentive pay, or career ladders.

233

Unfortunately, there is substantial evidence that the initial responses have not had the desired effect on solving the staffing problems. In fact, staffing problems have grown worse, reaching the crisis stage in some areas. In Los Angeles, for example, 75 percent of the new teachers hired for the September 1985 term were uncertified by state standards. In New York City at least 13,000 teachers did not have the minimum credentials. Misassignment of teachers proliferates. An estimated 40 percent of the math teachers in Florida are out of license. A headline in **Education Week** wryly summed up the national scene: "Shortages of '85 Vanish as Schools Hire Uncertified Teachers" (Currence, 1985).

Those hired also often lack not only proper credentials but minimum academic skills as well. The recent experience of the Baltimore school system illustrates the situation. Thirty-two candidates were hired as teachers although they failed the writing part of a newly implemented competency test. Given the lack of better applicants, the Board of Education had little choice. When it comes to teacher recruitment, something is wrong.

Future Prospects are Bleak

While initial efforts to solve the problems of teacher recruitment and retention have failed, prospects for the future are equally bleak. Specifically, indicators suggest that there will be continuing problems because of (a) teacher turnover, (b) increases in student enrollment and decreases in teacher education graduates, and (c) heavy competition for college graduates in non-education sectors.

Teacher Turnover

One projection states that staff turnover in our classrooms will be so great that more than half of our nation's two million teachers will have to be replaced in the next ten years. The recent report of the California Commission on the Teaching Profession (1985, p. 33), **Who Will Teach Our Children?**, projected that by 1990 the state will have a shortage of between 21,000 and 35,000 teachers based on current conditions. If the Commission's recommendations on reduced class sizes are adopted, the shortage of teachers will soar beyond 80,000. There is a similar prognosis for the rest of the country.

Increases in Student Enrollment/Decreases in Teacher Education Graduates

To further complicate the problems with teacher turnover and staffing, the elementary and secondary school age population will be increasing at the same time that the numbers of college graduates will be declining. In other words, schools will find themselves competing with other employers in the public and private sectors for personnel in a shrinking work force. The latest **Statistical Abstract of the United States** (1985, p. 27) predicts that by 1990 children between 5 and 17 will number more than 44 million, while there will only be slightly more than half that total, about 25 million, in the 18 to 24 college age cohort.

Even on the crest of a wave of educational reform, staffing problems still exist in schools. What are the prospects when faced with the demographic and fiscal facts of life in the coming years?

Competition for College Graduates

In the past, circumstances sometimes conspired to enable our public schools to recruit highly qualified teachers. In the Great Depression, a shrunken job market made teaching a highly desirable occupation. During the Vietnam period, many able men went into our urban schools as an alternative to military service. Also, until quite recently, the classroom represented one of the few professional options open to women and minorities.

However, it is unlikely that our schools will be the beneficiaries of any such gratuitous "good fortune" in the near future. They will get no advantage over other employers; competition for personnel will be head on.

TRADITIONAL SOLUTIONS TO PROBLEMS

If you ask any teacher how his or her profession can be made more attractive, you'll most likely hear these three suggestions:

1. Raise salaries
2. Reduce class size
3. Increase opportunities for collegiality and professional growth

These fine objectives represent the traditional bread and butter issues that have, from the start, made up the action agendas of teacher organizations. Conventional wisdom still has it that significant gains in these areas will elevate the status of the profession, enabling it to attract and retain high quality people who, in turn, will raise the level of our schools.

All of this made sense once upon a time. But, given the realities of the next decade, the old agendas simply won't work for the profession as it is now constructed. We can mouth the old slogans and raise the venerable standards of past campaigns, but the unyielding arithmetic of the future will defeat our best efforts. Even doing more along the traditional efforts of raising salaries and reducing class sizes will not work, as shown in the following discussions.

Raise Salaries

Consider salary increases. The average annual salary for American teachers in 1984 was $23,500. A 50 percent across the board increase would bring teachers somewhat closer to what people with college degrees earn in the private sector. Now $35,000 is a respectable but by no means outstanding professional salary. But even this modest proposal would mean a $20 billion increase in the nationwide education budget; hardly a realistic expectation on top of current expenditures.

Reduce Class Size

Let's suppose, too, while the spirit was moving us to go all out to improve our schools, we also decided to lower class sizes by 20 percent; not a great stride, but a step in the right direction. In New York City high schools, for example, this would mean lowering the average number of students per class from the current level of 33 to about 27 or 28. But even this modest reform across the country would mean hiring anywhere from 100,000 to 300,000 more teachers than we have now, requiring an additional $60 to $80 billion for wages. So what we're talking about is a total package of about $100 billion for more teachers and higher teacher salaries. Clearly nothing remotely approaching this figure will be available in the future to bring the salaries of all teachers up to a professional level.

As an aside, I should point out that if our schools entered into a bidding war for personnel with corporate heavy hitters, it might only succeed in raising the ante for top talent. It is unlikely that IBM will let itself be outbid for a promising mathematician by the Lonesome Valley School District.

New Solutions Are Needed

But our problem is not only economic. The demographic picture of the next decade also points up the futility of thinking along old lines. We talk about the need to replace half of our professional staff by 1995; this is one million people. We also talk about the necessity of getting high quality personnel. This is what we want. But what can we reasonably expect?

According to a U.S. Department of Education projection, about 981,000 bachelor's degrees will be awarded in 1986. This number is expected to decline to 922,000 by 1991 (**Standard Education Almanac, 1982-1983,** 1983, p. 181). If we were interested in recruiting only the better students, that is, from the top half of each graduating class, and need roughly 100,000 new teachers each year, we would have to claim from 20 percent to 25 percent as our share of the available candidates. This actually is a conservative estimate since it doesn't take into account any attempt to reduce class sizes or increase the teaching force to accommodate an anticipated increase in our student population. Where a master's degree is required, the crunch will be even greater.

Given the dynamics of our competitive economy, no matter how attractive a teaching career is made, it is utterly unrealistic to expect that a minimum of one out of every four of our better students will go into elementary or secondary school teaching. Nor, one might argue, is it desirable. After all, our society will still need doctors, lawyers, accountants, systems analysts, research chemists, journalists, and other professionals.

There is simply no way that in the year 1995 we will have 2 million teachers earning professionally competitive salaries who were in the top half of their classes. The bottom line is that our current school system is a kind of trap for our teachers and our students, and by extension for our country at large.

If we persist in duplicating or even expanding the structure now in place, fiscal and demographic realities will make it certain that we will continue to have marginal salaries, generally large classes, and teachers with low academic ability who will need more and more supervision and guidance. This, in turn, will perpetuate or even exacerbate some of the worst features of a teaching career. Any hope of increased professionalism will be impossible under such conditions. New solutions obviously are needed.

ONE VIEW OF THE FUTURE

If our current professional structure makes the old agendas unrealistic, it's time to change the structure. This section will include a discussion of (a) principles that could guide decisions and actions, and (b) suggestions for restructuring the school and the teaching profession.

Principles to Guide Our Decisions and Actions

As decision makers consider ways to improve the teaching profession, there are several principles that should guide decisions and actions. Whether the decisions address career ladders or other changes in the teaching profession, the principles will promote thoughtful deliberation.

Reexamine Ideas of the Past

It may be time to reexamine some of the ideas that we rejected in the past when conditions were quite different from what they are now. For example, I now believe that an effective career ladder program will be needed as part of a larger effort to recruit the kind of teachers that are necessary to restore quality to our schools. A careful examination of differentiated staffing programs attempted in the past would be useful at this time to provide guidance for decision makers. While differentiated staffing plans attempted in the past, for the most part, did not work, we can learn from past mistakes and recognize features that would contribute to the success of career ladders.

Most of the teacher career ladder proposals that I have seen, stripped of their rhetoric, are mainly schemes to give a handful of people more money than others. They represent a new attempt to establish merit pay. Though some of these plans offer teachers a degree of increased professional responsibility and are small steps in the right direction, the old administrative pecking order is still very apparent. I've seen little in any of the plans with the scope and imagination that would begin to address the problem of making teaching more attractive to the better college graduates. It's all mostly about a few thousand dollars more in pay and a modicum of increased professional responsibility. Furthermore, it's all tied up with the old assumptions about how schools should be organized.

Break Out of Old Modes of Thought

To do better we have to break out of the old modes of thought about what schools and teachers are supposed to be. Let's imagine, for example, that the United States was an impoverished Third World nation, too poor to have any sort of education system. Children went out into the fields when they were five instead of going off to kindergarten.

Suddenly, vast reserves of oil were discovered. We were rich and wanted to jump right into the 20th Century. We knew that the best way to accomplish this was through education, but we had to start our system from scratch. Is there anyone bold enough to argue that the system we have now is the one we'd choose?

Ask What We Want To Accomplish

Without preconceptions, we have to ask ourselves exactly what we want to accomplish (within realistic limits) and how that can best be achieved. Although we can't reasonably hope to restaff our schools completely with top caliber people, we can, if we create the right conditions, recruit a fair share of the talent pool and judiciously place them to influence the quality of our schools, in much the same way that private industry uses top management to reshape a whole organization.

Suggestions for Restructuring the School

How can the school and the teaching profession be restructured to solve these problems? Let me suggest a new sort of school structure that might enable us to rise above the unpleasant and demographic facts of life.

Many observers have described at length exactly what goes on in our schools. John Goodlad (1984, pp. 105–107), for example, in **A Place Called School**, broke down how teachers actually spend their classroom time. He noted that only about 50 or 60 percent of the activities could be called "teaching," and of that a large chunk of time was given to lecturing, all too often to apathetic, restless students. Clearly there must be a more efficient and effective way of using our instructional staff.

I believe that it's possible to restructure (and improve) our schools in the future with a vastly different staff mix from that which we now employ, with perhaps one-third or one-half the current number of career teachers. Those career teachers also will be highly qualified and highly paid. This can be achieved through a number of changes as discussed in the following sections.

Encourage Greater Use of Technology

First, we need to make greater use of technology. As Christopher J. Dede (1983) of the University of Houston put it, " . . . our labor-intensive position [i.e., as teachers] in education has caused us steadily to consume more and more of the consumer dollar, just as have all the other labor-intensive industries. . . . To get past this fiscal problem of being labor-intensive, we must find a way ultimately to use more technology in education" (pp. 23–24). This is another way of saying that the teaching profession as now constituted is pricing itself out of the market.

Video- and audiotapes, cable television, computers, and films offer the promise of more effective ways of communicating much of the information now conveyed, with only mixed success, through lectures. A one-time viewing of Jose Ferrer in **Cyrano de Bergerac** would probably have a greater impact on youngsters than a series of reading and homework assignments.

Free Teachers from Administrative Tasks

Also, teachers need to be liberated entirely from administrative and custodial functions that now take up a large portion of their time. Paraprofessionals in many schools now take attendance, proctor tests, do clerical work and supervise lunchrooms. Their role should be expanded to take in all such activities in all schools.

Encourage 3–5 Year Careers for Some Teachers

Suppose that in addition to increased use of technology and paraprofessionals, we encouraged bright college graduates to enter teaching for brief periods—three to five years perhaps. They might be motivated by the desire for public service on the Peace Corps model, or by the need to repay government education loans.

Draw Teachers from Industry for Short Careers

It is conceivable that large corporations might offer incentives for their own employees to go into the classroom for a few years to help make sure that educated personnel are in the pipeline for the future work force. These shortterm adjuncts would be trained and supervised by career teachers and would take over some of the normal classroom work. Although they would be extremely able people, they would be less costly for the system because they would be on the beginning salary steps and generally would not work toward a pension, unless they chose to remain in the profession.

Provide Professional Salaries

With a reduced corps of the new breed of career teachers in a reconstructed school system, we would suffer no loss of quality. On the contrary. Most likely our schools would be improved because, in addition to a more efficient use of staff, the salary budget would be spread among fewer people and we would be in a better position to compete for a respectable share of the top college graduates. We would be able to offer professional salaries for professional caliber personnel.

Change the Activities of a Teaching Career

But money is only part of the answer. Equally important is the question of what activities will make up a teaching career.

Our generation has seen a significant change in the expectations of employees across the spectrum of our work force. There is ample documentation that both blue and white collar workers are increasingly interested in more than economic benefits.

If we want better teachers, we're going to have to offer them at least two things: (a) greater control of their professional lives, and (b) a greater variety of opportunities to utilize their talents. Lacking this, we just won't get the kind of teachers that we need to raise the quality of our schools. As one commentator put it, "The problem [with teacher recruitment] is not too many children but too many adults who are seeking personal and professional satisfaction elsewhere" (McCurdy, 1985).

Provide Greater Control for Teachers. Efforts need to be made to broaden the influence of teachers within the new school structure. There is a growing demand for satisfaction on the job and for an increased say in how things are done. More and more employees want some sort of control of the conditions of their working lives.

American industry, perhaps belatedly under the pressure of foreign competition, has come to realize that this yearning can be channeled into more effective management practices. Consequently, many domestic companies have begun to imitate the Japanese practice of encouraging input from workers on all levels.

While managerial enlightenment has spread through much of our economy, our schools remain one of the last bastions of the old factory system. Back in 1917, William C. Bagley, a prominent educator, criticized the "factory plan" of American schools where the hierarchy of authority and responsibility turns superintendents into "foremen," principals into "bosses" and teachers into "hands or routine workers" who can't be trusted to do a competent day's work on their own (Callahan, 1962, p. 220). In nearly 70 years, administrative practices haven't changed very much.

The simple fact is that top quality personnel won't stand for such treatment. As Theodore Sizer (1984) put it, "Constant control from 'downtown' undermines the most able teachers and administrators, the very people whose number should be expanding. . . . Many of these most able folk will leave or have left teaching—or will never enter the profession in the first place" (p. 196).

Provide Greater Variety for Teachers. As things stand now, most teachers spend their careers doing essentially the same thing year after year with the same responsibilities that they had on the first day of their careers. Added to this is the cumulative stifling effect of dealing almost exclusively with children. One of the most widely documented causes of dissatisfaction among faculty members is the intense isolation caused by the lack of satisfying collegial relations.

What the teaching profession desperately needs is a way out of this; a ladder, if you will, to greater and more varied professional fulfillment. A recent report sadly noted that under present conditions a good teacher leaves no mark on his or her profession (California Commission on the Teaching Profession, 1985, p. 10). Currently, the only road to advancement leads out of the classroom into supervision. We have to give teachers the chance to make an impact as teachers.

Encourage a Variety of Teaching Strategies

The new school structure that I have in mind will broaden the scope of a teacher's influence and will liberate all of us from the notion that education has to take place in a self-contained classroom. The resources that I've mentioned will give career teachers the freedom to use a variety of learning strategies. They can conduct seminars or have more time for individual or small group coaching. They can also become facilitators connecting the student with the appropriate teaching tool. For example, teachers might outline chemical experiments for students to do in the lab or a program of research to be done in the library. In short, they will decide how their curriculum is to be taught and how the paraprofessionals and short-term staff can be most effectively used.

Reduce the Need for Supervision

As the quality of teachers increases, the need for supervision diminishes and ultimately should disappear as we know it. Highly qualified master teachers should run their schools like a partnership, in much the same way that a law firm operates today.

Allow Teachers to Participate in Policy Decisions

A fully realized professional career cannot be circumscribed by the walls of the school. Teachers need to be given more access to and greater control of the upper level policy making processes that influence what goes on in the classroom.

Establish a Professional Teachers Board

A key to professionalization is the power to set standards and policy practices. A Professional Teachers Board should be formed for these very purposes. I see at least four primary responsibilities of the Board.

First, the Professional Teachers Board should help upgrade and administer a tough, national teacher test. Such an examination would be devised initially by a blue ribbon commission of distinguished educators and others experienced in nationwide testing. At that point, a Professional Teachers Board would upgrade and administer the program. Admittedly this is a long-range prospect and would be done at a national level.

Second, the Professional Teachers Board should establish standards and assessments on teacher competence. Progress in this area could be made at the local or state level. Calls for professional boards to establish such standards are not new. For example, one key recommendation in the report of the California Commission on the Teaching Profession (1985) calls on the governor and legislature to abolish the current Teaching Standards and Board and create a new group comprised of a majority of teachers to "establish standards and assessments of teacher competence" (p. 15).

Third, the Professional Teachers Board should create panels of teachers on the district level to rule on the granting of tenure and on charges of malfeasance. The feasibility of such an expanded professional role for teachers has been convincingly demonstrated by the innovative peer review and counseling program developed through the collective bargaining process in Toledo, Ohio, where experienced teachers not only serve on tenure committees but also observe beginning teachers and intervene with suggestions or advice on classroom management or lesson planning for those having problems.

Fourth, the Professional Teachers Board should help open up other professional growth opportunities for teachers. For example, the way we usually choose our texts and write our curriculums is illogical and counterproductive. Often books and courses of study are mandated, frequently on a statewide basis, without consulting the classroom teachers who will have to use them. It seems to me only a matter of good sense to let people with recent classroom experience make the decisions about what to teach and what materials to use.

But I don't mean just choosing any teacher or group of teachers at random. There is a substantial body of scholarship on effective curriculum writing and textbook selection. Teachers with a particular interest in these areas should be trained as "specialists," whose work would be a supplement to their classroom duties. Similar training could be offered in other school-related areas. The Professional Teacher Board would devise and supervise tests for those who participate in such programs, and the teachers who pass would, in effect, become "board certified" experts who would serve as consultants in their areas of specialization as adjuncts to their teaching responsibilities.

Summary

There are many other promising possibilities for restructuring the school and the teaching profession. Once we agree on the underlying principles, I expect that others will offer their own ideas. But whatever we do, in one way or another, we're going to restaff our schools in the next decade, and, for the most part, the teachers that we hire will be in our classrooms well into the next century. We have a weighty responsibility.

To face this challenge we have to begin by recognizing the true nature of our recruitment problem and the fatal limitations of old assumptions. I'm confident that with good will and clarity of vision, we will then be able to muster the collective wisdom to reshape teaching into a profession that will excite and challenge enough bright college graduates to turn our schools around. We don't need a multitude, but we need good ones.

RECOMMENDATIONS

Teacher associations can do a number of things to help establish and maintain career ladders for teachers. As leaders in teacher associations at the local, state, and national levels become involved in the process of establishing career ladders for teachers, the issues discussed in this chapter and outlined below will provide guidance in making reasonable decisions.

1. Principles to Guide Decisions and Actions
   A. Reexamine Ideas of the Past
   B. Break Out of Old Modes of Thought
   C. Ask What We Want to Accomplish
2. Suggestions for Restructuring the School
   A. Encourage Greater Use of Technology
   B. Free Teachers From Administrative Tasks
   C. Encourage 3–5 Year Careers for Some Teachers
   D. Draw Teachers from Industry for Short Careers
   E. Provide Professional Salaries
   F. Change the Activities of a Teaching Career
      a. Provide greater control for teachers
      b. Provide greater variety for teachers
   G. Encourage a Variety of Teaching Techniques
   H. Reduce the Need for Supervision

I. Allow Teachers to Participate in Policy Decisions
J. Establish a Professional Teachers Board

REFERENCES

California Commission On The Teaching Profession. (1985, November). *Who will teach our children?*. Sacramento, CA: Author.

Callahan, R. E. (1962). *Education and the cult of efficiency.* Chicago, IL: University of Chicago Press.

Currence, C. (1985, September 25). Shortages of '85 vanish as schools hire uncertified teachers. *Education Week,* pp. 1, 16.

Dede, C. J. (1983). Tendencies for technology in the year 2000. *Education Media International,* pp. 23–24.

Goodlad, J. I. (1984). *A place called school.* New York: McGraw-Hill.

McCurdy, J. (1985, January 7). Crisis in quality. *Education USA,* p. 139.

Sizer, T. (1984). *Horace's compromise.* Boston, MA: Houghton-Mifflin.

Standard Education Almanac, 1982–1983. (1983). Chicago, IL: Marquis.

Statistical Abstract of the United States. (1985). Washington, DC: Bureau of Census.

Section III

SUMMARY OF RECOMMENDATIONS

Chapter 13

PRINCIPLES TO GUIDE DECISION MAKERS IN THE TASKS AHEAD

PAUL R. BURDEN

Career ladders may represent a significant advance in improving the quality of education and in satisfying teachers' needs for more status, recognition, salary, and varied job responsibilities. This book has focused on a number of issues that decision makers need to carefully consider as career ladders are being implemented.

This chapter includes a discussion of (a) outcomes of career ladders up to this time, and (b) principles to guide decision makers for the tasks ahead in implementing career ladders.

OUTCOMES OF CAREER LADDERS SO FAR

Since career ladders already have been implemented in some districts and states, it would be useful to look at the experiences within those jurisdictions in an effort to provide guidance for the implementation of career ladders in other districts. This section includes a discussion of (a) some generalizations that can be made about career ladders that have been implemented so far, and (b) some problems that have been experienced in those settings.

Generalizations

A number of school districts already have implemented career ladders. Some generalizations can be made based on the experience of programs currently in place (Cornett & Weeks, 1985).

1. Plans show considerable variation concerning who controls the program. Some plans have clearly defined state standards; others allow considerable local autonomy.

2. States are proceeding cautiously, lengthening time for implementation, phasing in programs, or experimenting with pilot projects.
3. The career ladder movement has clearly stimulated changes in procedures for evaluating classroom performance of teachers.
4. School districts and teachers are volunteering to participate in the career ladder programs, often in greater numbers than anticipated.
5. Teachers and other educators are involved in planning, analyzing, and revising career ladder programs.
6. Incentive programs are expensive and the total costs can be difficult to predict. If the programs are to achieve their objectives, funding over the long term must be assured.
7. Formal program evaluation of incentive programs is limited to date. It is important that plans be evaluated by outside persons. (pp. 8–9)

Problems With Career Ladders So Far

States and school districts are experiencing some problems as they adopt career ladders. It is critical that the problems in the adoption process be identified so that career ladders can be successfully implemented.

A review of news reports about the implementation of career ladders in a number of states reveals that problems include (a) a lack of comprehensive planning, (b) inadequate time to fully implement the program, (c) loosely defined transition steps to enact the career ladder programs, (d) the need to involve teachers in the planning process, (e) the lack of or inconsistent funding, (f) the use of quotas that require teachers to compete for a fixed number of positions or for a fixed amount of resources, (g) evaluation criteria and procedures that are inadequate for a variety of reasons, (h) a lack of teacher union involvement and support, and (i) fluctuating support from various political forces.

PRINCIPLES FOR THE TASKS AHEAD

If policy makers were aware of potential implementation problems, they would be able to make decisions that would minimize the problems. Topics for the sections that follow came largely from ideas presented in the chapters in this book and also from other sources including Cornett (1985), Hawley (1985), and newspaper and journal accounts.

Principles that can guide decision makers are listed and discussed in each of the following sections: (a) state and local control of career ladder plans, (b) the process of planning and implementing the change, (c) career ladder features, (d) roles of teachers and administrators, (e) decision management in schools, (f) identifying and evaluating teachers, (g) promoting the professional development of teachers, (h) improving the work environment of teachers, (i) costs/funding, (j) teacher association support, (k) evaluating the career ladder program, and (l) changes in the role of higher education.

State and Local Control of Career Ladder Plans

Principle 1   Identify the limits of control at the state and local levels.

Most states use statewide criteria to guide local districts in the design and implementation of incentive programs. Some states such as Florida, Texas, Tennessee, and Alabama take a more centralized approach where legislation outlines the program. Many states such as Utah and South Carolina have given local districts almost complete autonomy in developing programs by providing funding and issuing limited guidelines (Cornett, 1985).

If implementation of career ladders is to be orchestrated at the state level, certain conditions need to be present to have successful change. Anderson and Odden (1986) identified four conditions at the state level— but outside the state agency—that appear to be critical for successful implementation of school improvement programs, including programs such as career ladders. The conditions are (a) state pressure to change, reform, or improve education; (b) state respect for traditional balance between state and local control; (c) support from political leaders; and (d) discretionary money available to local districts and schools.

Anderson and Odden (1986) also identified five factors within the state departments of education that were found to be important to the success of the improvement programs. The factors were (a) political support within the department, (b) a collegial relationship with local school people, (c) adequate resources, (d) structure and organization of the state department, and (e) an effort to develop local capacity through technical assistance.

It is important to recognize the source of control for career ladders because decisions that will be made about the design and implementation of career ladders will be affected by the source of control.

The Process of Planning and Implementing Change

Principle 2 Develop an appropriate, systematic, and comprehensive change strategy that is founded on principles of change theory.

Principle 3 Involve teachers and teacher groups from the earliest stages to help design the career ladder plan.

Principle 4 Establish a time frame for developing and implementing career ladder plans.

Principle 5 Establish a clearly defined transition plan to implement the plan.

Principle 6 Provide for revision and reconsideration if experience should indicate that a change in plans would be desirable.

A number of concepts and principles concerning the process of change are discussed in Chapter 3, including organizational change, resistance to change, change as a transition process, and other related issues.

Career ladders are likely to be most effective if those they affect understand them and believe in their benefits. Career ladder plans will find greater acceptance among teachers if teachers can help design and redesign them (Cohen & Murnane, 1985).

As states design and implement career ladder plans, the necessary time to develop workable programs and reach consensus has become an issue of debate (Cornett, 1985, p. 8). Some states, fearing that momentum would be lost, enacted programs quickly (e.g., Tennessee, Florida, Texas). Other states proceeded under delayed time frames or started with pilot programs because of fiscal realities, opposition to the project, or a cautious approach. Pilot programs have been established in several states (e.g., Virginia, Maine, South Carolina, Arkansas).

Revision of the career ladder plan may be necessary once implementation is started. Based on the initial experiences with the Tennessee career ladder plan, George Malo of the State Department of Education suggested that states do the following as they move into career ladder programs: (a) clearly define "teacher" and identify who will be included in the program (e.g., Will non-classroom school personnel such as counselors and librarians be included?); (b) phase in applicants rather than attempt to place all teachers in the first year of implementation; (c) refine communications; (d) focus on the fact that the upper levels of a career ladder are for outstanding teachers, with other levels designed for those who demonstrate good teaching; (e) don't make changes in the first year of enactment since midyear changes almost always cause confusion; (f) don't have too many years needed for teachers to advance up the ladder; and (g) consider the use of local and state evaluators for those at the upper levels (Cornett, 1986).

Career Ladder Features

Principle 7   Select career ladder features with market sensitivity in mind.

Principle 8   Establish some type of differentiation in roles on a career ladder.

Principle 9   Consider altering the school decision-making structure with a career ladder.

Principle 10   Establish criteria to move up a career ladder that focus on knowledge and skills, rather than on competition among teachers.

Principle 11   Make provisions for teachers to move down as well as up the ladder.

Principle 12   Allow teachers to advance up the career ladder once they meet the predetermined criteria, and do not set quotas that limit the number of teachers at each career step.

Principle 13   Allow teachers to move up the steps of a career ladder quickly (fast tracking).

Principle 14   Select features of career ladders that both attract and retain teachers.

Principle 15   Require teachers to continuously demonstrate high performance to retain higher levels of pay and status.

Principle 16   Prepare for new relationships among administrators, supervisors, and teachers.

Principle 17   Provide salaries for teachers at the upper steps of the career ladder that are competitive with administrative positions.

Chapter 4 includes a discussion of many issues relating to career ladder features. The issue of market sensitivity relates primarily to teachers' base salary and extra salary that is provided as teachers move up the steps of the career ladder.

A basic element of motivation theory is that incentives must be considered attainable (Vroom, 1966). Awards based on comparison among individuals or limited in number will be viewed by many workers as beyond their reach. Furthermore, competitive awards will discourage peer interaction and social approval, both important to effective teaching (Rosenholtz & Smylie, 1984).

Since the focus of the evaluation system is on meeting predetermined criteria, teachers should be able to advance up the career ladder once they meet the criteria. In closed reward systems where quotas are set to limit the number of teachers who can advance to a given career ladder step, the focus is on competition and a high proportion of workers may believe their prospects of receiving an award are remote no matter how hard they try to improve their performance.

Roles of Teachers and Administrators

Principle 18 Define which teachers and non-classroom school personnel are eligible for participation in the career ladder.

Principle 19 Define the roles and rewards for each step of the career ladder.

Principle 20 Provide for a variety of responsibilities in a teacher's career along with opportunities for increases in salary, status, recognition, and authority.

Principle 21 Provide for gradual induction into the profession with opportunities for continual advancement.

A discussion of the roles of teachers and administrators is included in Chapter 5. School districts employ a number of non-classroom school personnel such as librarians, counselors, and speech pathologists and it should be clear whether they are included in the career ladder plan or not. The roles and rewards for each of the career ladder steps should be clearly defined.

Decision Management in Schools

Principle 22 Identify the limits of teacher decision making between areas involving instructional improvement and administration.

Principle 23 Prepare career ladder teachers for group leadership.

Principle 24 Make the organizational structure of the school reflect the increased decision-making capacity of faculty and the new responsibilities of career ladder teachers.

Principle 25 Prepare administrators to support school-wide decision making and to see advancing career ladder teachers as augmenting and complementing their instructional leadership role rather than competing with it.

A number of aspects of decision making are discussed in Chapter 6 including implications of effective schools research, responsibilities and role descriptions, organizational changes to support the new decision-making role of teachers on a career ladder, and preparation of administrators to support such changes. Teacher involvement in decision making represents an important part of a career ladder plan. Consequently, careful attention should be given to clarifying the decision-making boundaries of teachers and administrators and to the training of decision makers for group leadership.

Identifying and Evaluating Teachers

Principle 26 Maintain a density of leadership to deal with evaluation.
Principle 27 Establish clear, visible, appropriate, and detailed criteria for advancement in a career ladder.
Principle 28 Use alternative data sources in the evaluation of teaching and the performance of additional professional duties.
Principle 29 Use multiple evaluators in the evaluation of career ladder teachers.
Principle 30 Use formative and summative evaluation, and consider them as complementary rather than competing activities.
Principle 31 Have the same criteria and standards for formative and summative evaluation, but administer the evaluations separately.
Principle 32 Link the evaluation system to the staff development program.
Principle 33 Establish assessment measures and procedures that are seen to be fair and predictable.
Principle 34 Provide frequent evaluation, monitoring, and feedback.

Issues relating to identifying and evaluating teachers are discussed in Chapter 7. The criteria for teacher advancement, of course, should match the goals of effective instruction and the fulfillment of other professional duties. But even within schools, different educators have different goals (e.g., special educators, vocational specialists, mathematics teachers). The solution to this blend of goals seems to be a mix of general and situational criteria against which the teachers are measured (Hawley, 1985).

In states that have implemented career ladders, all plans have the common criterion of excellence in job performance, however defined, to determine who will be chosen to advance on the career ladder. Most plans require experience at each level (usually from two to five years), and some states additionally require academic or staff development credits for advancement. Leadership within the school and professional work outside the school are sometimes included. Increasingly, student achievement or progress also is a factor in determining teachers' performance (Cornett, 1985).

Teachers who have experienced performance-based pay often feel that the plan was administered unfairly (Porwoll, 1979). Therefore, guidelines should be developed to increase the perceived legitimacy and reliability of performance evaluations (Hawley, 1985).

Promoting the Professional Development of Teachers

Principle 35 Include inservice training or staff development as an integral part of the career ladder system.

Principle 36 Provide professional development opportunities in (a) improving teaching and gaining content mastery, and (b) knowledge and skills necessary to perform new duties as part of a new level on the career ladder.

Principle 37 Apply the principles of adult learning in the design of professional development programs.

Principle 38 Provide appropriate organizational support for the professional development programs.

Principle 39 Apply research-based knowledge about conducting staff development programs to the design of professional development programs in career ladders.

Promoting the professional development of teachers in career ladders is discussed in Chapter 8. Teachers may experience alienation and frustration if their evaluation information indicates that they are falling short of performance goals. The means and support for teachers to improve in their professional skills should be provided as a central component of a career ladder plan. The staff development programs also should be designed based on the knowledge of effective professional development programs and the principles of adult learning.

Improving the Work Environment of Teachers

Principle 40 Provide support for the continuing professional growth of teachers.

Principle 41 Recognize teachers' contributions.

Principle 42 Recognize the effects of the nature of the job assignment, the work environment, time, material resources, and staff support.

Principle 43 Allow teachers to participate in school management decisions.

Based on the recommendations in Chapter 9 and those from other sources, the principles listed above are presented to guide decision makers in improving the working conditions of teachers.

A number of the recommendations in Chapter 9 concerning improving the work environment of teachers are consistent with recommendations in **Developing Career Ladders in Teaching** (Association of Teacher Educators, 1985) and **Incentives for Excellence in America's Schools** (Association for Supervision and Curriculum Development, 1985). Both publications outlined ways that teachers can be rewarded through monetary means and through improving the work environment.

The results of a survey of NEA members reveal that a majority of teachers have problems with the resources and working conditions in their schools and want more say in the decisions that affect them and their students (Olson, 1986).

Costs/Funding

Principle 44 Economic rewards for high performance should be significant.

Principle 45 Identify all expected cost areas and carefully calculate estimates before implementation.

Principle 46 Select a model that will be used for determining teacher salaries on all career steps.

Principle 47 Arrange for sufficient funding.

Small economic rewards provide limited incentives to undertake risks and expend the energy to achieve new levels of competence. But, how large an award needs to be to motivate cannot be determined from available research. In the planning stage, all expected costs of implementing the career ladder plan should be identified and sufficient funds should be available. A model for the salary schedule to be used should also be determined before implementation. These issues are discussed in Chapter 10.

Teacher Association Support

Principle 48 Involve teacher associations in the planning, development, and evaluation of the career ladder program.

Principle 49 Have teacher associations at the local level formally endorse the career ladder plan that they helped plan.

The presidents of the National Education Association and the American Federation of Teachers discussed the issue of teacher association support in Chapters 11 and 12. A central theme in each chapter was to include teachers and teacher associations in the planning, development, and evaluation of the career ladder program. Without the support and involvement of the teacher associations, the success of career ladders may be in jeopardy.

Evaluating the Career Ladder Program

Principle 50 Teachers should help assess the plan.

Principle 51 Provide a mechanism for obtaining feedback on the progress and acceptance of implementation.

Those most affected by career ladder plans should also be involved in evaluating them. Teachers themselves would experience changes in their professional lives and would be in a position to assess the effects of a career ladder plan. Regular evaluation procedures should be established for this purpose and there should be the opportunity to make necessary changes in the plan based on information obtained through the evaluation.

Changes in the Role of Higher Education

Principle 52 Have undergraduate and graduate coursework (and clinical and field experiences) focus on the effective teaching behaviors that are required in career ladder evaluation systems.

Principle 53 Have graduate coursework focus on knowledge and skills needed by career ladder teachers to engage in mentoring, evaluation, and the performance of other professional duties identified in career ladder steps.

258 Establishing Career Ladders in Teaching: A Guide for Policy Makers

Principle 54 Work with school districts and state agencies to create career ladder programs.

Principle 55 Work with school districts in the delivery of professional (staff) development programs.

Principle 56 Work with school districts in conducting personnel evaluations.

Principle 57 Have the graduate coursework requirements in the training of administrators reflect the expanded role in instructional leadership inherent in career ladder programs.

Principle 58 Work with legislators and state agencies to alter policies as needed to enact and support career ladder programs.

Richard Swain of the Texas Education Agency noted that the career ladder program has caused higher education to become more sensitive to the real needs of teachers and school districts and to design programs accordingly (Cornett, 1986). Several of the principles listed above reflect the increasing focus on effective teaching behaviors for teachers and on instructional leadership for principals and other administrators. College coursework could be changed at the undergraduate and graduate levels to meet these expectations.

University teacher educators also could work with school districts in determining the features of a career ladder plan, in sponsoring staff development programs, in conducting personnel evaluation, and in evaluating the career ladder plan itself.

Higher education personnel also could work with legislators and state agencies to alter certification guidelines, teacher tenure policies, and entrance and exit requirements for teacher education.

CONCLUSION

Career ladders for teachers have been proposed in an effort to provide: (a) a formal procedure to recognize and use the full potential of master teachers, (b) a systematic way to provide exemplary models for beginning teachers, (c) different pay for different levels of teaching experience and expertise, (d) a system of promotion within teaching, (e) a career pattern to give teachers something to which they can aspire, (f) a means of attracting talented people to the classroom and retaining talented people in the classroom, and (g) a means of providing the profession with an avenue to improve its image and gain prestige (Burden, 1985).

Each chapter in Section 2 ended with a set of recommendations that related to the topic of the chapter. The principles listed and discussed in this chapter are intended to serve as guidelines for decision makers as they address the issues. The potential of career ladders can be achieved if decision makers give careful attention to the issues discussed in this book. Then the goals of improving the quality of education and satisfying teachers' needs may be realized.

REFERENCES

Anderson, B., & Odden, A. (1986). State initiatives can foster school improvement. *Phi Delta Kappan, 67*(8), 578–581.

Association for Supervision and Curriculum Development. (1985). *Incentives for excellence in America's schools.* Alexandria, VA: Author.

Association of Teacher Educators. (1985). *Developing career ladders in teaching.* Reston, VA: Author.

Burden, P. R. (1985). Career ladders: Retaining academically talented teachers. In H. C. Johnson, Jr. (Ed.), *Merit, money and teachers' careers: Studies on merit pay and career ladders for teachers* (pp. 197–207). Lanham, MD: University Press of America.

Cohen, D. K., & Murnane, R. J. (1985). The merits of merit pay. *The Public Interest, 80,* 3–30.

Cornett, L. M. (1985). Trends and emerging issues in career ladder plans. *Educational Leadership, 43*(3), 6–10.

Cornett, L. M. (1986, March). Implementing plans: Success and change. In *Career Ladder Clearinghouse.* Atlanta, GA: Southern Regional Education Board.

Cornett, L. M., & Weeks, K. (1985, July). Career ladder plans: Trends and emerging issues—1985. In *Career Ladder Clearinghouse.* Atlanta, GA: Southern Regional Education Board.

Hawley, W. D. (1985). Designing and implementing performance-based career ladder plans. *Educational Leadership, 43*(3), 57–61.

Olson, L. (1986, April 16). Teachers' work environment not "supportive," poll confirms. *Education Week,* pp. 1, 43.

Porwoll, P. J. (1979). *Merit pay for teachers.* Arlington, VA: Educational Research Service.

Rosenholtz, S. J., & Smylie, M. A. (1984). Teacher compensation and career ladders: Policy implications from research. *Elementary School Journal, 85*(2), 149–167.

Vroom, V. H. (1966). *Work and motivation.* New York: Wiley.

NAME INDEX

SUBJECT INDEX

267